THE SMALL-TOWN MIDWEST

IOWA AND THE

MIDWEST EXPERIENCE

WILLIAM B. FRIEDRICKS,

series editor

Iowa History Center at

Simpson College

RESILIENCE
AND HOPE
IN THE
TWENTY-FIRST
CENTURY

THE SMALL-TOWN MIDWEST

JULIANNE
COUCH

UNIVERSITY
OF IOWA PRESS,
IOWA CITY

University of Iowa Press, Iowa City 52242

Copyright © 2016 by the University of Iowa Press

www.uiowapress.org

Printed in the United States of America

Design by Richard Hendel

The University of Iowa Press is a member of Green Press Initiative and is committed to preserving natural resources.

Printed on acid-free paper

Library of Congress Cataloging-in-Publication Data
Couch, Julianne, author.
The small-town Midwest : resilience and hope in the twenty-first century / Julianne Couch.
    pages   cm. — (Iowa and the Midwest experience)
Includes bibliographical references and index.
ISBN 978-1-60938-405-0 (pbk), ISBN 978-1-60938-406-7 (e-book)
1. Small cities—Middle West.   2. Middle West—Social conditions—21st century.
3. Middle West—Economic conditions—21st century.   4. Middle West—History—21st century.   I. Title.
HN79.A14C68   2016
306.0977—dc23   2015031851

To Ronald,

who was there with me

even when he wasn't

there with me

CONTENTS

THE
SMALL-TOWN
MIDWEST

INTRODUCTION

"Iowa doesn't look like America anymore."

So declared journalist Katie Couric, when questioning why the Iowa caucuses are still the first important political event of the presidential campaign season. For more than four decades presidential hopefuls have come to Iowa to woo supporters with their temporarily corn-tinted messages. But *why*, Ms. Couric—and likely others—wondered. After all, Americans in the East, Southeast, and on the West Coast are more ethnically diverse, younger, and closer to the leading edge of rapid demographic shifts, compared to people in rural states like Iowa. By rights, those folks should have the first crack at shaping the course of a national election through their own primaries. Maybe it is time to accept that rural America's interests and concerns no longer matter to most Americans the way they once did in our nation's agrarian past.

On the other hand, although America's middle might not "look like" a lot of this country, it looks like an awfully big piece of it. According to 2010 US Census figures, 15 percent of the population reside in rural counties, spread across 72 percent of land in the Midwest and Great Plains. Though the population percentage is not a huge number, it does represent 46.2 million people who live in the region. For the first time in US history, however, rural counties in America, as a whole, have started losing population. The decline, first reported in 2012, is attributed to several factors, including the lower birth rate, the downturn in agricultural and manufacturing economies, and the fact that older people are choosing to remain in urban areas where they've lived and worked, rather than retire to scenic rural locales.

Some might look at those facts and think the region has declined to the point that there is little reason to pay attention to it, let alone worry when its economy is slow to recover, or consider whether it might benefit from infrastructure like rural broadband, or access to adequately funded medical care, or to public transportation, or to school systems that introduce children to a wide range of academic and creative options. They might argue that these concerns are suited to larger population centers. Now that agriculture is less labor-intensive than it was in the heyday of the farm town, the thinking goes, it is time to pool our resources and let small communities fade away, in the natural order of things. Small, rural agricultural communities in the middle of our country have plenty of life left in them, at least for now, because the people who live in them have discovered resources both internal and external to stabilize their roots.

That isn't to say there might not be some place people in small rural agricultural towns would rather live. But live there they do. They are willing to tax themselves to build recreation centers or bike trails, making themselves attractive to newcomers. They are willing to live in a small town but commute to larger cities for work, shopping, and services they can't obtain at home. They are willing for one family member to take a job in a larger town so the family has health benefits while the others farm the acreage or run a small business. They develop succession plans so that farms can be kept in families rather than sold for subdivision developments. They work long hours on efforts to plan festivals so that tourists will see their town in the Country Living sections of regional metropolitan newspapers, and make trips there a habit.

They count it as a success when a new family with two or three school-aged kids moves to town, and a loss when a family like that leaves. Some years a town might see its population bounce up a bit. Other years it might cope with a downturn in the regional farm economy and the ripple effect that has on the local implement dealer, and in turn the grocery store, and in turn the church collection basket, and so on down the line. In a town with little social beachfront to absorb them, these ripples of change can become scouring waves.

Yet a core of people stays in place and maintains. There's a trait that town leaders and everyday residents have in common: they take what remains and make do. In spite of downturns or difficulties, they make it work, whether because of duty or fear of letting down previous or future generations, or of letting themselves down. To me, that is resilience.

The late Elizabeth Edwards is often quoted as saying, "Resilience is accepting your new reality, even if it's less good than the one you had before." I would add to that definition a collective sense, thinking about how a place accepts its new reality of shrinking populations or hard economic times, or both. Yet resilience of place doesn't exist if people see themselves simply as inhabitants there. It exists if people see themselves as stewards, understanding they are responsible for knowing the place's story, its challenges, and striving to keep the collective porch swept. If they don't see themselves in that way, those trips to bigger cities might be one-way trips. A town that doesn't come together to plan how to keep the doors open, and then see those plans through, is likely to falter, and lose population to the point that it cannot be sustained.

I have been a Middle American all my life and have seen towns both flourish against the odds, and collapse with a farm crisis or energy bust. I was born and raised in Kansas, lived for seven years in Missouri, spent twenty years in Wyoming, and now have settled in Iowa. From these vantage points, I have considered qualities that make people stick to small, rural places. But I wanted to do more than just consider. That's why I decided to visit nine small communities in five states from the Rocky Mountains to the Mississippi River, the boundaries of the region I've called home for more than a half century. I wanted to compare notes on why we live in small towns of this region, in spite of the challenges that come from depopulation and distance.

All my years of driving back and forth between those states and my family's home base of Kansas City have meant a great deal of time traversing Nebraska. So Iowa, Missouri, Nebraska, Kansas, and Wyoming are the five states I chose in order to write about places I know and about things I understand: friendly small-town sidewalk chats; lost keys found dangling in the car door; combining lots of ways to make a living, sometimes simultaneously; discomfort with change and distrust of difference; longing for culture beyond high school musicals; shortage of affordable quality housing and good jobs; eye rolls at each mention of that condescending term "flyover country"; the repercussions of being seen as a political monoculture; personal identification with a place dismissed as a commodity colony; and stirring pleasure at the hint of a trend that to young people, rural is becoming cool.

In general, I've learned from these conversations that although the rural Great Plains and Midwest region is losing population, the town borders are porous and open to new possibilities. People are able to keep two concepts alive in them at once: permanence and mobility. That is, people are thinking of themselves not as part of a town of a thousand and shrinking, but as a town of a thousand that is not too far from a town of five thousand, where they can go when need be and if they have the resources. And those five thousand can access the town of twenty thousand at the other end of their county, and so on. It helps if a small town is the county seat. It helps to have more than one steady employer, like a small manufacturing plant, a nursing home, a regional hospital. It helps to have a school. It helps to have a grocery store, a motel, a place to buy gas.

Based on 2000 Census statistics, the US Department of Agriculture Economic Research Service (ERS) described the proximity of people in the Lower 48 to goods and services by the acronym FAR: Frontier and Remote. FAR refers to varying degrees of remoteness relative to the time it takes to drive to urban areas of various populations. Level 1 means you are remote from urban areas of 50,000 people but that there are plenty of smaller cities nearby. There are 18 million people living in Level 1 FAR areas, where most goods and services are easily accessible. Level 2 means you are far from urban areas of 25,000 people, but again, somewhat smaller towns are nearby. Level 3 means you are far from urban areas of 10,000 people, where smaller towns are nearby but are not exactly burgeoning with goods and services. At the most remote end of the spectrum are the 4.8 million people who live in Level 4 FAR areas. These are far from urban areas of 25,000 people. It takes folks in Level 4 FAR areas a little while to reach a movie theater, a longer while to kick tires at a car dealership, and quite a poke to board a plane. They are officially considered "rural."

Most communities featured in this book are Level 3 or level 4 FAR, and all range in population from less than 100 to approximately 4,000. The highest count of people per square mile in the counties I visited measures at thirty-one. Compare that to a modestly sized Midwestern city in my interest area, like Omaha, with 3,247 people per square mile. To many people in small rural communities, myself included, that is about 3,227 square-mile people too many. We can't live without cities, but that doesn't mean we want to live in them. After all, we can visit whenever we want. Then we can go home. By saying "we" I do not suggest that people featured in this book fully represent their town, or that the towns are stand-ins for their states, or that the states are proxy for the entire region. But their voices tell a story familiar to anyone who might go there and listen, on any given day.

I selected towns through a combination of map studying, Internet searching, calendar consulting, and dart throwing. Other than towns represented in the first and last chapters, I literally did not know a soul when I began my research. I selected towns to visit partly because they were accessible to me, meaning I could drive there in my 1996 Toyota. Another sort of accessibility was of the logistical sort. I chose places that had a motel where I could stay, and public places I could visit, such as county courthouses, libraries, or restaurants. Also, I didn't want someplace that was a small town in name only, just an exurb ready to be swallowed by a swelling metropolitan area. I wanted towns off the beaten path where I had quick access to solitude and public lands. And no interstate highways. And no Walmart.

In addition, I wanted my collection of towns to have a variety of core economies that distinguished them from one another, such as a college or a quirky tourism niche. I also wanted geographic diversity between the communities chosen for each state. Once I selected a town, I made contacts in advance, either through cold calls, chatty e-mails, or connections of friends of friends on social media. Without exception, I found people to guide me, such as chamber of commerce directors or economic development specialists. Their positive spins were sometimes offset, sometimes affirmed, by local newspaper editors who could speak objectively about the sort of stories they'd covered over the years, and what nagging problems still dogged the community. From there, I could meet town leaders, business owners, parents of young children, and the always helpful folks who like to chat in grocery store lines.

The area from the Rocky Mountains to the Mississippi River is a span of some 900 miles. I drove four times that distance in nearly three years of research. I visited two towns along very different stretches of the Mississippi, and two towns near the Missouri. I went to one town on a natural lake, two towns on the High Plains, one in the southern Flint Hills, and one at an elevation of 8,400 feet. Each had its own form of natural beauty. For this, there is also a scale. Like the FAR measurements, the Natural Amenities scale was developed by the ERS. Although I still believe that beauty is where we find it, I cannot disagree that certain physical characteristics like warmth and sunshine do enhance an area as a place to live. Almost everywhere I visited ranked in what can be described as the "blah" level according to the amenities scale. Yet the people I spoke to knew that in the blink of an eye, they could be out of town and in the country, enjoying sunsets or fishing in a stream, or just driving around, enjoying uncrowded natural spaces.

The first town I write about does score high on the Natural Amenities scale. That is Centennial, Wyoming, population 270 (as of the 2010 Census), located just about twenty-five miles west of Laramie. Centennial is in Albany County, population 37,422, the vast majority of whom live in the college town of Laramie. Albany is a large county, though many in Wyoming are bigger. It covers 4,309 square miles, with a population density of eight people per square mile. Centennial is an unincorporated mountain town, home to equal parts wealthy folks with vacation homes; commuters with the mental toughness to endure icy roads during the endless winter; and people who are perfectly happy living in their cars or rustic cabins so they can play in bands or just get away from whatever it is they want to get away from. The place fights to throw off its image as merely a Laramie party stop, while also resisting going the way of too many Colorado ski towns whose agricultural roots have been tilled into oblivion by tourism and wealth. I chose to write about Centennial because of my personal connections and my perception that people there have formed a highly creative and diverse but not commercialized town.

Beyond the 106th meridian looking west toward the Continental Divide, Wyoming does not fit into most definitions of the Great Plains. But looking east, the viewscape sweeps down across the vast valleys and cattle ranches of the Laramie Basin and beyond, to the grasslands of Nebraska. I selected two locations in that state to visit. One was Bridgeport, population 1,522 (as of 2013), located in the western panhandle. Bridgeport is in Morrill County, with about a third of the square miles of Albany County and about one-seventh its population. The density there is four people per square mile. It is not far from either Colorado or Wyoming and I wanted to see how those very different states influenced the politics and culture of this community. Morrill County aggregates much of what I expected to discover: political conservatism, young people who desire to raise their children near their grandparents, a focus on cultural heritage, and deep ties to surrounding lands. I also noticed a burgeoning ethos for land conservation and sustainability and an effort to reclaim less productive farmland for wildlife areas and conservation easements.

I decided to continue my consideration of the High Plains, so I put off visiting my second Nebraska town. Instead, I headed for Norton, Kansas, population 2,880 (as of 2013), located in the far northwestern part of the state. Kansas counties are comparable to one another in size, but expand a bit as one moves west. Yet Norton County is still only 881 square miles. It is home to 5,671 people, with a density of seven people per square mile. I was curious to see how a town is reinventing itself in a world where farming is so highly automated that its residents need to find other ways to make a living, if they are to stay. The town of Norton is the county seat and the site of a medium-security state prison housing approximately 700 inmates, so the town has both a steady employer and an influx of visitors. A highly conservative, church-based culture is sometimes at odds with, but mostly energized by, the changes in town.

From Norton I visited a second town in Kansas. Sedan, population 1,088 (as of 2013), in the highly scenic southeastern region, is the seat of Chautauqua County. That fact has done little to stabilize its population. The county itself sees its 3,369 persons spread across 645 square miles, with a density of just under six people per square mile. I selected Sedan because it is near the Oklahoma border, and people there are as likely to affiliate with Bartlesville as with Wichita. Though the region once sat on rich oil and gas reserves, local oil fields are nearly played out. Chautauqua is part of what Kansas calls its Rural Opportunity Zone, so developed to aid counties suffering significant population loss. While some residents take kindly to state-sponsored entrepreneurship programs, others resist government involvement, regardless of how acute the need.

After my visit to Sedan it was time to head north again to Nebraska, this time along the Missouri River, near the South Dakota border. My focus was on the town of Niobrara, population 257 (as of 2013). I treated the area of Knox County as a collective rather than focusing on one town. That's partly because the county seat of Center has a population of only ninety-four. I took a broader look at the 8,710 county residents, scattered across 1,140 miles and with a density of just under 8 people per square mile. Within Knox County lies the Santee Sioux Reservation, and its 173 square miles of tribal land. The presence of Native American persons gave me a chance to bring their voices into this rural story.

Following the Missouri River, I visited the northwestern-most county in Missouri: Atchison. There I focused on the town of Tarkio, population 1,516 (as of 2013), whose economy once centered on a private college and a meat-packing plant, before they both closed down decades ago. The county itself is small in size: just 550 square miles. It is also small in population: just 5,685, with a density of ten people per square mile. It has rich farmland, which in recent years has spent much of its time under the flooding waters of the Missouri. Some blame the flood-control programs of the US Army Corps of Engineers for these agricultural disasters. Atchison County, consisting mostly of Tarkio, Rock Port, and Fairfax, has, in recent years, lost population more dramatically than any county in the state.

From Atchison County I cut a diagonal line nearly to the antipode of Missouri. I visited New Madrid, population 3,031 (as of 2013), which is the county seat. The county is small, at 687 square miles, but with a comparatively whopping population of 18,956, living twenty-eight people to a square mile. I wanted to visit a Mississippi River town and compare the culture of this more southerly community to the river town where I now live. The African American population here is comparable to the national average—that is to say, much larger than in most other small rural towns in the Midwest and Great Plains region. This part of Missouri seems much more culturally connected to neighboring Kentucky than to other bordering states like Illinois or Kansas. Not a few of the stories focused on problems of crime, drug abuse, poor health, and entrenched racism. However, the town just came into an enormous sum of money. How it uses the funds might make a difference in those problems.

From New Madrid I traveled to my newly adopted state of Iowa and found Emmetsburg, population 3,811 (as of 2013), the seat of Palo Alto County. Physically, that county is just a bit smaller than New Madrid County, at 569 square miles. The county's population is 10,147, with a density of seventeen people per square mile. Emmetsburg is the largest town I visited. I selected it in part because it has a casino, several agricultural and industrial employers, and a modest-sized community college that attracts international students and people of color. I was especially interested in the college because it would mean there are younger people in the community. There also are a larger number of Hispanic residents here than in other areas I visited, a demographic shift in this part of the country, as it is elsewhere in our nation.

I end my story in Bellevue, Iowa, population 2,172 (as of 2013), where I moved in part because I've long been obsessed with the Mississippi River, and in part because technology gives me the freedom to work from anywhere. I'm watching this farm town figure out if it wants to be a tourism center bolstered by a scenic byway and river traffic, or if it wants to be a bedroom community of Dubuque, twenty-three miles distant, or if it wants to put in an industrial park and compete with its neighbors for agribusiness entrepreneurs. Bellevue is not the seat of Jackson County, population 19,848, with a population density of thirty-one people per square mile. Not a fan of crowds, I'm happy almost a third of them live in the county seat of Maquoketa, keeping that town's population stable and by trickle down, Bellevue's.

I once explained my plans for this book to a literary acquaintance in New York City. Her response was, once I've written about one town, what on earth would I have to say about the others? Everything to say about small towns would have been exhausted after the first chapter. The opposite turns out to be true.

There are distinct differences between the communities in this book and between this region and other areas of the country. So in order to ground my thinking in contemporary research on regional culture, I read works like Robert Wuthnow's *Small-Town America: Finding Community, Shaping the Future*, and Patrick J. Carr and Maria J. Kefalas's *Hollowing Out the Middle: Rural Brain Drain and What It Means for America*. Yet I approach my stories of these places not as an economist, social scientist, agriculturist, or custodian of any particular wisdom. Instead, I approach my stories as an interested traveler. I'm noticing how people in small towns look to larger towns and cities for what they need while at the same time shaking the dust off those "big crowded places" as soon as they get back home. I'm also reflecting on how people in larger towns and cities look to small towns for reassurance that the corner-stone on which their cities were built still stands, and for the hope that maybe one day they can return to their grandparents' home place, even if just for a B&B weekend or a pumpkin festival. And then get the heck back to "civilization"! Sometimes small-town folks decide it is time to head to the city and stay. Sometimes metropolitan folks decide they won't be missed and relocate to a smaller town. An America without this porous but hardy membrane of culture would be unworkably stagnant, to my mind. Rural Middle America might not be diverse in the way some people think of the term, but for many reasons it remains both resilient and hopeful. And in that way, it really does look like America.

1 CENTENNIAL, WYOMING
LEAVING THAT FOREVER PLACE

Wyoming is the least populated state in the country and the tenth largest in size. However, at six people per square mile, it is not last in density. Alaska has it beat, at 1.3 people per square mile. Wyoming has a few "big cities," with Casper and Cheyenne both around 60,000 residents, not counting their surrounding suburban communities. Many of Wyoming's towns of all sizes have swelled in recent years due to booms in energy extraction: coal, gas, and uranium. When I moved to the state in 1992, Wyoming's population had been in a brief decline due to a bust in the energy economy, dropping it to about 430,000. However, the period between the 1980 and the 1990 Census was the only time the decennial census registered a population loss. By 2000, it had grown by 8.9 percent. By 2010, the energy economy, in spite of the global economic downturn, had still attracted or retained enough people that the population was up another 14.1 percent. In 2013, it had about 582,000 residents.

Wyomingites describe their state in myriad ways. One label they are sorry that fits is the Suicide Capital of America. With 23.2 suicides per 100,000 people in 2010, Wyoming had the number one ranking in the country for that dishonor. According to Wyoming Department of Health (DOH) statistics, in 2009, suicide was the fifth leading cause of death. To be fair, suicide was the cause of only 127 deaths, or 2.9 percent of all deaths from specific causes. The Wyoming DOH cites access to firearms and "regional context" as components that explain the high suicide rate in Wyoming and other western states. Regional context includes things like an attitude of self-reliance, and poor access to mental health care and intervention because of the vast spaces separating people from one another. Suicide isn't confined to financially ruined ranchers, or drunken oil field workers, however. It affects Wyoming's elite, such as one powerful oilman and philanthropist. His name, and money, are behind numerous efforts and edifices around the state, down to the playing field at the University of Wyoming football stadium. Even he chose a self-inflicted bullet as a solution to the problems he suffered after back surgery, his family said. The notion that people are suffering with no recourse to help belies, or perhaps underscores in this man's case, the notion of independent individualism. Self-reliance and wide-open spaces appeal to many people—after all, that's the "cowboy" image—so it is a cruel irony when those things lead to self-destructiveness.

Wyoming's unofficial nickname is the Cowboy State. This might be a good fit but there are many people in the state left scratching their heads, for they neither care about the University of Wyoming Cowboy or Cowgirl sports teams nor live an agricultural lifestyle. Some with more urban sensibilities were rankled when in 2010 the state adopted an official ethics code known as "Code of the West," espousing colloquially expressed principles such as "be tough but fair" and "ride for the brand," which, while admirable, seem straight out of Owen Wister's *The Virginian: A Horseman of the Plains.*

The state's official seal calls it the Equality State, a label that in part references the fact that Wyoming was the first state where women were allowed to vote in public elections. Many around the country cringe at the irony of the equal rights label. The shadow of Matthew Shepard, a gay man brutally murdered in Laramie, still darkens Wyoming's reputation, making it seem that intolerance is the state's chief value. Although equality is a work in progress there, as it is the world over, most people in Wyoming have a kinship with their fellow Wyomingites. A common expression is that Wyoming is one small town with really long streets, since everyone is assumed—rightly or wrongly—to be family, or at least neighbors.

Residents sometimes refer to the state as Big Wonderful Wyoming, or just Big Wonderful for short. Newcomers sport bumper stickers that read "I'm not native but I got here as soon as I could." Wyoming's official tourism slogan was, for many years, "Like No Place on Earth." Grammar sticklers argued it should rightfully say "Like No Place Else on Earth." Instead, it was eventually changed to "Forever West." It is as if when one crosses the eastern border at Interstate 80, Aaron Copland's "Rodeo" should be blasting out from speakers hidden in the sagebrush. Coming into Cheyenne, visitors encounter that city's slogan: "Live the Legend." Forty-five miles later, coming into Laramie, billboards announce this as a place of "Real History. True Adventure."

To me, the most meaningful tourism slogan was coined in the 1970s: "Wyoming Is What America Was." Those words conjure a sense of wistful nostalgia textured by values worth restoring and fighting for. A safe haven in a world gone to pot. Spend enough time immersing yourself in the state and you might believe it is true, as I admit without hesitation I still do. Wyoming comprises a vast landscape of rock and desert, scrub vegetation and hardy forests, divided into twenty-three counties, one Indian reservation, and more than 30 million acres of federally managed public land. Between that federal land and another 3.8 million acres of state land, approximately 50 percent of Wyoming is publicly held. I've explored a significant portion of these public lands, and have been to virtually every town that is on the Wyoming map, and several places that aren't. In spite of Wyoming's sometimes reckless boom-and-bust cycles, its disturbingly careless environmental degradation, its real struggles, I love it, beyond any place else on earth.

———————

I'm not quite sure how I first met Nancy Waldman Taft. It might have been at an art show in Centennial, where she was one of the organizers. It might have been at a library event she helped organize. It might have been at a festival at the UW president's official mountain retreat in Centennial. She was an organizer of that, too. Since I moved to Iowa in 2011, we've managed to keep up with the broad strokes of each other's lives. But it wasn't until someone forwarded me the Centennial e-Post did I realize Nancy was also involved with that online form of communication that keeps newcomers, part-time residents, and locals in touch with each other.

The e-Post covers summer news like what wildflowers are blooming in the mountains, what bands are playing in various bars, what local fundraisers are being held for organizations and individuals in need, and what nearby locations are being evacuated because of forest fires. In late fall the e-Post lets residents know when Highway 30, the road through town and over the Snowy Range summit, has been allowed to close for the season due to snowfall. In the winter, the e-Post publishes photos of blizzards and the winter recreation they beget. Then in late May, the e-Post announces when the highway has been cleared of snow by the Department of Transportation, which does its best to keep the road open despite stubborn blizzards that can strike at any time of the year.

It didn't take working on the e-Post for Nancy to know what was going on around town. She is one of the most involved citizens of this community, maybe because she knew she'd need to be in order to make friends in her new town. She and her husband, Kirk, have lived all over the United States and even in Germany because of his Air Force career. For a few years he taught Air Force ROTC at UW in Laramie. Nancy has degrees in environmental conservation and public relations. When the time came for him to retire, they realized that Laramie had been their favorite place of all. During a return visit in 1997 they were cross-country skiing near Centennial and noticed a For Sale sign. It was for 13.9 acres of sagebrush. They bought the land, built on it in 2002, and have called it home since 2003.

An unincorporated community, Centennial for many years claimed to have 100 residents. That was a clever tie-in to the origins of its name, chosen because the town was founded in 1876, the same year as the centennial of the signing of the Declaration of Independence. But then, just a few years ago, Centennial's population nearly tripled, overnight. That's because the US Census Bureau revamped how it counted people in cities, towns, and villages. It created the category of Census Designated Place, lumped the people scattered up and down the Centennial Valley into one of them, and put up a new sign: Population 270.

"Everyone was shocked when the highway department came through and switched out those signs," Nancy told me. Not so shocked that a few quick-thinking bar owners didn't run outside to ask if they could have them. Now those signs hang proudly in these public places, relics of a version of their town no one truly believes is past.

Centennial is close enough to Laramie that a good portion of its residents work there, or used to before retiring to Centennial, as the Tafts had done. But that doesn't mean residents think of themselves as living in a Laramie suburb. "Nobody here believes we are a satellite of Laramie," she said. "You have to be tough to live in Laramie, but you have to be downright rugged to stay long in Centennial." First, there's the frequent high winds, which are always present in Laramie but much more intense at 8,200 feet, at the base of the mountain. Nancy recalls one winter day when the weather station on her home computer registered oo. She knew with the howling winds outside her door that measurement couldn't be right. Then she realized that the wind readout only had two digits. It should have said 100.

"The wind comes screaming down the highway from the mountain," she said. "In winter, our windshields get cracked by flying rocks. During spring, everyone tells winter survival stories, because surviving winter is a badge of honor."

Centennial has long been understood to be a place people go to get away from something, and not just temporarily. There is something about the forlorn appearance of wood-frame homes scattered in what appears to be a haphazard way up the hill toward the mountain that strikes the untrained eye as a place where no one cares about outward appearance. An empty police car, now shrouded in overgrown vegetation along the highway, for many years fooled drivers into thinking Centennial actually had an officer ready to hand out speeding tickets. Besides the Snowy Range Scenic Byway designation sign, the most visible sign on the highway is a big yellow diamond-shaped sign: "Watch for Pedestrians." Besides the theoretically outdated population signs, other telling signage hangs in local bars. "Centennial: One square mile surrounded by reality," reads one. "Broke? Unwanted? Unemployable? Come Home to Centennial" reads another, in a mild jab at the cheerleading efforts of other communities trying to recapture their expatriates.

Some people settle here for the astounding natural beauty of the area, the aspen and hummingbird summers, the tracks of moose and elk on winter snow, the sprawling ranchlands of the valley dotted with cattle and antelope. Some of these ranchlands have been broken up and developed into housing over the years, such as the cluster of subdivisions known collectively as North Fork for its proximity to the North Fork of the Little Laramie River. There's also an area called Aspen Country, a favorite dwelling for UW professors. Nancy Taft, who lives in North Fork, says these two groups have come to be known as the Forkers and the Assers, in the lovingly disparaging tones of locals who would not take well to outsiders using these terms.

For many in Laramie or Cheyenne, Centennial is the place to stop on the way to and from the mountains, or as a destination to one of the town's unassumingly entertaining bars or cafés that serve really good food. The town includes an historic hotel, a public library, a two-room

To watch for pedestrians is good advice for drivers along this highway, which locals view more like a neighborhood sidewalk than a road. Photograph © Julianne Couch.

public school, a gift mercantile, a church, and a business that makes log homes. It has a part-time post office, and the Friendly Store sells a few groceries and necessities, along with gasoline. That's about it. In spite of, or perhaps because of these limitations, it has retained its core of old ranching families and attracted individuals of means to settle there, at least as part-time residents.

There are few places to work in town, but some people who live in "downtown" Centennial seem to function just fine with minimal employment at the places where they'd be hanging out anyway, like the restaurants and bars or ski area. Some people come here, or stay here, because they are attracted to a town where there are no zoning laws and they can pile as much detritus in their yard as they want. It seems to amuse them to irritate individuals who spend large sums on large, fancy "log homes."

Other than littering, if that term can be applied to accumulating junk on one's own property, there isn't much crime in Centennial. The town is so small that its statistics are lumped in with Laramie's. That is why it was so surprising during the summer of 2014 when a local pastor summoned emergency personnel after sustaining a gunshot wound. He told authorities a would-be robber in a ski mask and camouflage had stopped at the church to steal funds, and in the struggle, the gunman had shot the pastor, with the pastor's own gun. It wasn't too many days later when the local sheriff announced that in fact the pastor had attempted to harm himself, and that there had been no attempted robbery, and no gunman in a ski mask. The tone in the Centennial e-Post had moved from sadness over Centennial's perceived loss of innocence to unspoken acknowledgment over the troubling incident that had affected one of their own. According to authorities, the pastor admitted making up the burglary story and apologized, saying that he had some personal issues to work out for himself.

Long before this incident, I made my first trip to the Laramie area as a tourist in the late 1980s. While there I heard about an open wedding reception at the Trading Post Saloon in Centennial, and I didn't want to miss it. The Trading Post is a combination local bar, famous for live music, and restaurant, famous for steaks. On that night the groom was playing in the band, made up of some of his buddies who'd been making music there for many years. The bride, whom I recall dressed in traditional white, was dancing in rotation with a bar full of Centennial regulars, plus some extras. Some were in tie-dye, others in cowboy boots, some in standard wedding-guest attire, and some, like me, nerdy in Midwestern tourist shorts and tennies.

Wyoming, and the Rocky Mountain West, is full of these scattered mountain communities, unincorporated, not concerned about attracting industry or about the brain drain of young people. Most people just want basic services, and sometimes not even that. Some rural properties in the mountains were built on national forest land and are allowed to retain private ownership. Many of these properties are not on water or sewer lines and don't have wells. People haul water in to their mountain cabins, and pack out trash. They have outhouses. Often there is no cell phone service. If an emergency occurs, it can be a long wait for a sheriff or a volunteer first responder.

One thing Centennial has that thrusts it into the "real" world is Laramie. Residents can insist they aren't an exurban community, but that argument loses some air when one considers that if one wants groceries or goods beyond the slender offerings at the Friendly Store and the seasonal farmer's market, one goes to Laramie. If one wants to visit a doctor, or a shoe store, or send their children to school beyond the sixth grade, they need Laramie. And if they need to interact with Albany County government, they go into Laramie, the county seat.

Nancy says people sometimes look around the ramshackle structures of downtown Centennial and ask her why the place even exists today. "There are still mines up in the mountains and people are still panning for gold," she points out. "So, the ranching, the gold mine, the tourists have kept the place going." Also the National Forest adds recreation into the mix with hiking trails and skiing. In fact, for many years the skiing had an international reach, spawning a winter recreation event called the Norwegian Olympics. This free-for-all was organized in the Snowy Range by the numerous Norwegian students who attended UW to ski on the team. They had plenty of American friends and other Norwegian students who willingly participated in innocent fun through events like naked ski jumping. The Norwegian Olympics was eventually curtailed because of the unabated drinking that often took place, followed by the unfortunate driving back into Laramie by people who had no business behind the wheel. This is just one example of the sort of partying common in the mountains. Once Wyoming made it illegal to drink and drive in 2007, things calmed down a bit.

"The party reputation has been difficult to fight if you are trying to do other things," Nancy said. For example, in recent years, locals have promoted Christmas in Centennial as a family friendly event. For the first few years attendance was poor because potential attendees from Laramie and beyond laughed at the idea that there was anything in town besides bars. Rather, the event promotes the local gift shops, craft vendors, and includes a puppet show, a snowman contest, and a chance to visit Santa at the library. There's a fairly good following now, although attendance is dictated by the weather. "Some years you couldn't see across the highway, other years it was 50 degrees. If the weather is too nice, they all go to Fort Collins," Nancy said, referring to the city of 100,000 people more than an hour south in Colorado.

The fact that there are factions of residents, from the permanently underemployed to the retirees in the exclusive subdivisions, doesn't mean social classes have no contact with one another. In fact, social strata are flattened in a community of this size because it takes a certain amount of cooperation among a certain amount of people to do the most basic things. Sure, there are unfortunate situations where groups don't mix as well as they could. Like when a man said to have ruined his health by drink needed medical care for an unrelated condition. It was mostly through the contributions of those who could little afford it that funds were raised for gas money to transport him back and forth to Laramie for treatment. Then there was the man who moved to town from "back east" for the great skiing, but almost immediately began a campaign to clean up downtown Centennial. That made everybody mad, Nancy told me. "We thought, 'It looked like this when you moved here.'" That person gave up his efforts and few have tried since. There are also political disagreements, in spite of the fact that this unincorporated town has no formal local governance, only neighborhood associations. But that doesn't stop people with strong political opinions from voicing their views whenever the opportunity presents itself, sometimes polarizing the very people who depend on each other so much in this often challenging environment. But at least they are talking, at the neighborhood associations, or over dinner at the Trading Post, or at a fundraiser for the library.

In many ways, Centennial is no different from other small towns. It has the same set of problems of other communities struggling with demographics, but with a twist. Centennial has younger people. But many of them work in Laramie and have very busy schedules. Others are part-time residents who are there just in summer or winter. All community events in town are organized by volunteers. That's true of the museum board, the library, the Volunteer Fire Department (VFD), and the mountain rescue crews who search for lost snowmobilers.

Nancy and her husband are both involved with the VFD in Centennial. She told me there are lots of people who live in Laramie who'd volunteer on the ambulance, for example, but their response time from that distance would be too long. The youngest firefighter who lives in Centennial is fifty-eight, Nancy said. The youngest EMT in Centennial is in her early sixties. There is one in her early seventies who has had joints replaced and is still driving the snowmobile to rescue folks who stray off the trails and get lost. They would gladly take seasonal snowmobile rescuers if they would go through training. Same thing with firefighters. "Only here in summer? Great. But you can't just sit in the truck and drive. You have to have training," Nancy said.

One person who knows plenty about firefighter training is Tom Kern. He is the long-serving chief of the Centennial VFD, and has been a member since 1968. We spoke on a morning while he was idle (a rare occurrence), waiting for the dew in his hay meadow to dry. He'd been called away from putting up hay the day before to check a report of smoke at Lake Owen. It had been a false alarm, which was good, but it cost him two hours of work, which was not. In between ranching and the VFD, he also works as an electrician/fire-alarm tech at UW.

Tom notes it took some practice to balance the elements of this busy life. He and his wife, Andrea, have been married forty-four years and have three grown children. Two live in Laramie, and one in Steamboat Springs, Colorado. "When we were first married, I got hurt on the ranch a couple times. So Andrea decided she better get EMT training." Tom was already on the VFD. "Life hereafter hinged on the telephone. All calls came in on a phone tree, so when it rang it wasn't good."

Tom grew up in Laramie. He'd spent his boyhood helping his dad put up hay in the summer for local ranchers. Then when Tom was seventeen, his dad bought their own ranch and moved the family there. His father has since passed away, but Tom and his brother have the title to a section of land, which is about 640 acres. Plus they have a grazing lease for 16,000 acres on the national forest. They drive the cattle up there in early summer to graze, with the idea of driving them back to the ranch come fall. "Sometimes the cattle beat us back home," Tom said. "They're afraid they'll see a bear."

The ranch is not directly on Highway 30, the road connecting Laramie and Centennial. Rather, it is off Highway 11, which cuts along the face of Sheep Mountain into the heart of the Centennial Valley. "It is beautiful in summer but tough getting around in winter," he said. Rural people in the wintery Rocky Mountains use snowmobiles for necessity, not just for recreation. "My wife didn't do much snow machining until we were married. The first year was a winter of snow machining in and out for a full three months. When the kids were in school, she had to snow machine them to the bus stop. She doesn't see much beauty in snow machining anymore."

In spite of large ranches, people do have neighbors. Tom knows many ranchers who have sold their places for development. "When we moved out here there were three families. They had young kids then who are now running their parents' ranch. The rest have changed hands three or four times." The wealth coming into the area is noticeable, he says, though maybe not so much in downtown Centennial. "The big money is coming in and buying up ranches, tearing everything down and building new." One nearby ranch has sold three times, Tom says, and the newest owner has been here six months and works for one of the big oil companies. Another ranch was also purchased by an oil company executive, and so far, they are maintaining it as a ranch. On another ranch recently purchased by a wealthy newcomer, most of the existing structures were torn down and replaced by bigger and better. "One night it was 27 below zero," Tom recalls. "The brand new shop caught fire, so the VFD went there, and wound up freezing the pump on the truck. We did put out the fire. He was so excited he wrote us a check for five thousand bucks. We appreciate that guy."

Other ranchers are also generous with donations to the Centennial VFD, he says, because they understand the value of the service and the difficulties in maintaining it. There are issues of equipment, which Tom says can run $3,500 each for an air pack, $2,400 for bunker gear (the outer protective clothing), and $5,000 for a radio. Then there is the matter of recruiting and training firefighters. Tom says twenty volunteers is a good number. "But sometimes there are too many sets of bunker gear sitting around the wall. As people get older, they don't want to be tied down to a pager. It is reaching a serious point. People will have to step up or do without." That means the time might come when a call for a grass fire or a heart attack or a 3:00 a.m. shop fire on a double-digit below-zero winter night might be met first by a crew from Laramie. Those are well-trained and well-equipped crews. "But they'll be twenty-five minutes behind schedule. People will be in trouble."

Training to fight structure fires can take eight or nine months, he says, which then gives a firefighter credentials to work anywhere in the United States. And after only a few weeks, people can receive adequate training to begin work as a wildland firefighter, providing they go out with more experienced firefighters. Tom's days of going out on engines to fires in places where more help is needed around the country are behind them. "I've had enough going across the country, sleeping on the ground. It is time to let younger guys have fun." Tom tried to give up the position as chief, but the crew wouldn't let him. As to the future, Tom is certain his ranch will remain in the family and not be sold for a subdivision. For one thing, his father had always been adamant the ranch not be split up for development.

"People are moving up here because the Snowy Range is in the top five areas for snowmobiling. There's also the ski area, and in summer the range is popular for fishing and hunting," Tom says. "In summer, it draws oohs and aahs. People say, 'I gotta move up here.' That's good until you try to sell. Then you think, 'Is there anybody who wants to buy this place?'" Tom's brother has two children, so between the five offspring they'll be able to decide one day how to share it among them.

When I was hatching my plan to move to Wyoming, I'd never given any thought to moving to Centennial. But had I been so inclined, I would have contacted someone like Diane Watson. She's an associate broker with Advantage Real Estate, which is the only real estate agency with an office in Centennial. She moved there some twenty years ago. She started out in California working for a technology business, and then decided she wanted out of the area. So she spent some years in Albuquerque, New Mexico, but also wasn't comfortable with the growing population there. She had a friend in Laramie and liked the place. So she drew a circle on the map around Laramie and looked at the possibilities that fell within the circumference. Centennial seemed as good a choice as any, so that's what she picked. Now she lives a mile south of town on the "mortal remains" of an old ranch. "It is falling down, but I keep propping it back up."

I am no longer surprised when people tell me they moved to a certain place guided by the landing of a thrown dart. Sometimes they use that expression figuratively, other times not. I knew a woman in Laramie who picked that place after her map was penetrated by a pen knife. Here in Bellevue, I know at least one actual dart-map thrower. And a lot of people who were just driving around and were unexpectedly caught in the force field of a place they knew little about, realized resistance was futile, and allowed themselves to be absorbed.

Diane says she has no regrets about her move. For one thing, she feels at home. Centennial is a combination of people who are like her and her husband, Diane says. They've lived full lives in other places but are hermits at heart who enjoy their own company. "People like us tend to gravitate to places like this." Diane hears from a lot of people who are searching for what she's found. Now that rural property listings are available online, people have a pretty good idea of what they are looking for in a home before they contact her. Often they are looking for a part-time residence to which they can retire full time, one day. Many are from Texas, Nebraska, or Kansas, and are looking for a way to escape the summer heat.

"People are just basically looking for a place to play," Diane said. For most, the decision is also price-driven. Real estate is limited, and land to build on is scarce. The Medicine Bow National Forest looms to the west, meaning virtually no property is for sale there. "If you are the kind of person who is happy to sit and read a book, you'll be fine. If you need to be entertained, you won't be. There aren't so many people like that. People who decide to settle here are a congenial and content group."

To Diane, congenial and content people do the sorts of things they do in Centennial. They join service organizations to help their neighbors. They welcome newcomers and help them assimilate, and then leave them alone. On the Fourth of July, they shoot off their own fireworks. They used to shoot bottle rockets back and forth across the highway at each other until Albany County law enforcement discouraged that practice. Now the VFD brings their trucks just in case any of the curing grasses of summer catch fire. In times of drought and high fire danger, the Forest Service will issue burning bans, which includes fireworks. Although some nonlocals and locals alike disregard Forest Service road-closure signs when it suits them, forest-fire prevention is a goal most people have the sense to share.

Diane had a term for this part of the country that I'd never heard before but made me laugh with recognition: "Turnaround Country." That's the spot where the national television weather forecasters stand in front of the map. They face one way to point out weather on the East Coast, and then turn around to describe what's happening on the West Coast, blocking the center of the country. "That's ok. If we want to know what the weather is we can look out a window. We're reasonably competent out here."

That competence starts early, with the schooling of young children. One room of the two-room schoolhouse is for kindergarten through third grade, while the other is for fourth through sixth. Albany County has avoided the tide of rural school consolidation, and in fact, operates several rural schools, necessary across its 4,309 square miles, where the towns can be counted on one hand. "There is a wonderful mix of parents from the local service industry in town, to university employees, to the ranch families in the valley," Diane said. "The kids all seem very comfortable with each other and get to go on trips into the mountains for skiing and other activities." She believes the children who go to school in Centennial are highly qualified for junior high school in Laramie. One thing she cautions parents about is the combination of poor roads and the very busy schedules of most middle and high schoolers. "Not only will the parents do a lot of hauling kids into town for sporting events, they'll eventually have to face the idea of letting the kids drive on their own as they grow up."

One young woman who grew up in Centennial, Lindsay Stoffers, has plenty of memories of that sort of thing. Now in her early thirties, Lindsay just missed attending Centennial Elementary School when her mother relocated from Laramie the summer before Lindsay started seventh grade. Mother and daughter moved into a little log cabin. "I remember being disappointed when it first happened," Lindsay said carefully. "I didn't appreciate small town Centennial." She was involved in cross country, basketball, and other activities at school in Laramie. "From the get-go, Mom commuted me into town every day for practices and school. When cross country running season started I had six a.m. practice. That meant we were up super, super early to leave Centennial in time. The drives were out of control during the winters. There was one night after basketball practice that I had to open my passenger side door to let Mom know if we were still on the road or not."

The day I met with Lindsay, we visited at Night Heron, a combination coffee shop and used bookstore in downtown Laramie. Each summer since moving to Iowa, I visit Laramie for a few weeks. Each time I'm amazed at how the town has grown, with new apartment complexes crowding out the local antelope herd that used to graze on the ridge behind my neighborhood grocery store. And when I go downtown, I am both pleased and a little concerned to see the beautiful historic district fills its storefronts (that's the pleased part) with stores where few besides tourists would shop. And when I have to stop in at Walmart because I realize I've forgotten to pack some little needed item, I feel like I'm in a foreign land. I recognize no one there. But at least at Night Heron I recognize a place that had long been an independent bookstore, just run by a different owner and with a different name. Sitting with me in that same space I first visited more than twenty years ago, I listened as Lindsay told me she was closing on the purchase of her own house later that afternoon, just across the train tracks from where we sat. She was just two years younger than I was when I moved to Laramie, and I couldn't help project myself into her life, just a bit.

Lindsay's upbringing was much different than mine, however. For one thing, I didn't have mountains and an alpine lake in my backyard. Now that she's grown, Lindsay appreciates those things in a way she didn't as a child. Her perspective was also shaped by the fact that after college she traveled internationally, spending two years working and living in India and South Korea. When she came back she wasn't sure what she wanted to do with herself next. She stayed with her mother and got a job at the Century Bar, part of the Friendly Store complex. "That was an interesting job to get to know everybody in different ways," she recalls. Like most bars, the Century Bar has its regulars, and they've been regulars for a very long time, in some cases. "I was so worried that things had changed when I came home, but everyone was still on the same barstool telling the same stories. I recognized that I appreciate and love Centennial but I have to be cautious where I spend my time."

Since those days, Lindsay has gone back to school, earning a master's degree in counseling. Her study of that field has given her the vocabulary and the professional distance to describe her beloved town like a family. "This is a solid community," she starts out. "But with any family there are good things and problems, too. There are groups of people that primarily spend the majority of their time in the bars. Other groups come for retirement and to go to the mountains. They are using those parts of the town. There are not cliques but interest groups, people live here for different reasons. It is an easy way of life."

Lindsay is not yet on the verge of settling down and raising children, but when she does, she says she would love to raise them in Centennial or a similar mountain town. "There was no 'nature deficit' for me growing up. When I have a family one day, I'd appreciate being able to have a space like that. What I love so much about Wyoming is that there are still places you can go to get away from chaos."

She might not meet the man of her dreams there if the slogan she's heard about her male-dominated town is accurate: "The odds are good, but the goods are odd." She says that somewhat tongue-in-cheek, of course. She's proud to be from Centennial. After all, not many people can say they are. There are legions of "wannabes" from the out-of-state part-timers, to the waves of church groups who take up residence in the area and bring their followers in for retreats. These newcomers don't always sit well with many in the community, she says, because their motives are not understood or trusted.

Religious groups and other organizations do congregate in this area in part because of the natural beauty and capacity to get away from chaos. Centennial does not seem preoccupied with announcing the number and variety of Christian churches in town. But these mountains and forests attract people like Lindsay, who are more apt to describe themselves as spiritual than religious. And they attract writers, visual artists, musicians, and performers of all types. For a time, the writer Annie Proulx lived in Centennial. She's most famous for being the author of the short story "Brokeback Mountain," upon which the film of the same name was based, featuring the love between two cowboys. And James Michener, author of the historical saga *Centennial*, based some of his story on this area of southeast Wyoming. He was greatly admired here and became friends with Pat Self, who with his wife, Nici, operated the Old Corral restaurant, a bar and steak house that generations of Wyomingites still revere. Their son Murray Self, widely known as Murf, along with his wife, Linda Taylor, operate the Trading Post.

This is the place where I attended the open wedding reception many years ago. It is also a spot where one can hear the Centennial-based band Mumbletypeg. They describe themselves as a "psychedelic/jam/rock & roll band created in a makeshift lab in the mountains of Wyoming."

I visited with two of its members about Centennial culture. Bliss Ragsdale is a Wyoming native and theater professional who after many years in Centennial returned to what is known as West Laramie. More about Bliss later. His bandmate, Ed Barbier, is an economics professor at the University of Wyoming. He obtained his PhD in economics from Birkbeck College at the University of London. Later, he and his wife, Jo Burgess Barbier, held academic positions at the University of York. He is American; she, British. They lived in a very rural area of North Yorkshire, a forty-five-minute commute into York. They wanted to live in a rural small town, a "typical" English village, which he says are disappearing rapidly. They built a cottage and were living where they wanted to be: out in nature, away from cities, where they would raise a family. Ed had a young daughter from a previous marriage, and then the couple had another child born in York. The family moved to Centennial from York in 2000, when Ed accepted his position at UW. Since moving to Centennial, they've had two more children. The two youngest attended school in Centennial until they reached the age to transfer to Laramie. It might have been more convenient for this university couple with young children to find a nice home in town. But Ed says they were used to being away, in a small community, with a pretty drive in to work, with neighbors who were near, but not in a suburban or urban or even small-town setting.

Ed's niche is an environmental economist whose main expertise is natural resource and development economics, as well as the interface between economics and ecology. A small mountain settlement at the base of a resource rich national forest, looking down on a vast valley of sprawling ranchlands toward the bustling college town economy of Laramie, seems a perfect spot for him to consider both the joys Centennial provides and the pressures it faces. That pressure he says is mostly in the form of the vastly wealthy individuals who have discovered the place.

At the end of their careers, people want to think about where to be and where they want to live, Ed says. "Wyoming is attractive for nostalgia, has an appeal to people who see it as the Old West. They have this dream from John Wayne and western movies." He's noticed people who are attracted specifically to Wyoming like it because they don't want to pay taxes, which works out because Wyoming collects no individual or corporate income tax. Ed cites another concept economists and political scientists are tracking, called clustering. "People want to live with people who are like them." He points to Colorado, which has shifted quickly to be a politically blue state, due to a combination of Hispanic immigrants, an influx of liberals who prefer relaxed social policies, and workers who seek green industry jobs in the Denver area. "In the case of Wyoming, it is pretty much all red." Although wealthy individuals want to be close to Denver, they might not want to live there full time. That makes Centennial, a few miles over the state line, a convenient choice. "They escape a blue state to come to red state, with low state taxes, and they are welcomed."

Centennial, however, is nobody's idea of ski-resort-to-the-presidents Jackson Hole, located in the wealthiest county in the state, Teton County. Albany County ranks fourteenth wealthiest out of twenty-three counties. Ed has noticed social stratification, which he senses has always been present in Centennial's long history but is based not on wealth but on lifestyles, such as miners versus ranchers, or loggers versus greenies.

"A lot has been written about income equality and wealth concentration," he says. "No economists deny it; the statistics are clear. It isn't just the one percent, but the five and ten percent." A lot of money and wealth is being accumulated by a small group of people. Some of the wealthy newcomers who've built a second or third or fourth home are hardworking, good people, Ed believes. "Some are not so nice. Some want to change things, some are retired, but wealth is starting to affect community, drive up prices, making it harder for people with any kind of family to live there because of the expense." He's noted that more often people are calling in the sheriff if they don't like what's going on around them. "People used to let people live and let live, but that attitude is increasingly moving in another direction."

Ed has observed that in the absence of a town governing body, power lies on two fronts. One is the business community. All are at least partially female-owned. As an example of their power, the bar owners decided they were tired of cigarette smoke. They didn't introduce a protracted and bitter fight over it, as Laramie did. They just banned it. The other seat of power lies in the various neighborhood associations. The core of Centennial is the strip of business and houses. It is the section of town where someone gives directions to their homes with words like "the blue house" or "the place with all the junk in the yard." But the core area is now dwarfed by the subdivisions. Ed has not heard of the county putting forth any pressure on the community to incorporate, but he feels it is possible they will do so if Centennial continues to grow and sprawl. I remarked that I thought keeping Centennial as it is would be a good thing. Ed agreed that kind of looseness has given Centennial an organic free-for-all feel, which many of us relish. "At the same time it means there is no cohesiveness. Those of us who care feel a loyalty, though others don't have to."

Whether hippie colony or moneyed resort, Centennial's future is at a crossroads. Will the area ever develop enough that it turns into a ski resort like Breckenridge, Colorado, or similar areas once haphazard and now a resort with enough western memes to keep the tourists satisfied? "More likely, it will remain what it has increasingly been turned into: a safe place for people who want to visit, feel happy, feel safe, and that looks clean," Ed said. "It'll become more commercialized. It'll be attractive to outsiders, with a more homogenized feel to it, that doesn't rock the boat or politically upset people." He refers in part to the look of many western towns, which are rustic to the point of dilapidation. But that doesn't mean people don't have pride of place. Old timers have properties filled with the detritus of a life spent there: old cars, broken agricultural equipment, cast-off material goods too cumbersome to haul to a landfill. Arrivals from other parts of the country bring their Eddie Bauer aesthetic with them: log homes, chain-saw-carved bears on the porch, cute painted bird feeders. But to fit in, they know subconsciously at least, they need to have a certain amount of junk. So they prowl antique stores and farm auctions for rusty bits of broken plows, wagon wheels a few spokes short of trustworthy, or little handcarts reminiscent of emigrant trails. They scatter these decorative markers around manicured lawns to show that they belong, or at least they know how to fit in.

One of the things people enjoy about present-day Centennial is the concentration of quirky, exceptionally talented people who gravitate there either to be alone, or to be surrounded by creativity, or both. There are Nobel Prize winners in town, and loner artists, and wealthy people who got that way by being very, very good at some particular thing.

Ed Barbier's Mumbletypeg bandmate Bliss Ragsdale is a staple of Centennial life and represents one of its most dynamic components: brilliant, quirky, and very good at a lot of things. However, unless he is keeping a very deep secret, Bliss is not wealthy. Ed says Bliss represents the "low ambition creative types" who are some of the brightest people he knows. They once filled Centennial but are slowly fading away, "in some cases priced out, in other cases, sadly, dying out."

Bliss tells me he moved to Centennial in the summer of 2001 as an alternative to "living in a van, couch surfing and the like." After a "rocky breakup" with a band in Laramie, he drove his barely functioning van/ home to Centennial and parked in front of a friend's house. There, he stayed for many months, until buying a Jeep and a camper and moving to a campground in the Snowy Range.

Bliss and I arranged to meet one afternoon in Laramie's Buckhorn Bar. We share the same taste in saloons, which runs to the unpretentious, where Pabst Blue Ribbon in sixteen-ounce cans is frequently on special. You can get a mixed drink at the Buck. Just don't ask for wine.

Bliss told me he grew up and attended high school in Green River, Wyoming, in the southwestern part of the state. He went to Western Wyoming Community College, where he says he became "the theater person I am today." He realized that there was more to theater than being an actor, so he decided he'd also focus on technical theater and on directing. Then he returned to Laramie to major in theater but felt pressure to decide between acting, designing, or being what his professors termed a *rock & roll star*. "What's the difference?" he wondered. So, he quit school, played in some bands, went back to Western Wyoming, and teched or directed more musicals. He developed his aesthetic at this time, which held in part that all sorts of arts, including theater, were inappropriately predicated on competition.

He sees some competition as healthy when its purpose is to give people a chance to receive the recognition they deserve for doing good work. But he thinks it takes a toll on younger people trying to figure out what kind of artist they want to be. "When kids from small towns go to college and want to be actors it's because they want to get out of there. When people who are looking for a way to get a break are forced to fight each other for opportunities, they'll ignore the idea of doing art for the art's sake, and nobody tells them they are wrong."

In his early forties now, he's done just about everything in theater, including developing venues. One of these was the Centennial Community Theatre, which he established in the late 1990s, operating out of a large back room at the Trading Post, collaborating with Linda Taylor and others. I was in the audience for their first show, a production of *Harvey*.

"We built lights out of coffee cans," Bliss recalls. "For a dimmer we had a light switch and two power strips." For actors, he found a group of people who had the same experience with theater in Laramie he'd had and were ready for a change. They did shows there for eight summers. He started pushing to bring the company to Laramie, partly because Murf and Linda were hoping to sell the Trading Post. "Laramie represented the application of sheer math: more people to audition, more to come to the show." They dissolved the Centennial Community Theatre and with another group of people he established the Albany County Theatre Company in Laramie. "To make a long story short, we put on good plays that not enough people wanted to see."

He's gotten out of the theater business in Laramie, for now. Instead, he's thinking of putting together an outdoor show, maybe even a melodrama. And then, there's his movie in progress, a horror picture called *Firebox Lake*. Bliss describes his film as a "Scooby-Doo episode with a really high body count." In the average action movie, he calculates, hundreds of people die. But in horror movies, an average of only five people die, he says. "I want to up that. I kill ten people by page five. The opening scene is a slaughter-fest." If all this sounds horribly twisted and graphic, Bliss is quick to point out it is actually intended to be funny. He's been working on and off on the project since 2000, and in 2014 decided it was time to get something done on the film. "It has been going on so long people are starting to make fun of me," he says.

In addition to the slaughter sequences, Bliss has also filmed some scenes in the Trading Post. He invited anyone who wanted to be an extra to come to the bar and just act natural while he filmed. He's also planning to shoot a crowd scene at the lake, with people gathered around a fire pit awaiting the law. He's content to film in tiny Centennial, where he knows the actors and knows the locations. Furthermore, he can film on private land owned by his friends there without having to pay the special-use fees that would be charged were he to film on forest lands. "Also, I prefer to film as far away from other neighbors as possible," he said, "because of the screaming."

He recently codirected a play in Las Vegas and says people there kept asking when he was moving there. "Yes, I could work there, but where would I live?" he asks rhetorically. He owns his house in West Laramie and says if he had extra money he'd rather use it to travel. Besides, he has a dog, some cats, enjoys playing flute and guitar in the band, and likes small towns. He's not married, he says, because he's married to a "pseudo career." Furthermore, not having kids allows him to make "rash decisions." But with a vivid memory of winter even on this warm June afternoon he says: "Being a snowbird is starting to appeal. I could rent out the house to college kids and live in the Caribbean in winter."

Snowbirding is a good remedy. But being a part-timer robs one of a certain amount of cred, that one is able to last not just one Wyoming winter, but can reckon them by the dozens. Yet snowbirding is less drastic than moving away entirely. There were few moments more traumatic for my husband and I than when we took those Steamboat the Bucking Bronc license plates off our cars for the final time, replacing them with their serviceable yet bland Iowa counterparts.

Our friends Brian and Dana Eberhard know that trauma, too. Originally from California, they decided to give up their rat-race professional lifestyle and move to the ski resort town of Steamboat Springs, Colorado. Brian wanted to study for a second bachelor's degree to become a high school social studies teacher. They found themselves spending much of their free time in Laramie and Centennial. They made the move to Laramie and bought a house. He enrolled in college at UW. They got involved in civic organizations, such as Rotary. During that time, they fell in love with the place.

Dana started life as a horse-obsessed little girl and is now a horse-obsessed adult woman. Being in Laramie allowed her to keep her horse and ride in the mountains and plains with her many like-minded friends. Brian's main outdoor exercise is cycling. He can be found riding along the shoulder of the highway on his way to the type of peaks some cars even have trouble summiting, let alone cyclists. They both love to cross-country ski. They love to listen to live music and in fact, Brian has played bass with many of the local musicians. Over the years they've gotten to know and love the diverse and some would say off-beat folks who populate Centennial. Now that Brian has finished his teaching degree through the doctoral level, I imagined they'd be perfect candidates to live in Centennial, either downtown or in one of the subdivisions. And Centennial would likely be happy to have them.

"We talked about living in Centennial because we love it up there, but there were barriers," Dana explained. "Brian needed to be in Laramie so much for school. The commute is not prohibitive for some, but for us it was. It wasn't like we didn't have what we loved in Laramie. Centennial is darn remote, especially in winter. But in Laramie weather doesn't matter. I can still get to Safeway and buy cilantro."

Brian explains what it is about Centennial that appeals so much, that draws them to spend most New Year's Eves in the small, thin-walled rooms of the Friendly Hotel. "We enjoy being with the local people who live at the 'bottom end' getting by working at restaurants or the ski area, or working a mining claim in the mountains. They are young and creative and highly intelligent. They want culture and theater and music and they create it themselves. They have homemade entertainment."

Eventually, the Eberhards faced a time when they had to retire their Wyoming license plates. Brian took a teaching job at a small college in Illinois. Now they spend a few months each summer in Laramie, then head back to Illinois for the academic year. This arrangement is not ideal. Brian finds not being fully engaged in their Illinois home almost as difficult as being away from Laramie. "We are disconnected from both. We want to be totally connected to a place and not commute. We did that already, working in California. I want to walk to work, and walk back home for lunch."

They don't know what the next few years will hold, but no place can ever equal Laramie. Not Los Angeles, nor San Diego, nor the high schools in small California and Nevada towns where they lived while Brian taught. "We have lived in places equally as beautiful as Laramie and were closer to our families, but the communities themselves, if you took away proximity to family, didn't live up to what we found in Laramie, which was the people," Dana said. "There is a breadth of human experience in Laramie that for a town that size is really interesting. For us, Laramie is home."

I imagine Nancy Waldman Taft will soon know that feeling of comparing the rest of the world to Wyoming. She and her husband, Kirk, have decided the time has come to try to find a buyer for their Centennial property and move on. "We thought this was our forever place and that we would never want to move again. But we're itching, we're restless for a change. It's nothing against Centennial. Something else is pulling us away. It is time to trade mountains for oceans."

Hearing those words, I felt sad for Centennial that it was losing two such dynamic and important members of its community. But I also felt a twinge of relief, that someone else understood the unsummoned siren that had called me, in spite of what I always thought would be a lifetime within the Big Square Wonderful. Like me, she understands that boundary walls are porous, only temporarily impervious. It is the job of boundaries to invite exploration of their edges. They tempt us to climb on top and embrace what lies beyond. They are their own invitations to a leap.

BRIDGEPORT, NEBRASKA 2
WHY WOULDN'T YOU WANT THIS?

Even though I can count the years until retirement on two hands, I still have trouble figuring out what I want to be when I grow up. When I was young, my mother coached me past some marginal life choices by saying, "Well, it was a good *experience*." Now I hear my own inner voice, suggesting that by my age, whim and experiment should give way to purpose and proof. Yet here I sit, thinking maybe I should buy a mandolin. Or study Gaelic. Or take a class in earth science. Lying awake in the wee hours, I consider what it might be like to live in Oregon or Rhode Island.

I wonder whether people who live in places bordered by beaches know about sands far away, lying deep beneath prairie sod. Well-drained but nutrient-poor, sand prairies provide home for things that are good at surviving on not much, such as bluestem, sedge, and shrubs, and the wildlife they support. I wonder if that ecology applies to humans there, too. I wonder if knowing the ground beneath us is porous gives us permission to enter the free draining sand and go where gravity takes us.

When I was preparing to leave Wyoming for Iowa I wrote a song to play on my guitar with a group of friends at our monthly jam session. I called it simply "Goodbye To." I contrasted what I was leaving with what I was headed for. I wrote lines like: *Goodbye to men named Cody and women named Cheyenne / goodbye to western meadowlarks, who know who I am / hello red cardinals, berries in the snow / goodbye all my old friends, it's time to go.* I tried to put a dichotomous spin on my relationship to these two worlds. Now I jokingly tell people that I'm not from Iowa, or Wyoming: I say I'm from Wyowa.

Nebraska is a bit of a conjoined entity, as well. The large rectangular section is akin to the row of states it is in: North Dakota, South Dakota, then Kansas, Oklahoma. Mark Stein, in *How States Got Their Shapes*, reports that early Nebraskans didn't want that rugged part in the southwest that was hard to farm or build railroads on. Plus it was full of unruly miners, so they gave it over to

Colorado. The panhandle section that remains thrusts itself into the West, sort of like I did when I moved there in 1992. Maybe that is why whenever I go to that part of Nebraska I feel both foreign and at home.

———————

It seems required of anyone who has driven across Nebraska more than once to assert that nothing is there but cornfields. I'm pretty sure I've heard the same sentiment expressed even by those who've never set a tire or a foot into the big rectangle. It's as if Interstate 80 across Nebraska has achieved superhero status, its superpower being the ability to lull travelers into a trance. Driving all 455 of its miles from east to west is to go from the cornfields of Iowa to the high basins of Wyoming. There are some fifty exits off the interstate, but other than Omaha, few cities or towns greet travelers at the other end of those exits, only their motel and fast food tentacles. But the interstate does have scenery to offer, if you look. It will take you through rolling hills, valleys, and plains. You will flirt with the Platte River, through whose basin some of the interstate's route wends. Two-thirds of the way across Nebraska you'll cross into Mountain Time and see dissected plains, eroded by water and wind. When you finally near the northeastern tip of Colorado you'll assume you are about to leave Nebraska. Instead, you'll be entering the panhandle, eleven counties taking up more than 14,000 square miles, home to about 88,000 people.

One major town in the panhandle area is Ogallala, population 4,737. The town is technically just east of the panhandle, but I include it because that's where you can exit I-80 and veer north onto Highway 26, which diagonals the panhandle region. Although I-80 does parallel historic emigrant trails, it is hard to feel communion with prairie schooners and the like while gripping the steering wheel against the breeze-wake of passing semis on the interstate. Doing sixty-five instead of seventy-five is a slightly better way to consider the emigrant experience along the Oregon and California Trail, and the Mormon Pioneer Trail.

Other major panhandle towns include Alliance, Chadron, Kimball, and Scottsbluff-Gering, the pair of which forms the seventh largest urban area in the state, at about 24,000 residents. Just a little west of the midpoint along Highway 26 between Ogallala and the Wyoming border is the town of Bridgeport, population 1,545. Bridgeport is the county seat of Morrill County. The county's population in 2012 was 4,889, which is about a thousand less than it had in 1970.

Because the panhandle is more than the sum of all its parts, I wanted to talk to someone who had a role to play in each community where it was and helping it reach its goals. That led me to Chuck Karpf, executive director of the Panhandle Area Development District and the Panhandle Resource Conservation and Development, Inc. Chuck is from Morrill, Nebraska. He went to college in Grinnell, Iowa, and then went to work in Omaha for twenty-five years before returning to the panhandle. He has been involved in rural development and entrepreneurship for most of his career. The two organizations share him as their director, but they are separate, with separate boards and separate operating philosophies. They each have their own 501(c)3 designation and operate separately, although they try to work together, as well. They are committed to assisting local communities through five areas of focus: economic development, recreation and tourism, natural resources improvement, community improvement, and education.

Chuck's dual roles mean a double opportunity for him to affect change. "We are a convener for regional action," he explains. "That means taking a 30,000 foot view of a community and what they'd like to see happen." He helps communities put together a comprehensive plan based on surveys and other data. A comprehensive plan is required in order to receive block grant funding, he explains. "Some just do a plan and put it on a shelf and never look at it. If a community uses it properly it helps the community progress. Otherwise, they just keep doing what they were doing. In other places you might as well use it as a doorstop. But Bridgeport is one that pays attention to it. The city administration brings it back to the city council every few months and looks at where they are."

The Bridgeport City Council needs to work on many issues, including demographics, housing, and economic planning issues, Chuck says. There has been an increase in personal incomes but many people there are still poor. The median family income in 2012 was only 77 percent of the statewide median, but that is up from 2000, Chuck says. Transfer payments, such as Social Security, constitutes one-fifth of income in the county, and personal poverty is double the statewide rate. As far as demographics, the population has peaked, Chuck suspects, and the population of those sixty-five or older is greater than the state or national averages. Bridgeport also offers some diversity, with 77 percent white and 20 percent Hispanic residents. This is a fairly typical breakdown of the panhandle region, according to state statistics.

Not wishing to overburden people with too much data, Chuck's group presented a few goals to Bridgeport officials that arose from the planning process. One: market the town as a family friendly community. Two: improve economic vitality and per-capita income by bringing jobs that pay living wages, not just minimum wage. Three: accommodate the needs of the aging population, such as by expanding the nursing home. The other two goals are to provide quality public services and to develop efficient land-use patterns.

Compared to those towns that use their strategic plan as a doorstop, Chuck believes Bridgeport is in better shape because it has good leadership. He cites a newly built community center as an example of what can happen when people take a chance and invest in their future. "The community center went in with a lot of debt, through fees and taxes. Now it is a gorgeous facility with an indoor gym. Facilities like these do not pay for themselves, but they're all quality of life issues that people expect and want." His conclusion about the region's prospects in the face of depopulation and the aging of those who are left? "Rural America has been doing the same thing for years and I don't think those things are going to change," he starts out. He chooses his words carefully as he considers how rural Nebraska could plot a different course. "Maybe by increasing incomes, we would worry less about population and instead about wealth of communities. Everyone wants lower taxes, but maybe that's not the answer. We already have low taxes, yet states with higher taxes grow faster than we do. Maybe we look at something else."

To contemplate a point that seems removed from the Nebraska Panhandle, consider research from the University of Utah about urban sprawl. Researchers are looking at cities and counties that constitute metropolitan areas with no fewer than 200,000 people. They are evaluating four main factors: development density, land use mix, activity centering, and street accessibility. After evaluating these factors, researchers calculated a Sprawl Index score. The higher the score, the more compact. New York City ranked number one for compactness, while Hickory, North Carolina, was the most sprawling of metropolitan areas measured. It turns out that it isn't so much population numbers, but whether the people were densely packed together or far flung. Compactness correlates to many positive features connected to quality of life, at least when people are numerous.

The Nebraska Panhandle is not a metro area, nor is it compact. It is not the sort of place that would be studied by researchers interested in urban sprawl, but rather, in rural sprawl. Morrill County has a population density of four people per square mile. It is obvious that a rural county would not be compared by the sort of criteria as their urban counterparts across the country. But rural areas and small towns are constantly compared to their nearest metropolitan neighbors, and that comparison is sometimes self-inflicted. Small towns need that next bigger fish to get goods and services not available at home. Bridgeport compares itself to Scottsbluff. Scottsbluff compares itself to Cheyenne. Cheyenne, to Fort Collins. Fort Collins, to Denver. What do they have that we need? What do they have we'd just as soon they keep to themselves? That comparison flow can also be reversed. What did we used to have that is gone now because of the Walmart in X, or the factory closing in Y, or the consolidated school in Z?

Steve Frederick, as editor of the *Scottsbluff Star-Herald*, has had more than twenty-five years to observe how people in various sized communities in the panhandle face those questions, and how they set about answering them. Compared to other small panhandle towns Steve has observed, he considers Bridgeport a "going little community." He grew up in Oregon, and when he was starting out in journalism, Oregon was economically a dead end. "There are only so many newspapers, and all those jobs were locked up. I was never going to own a home or work for a bigger paper unless it was in a big city." So he left Oregon. When he came to Scottsbluff, Steve says "everything opened up." He was able to buy a house, raise a family, and work his way up from copyeditor to editor-in-chief at his paper.

Although he is glad he made the move, he said he is still considered an outsider. That fact speaks to both the cohesiveness of a community whose individuals have a lot in common, and the difficulty those commonalities present to those who wish to inject new ideas. Although the small towns and large communities of the panhandle have different challenges, they do hold together as an identifiable region. For instance, compared to the rest of Nebraska, the panhandle has a more western influence. "This is cattle country," Steve explains. "More than fifty percent of our economy is based on cattle. This is real cowboy life, not Hollywood cowboy life."

He also sees some similarities and counterpoints to Wyoming. That state is every bit as Republican and conservative as Nebraska, but there is a difference, he believes. "In Wyoming, more people are libertarian, iconoclastic, and just want to be left alone. People there don't wake up thinking about politics. In Nebraska, politics are way more dogmatic and conformist. If you aren't a Nebraska Cornhuskers fan, or if you are a Democrat, keep it to yourself. They don't want people wandering off the reservation, politically."

People in the state must have an inkling they do tend to be a bit intense, and it is something they are working on. As a start, the tourism commission adopted "Nebraska Nice" as its state slogan. They say it is partly to conjure the pleasant feeling people have when they recall their latest vacation in the state. It is also a reflection that people here are nice to visitors and each other. Steve Frederick says people mostly are in fact quite nice, because most of the time they remember not to talk politics.

However, one result of strong feelings being hog-tied by niceness can be that innovation is stifled, Steve believes. "They've seen depopulation and don't feel anything can be done to substantially improve things. People who are new to the area, or people who've left then returned, tend to be the ones presenting the innovative ideas." Yet those ideas are sometimes resisted. For example, downtown Scottsbluff once had stoplights at every intersection, which added up to a half dozen or more. The city took them out and added other traffic control features to create a more walkable downtown. The farmers market is held in that space now, making it a social event for the community. Yet the paper received letters complaining the changes made parking too hard. "We have a much better downtown now, but some people are against 'newfangled' ideas," he said.

In another instance, some people resisted the renaming of a road through town to Old Oregon Trail, which was dreamed up as a tourism effort to spotlight the town's position along the historic trail. But a few people objected to having to change their physical address on business documents, so the road changes names back and forth to accommodate them. "Why wouldn't you want your business to be on Old Oregon Trail?" he wonders.

As a newspaper editor, Steve knows about all controversial issues that have faced the region in his time there. Some involve the sort of bickering that takes place in any town in a democracy, when people feel strongly and need to compromise to get anything done. One local issue that has a larger tourism impact has to do with the Scottsbluff National Monument. The monument is focused around an 800-foot bluff. This landmark has been important for people from Native Americans to emigrants on the Oregon, California, and Mormon Trails, to modern travelers.

Most visitors only see the monument from the road. But park visitors can actually climb the bluffs for an aerial view. Others have a semiaerial view because they've built homes on slopes lower than the bluff tops but still higher than town. From there, a fine view of both the monument and of the ever-growing Gering landfill presents itself. Many folks say the landfill is intolerable in the viewscape of this historically significant place. But it has been there since the 1940s, and people knew it was there before they built their homes with it visible from their porches. The city council reviewed the possibility of relocating the landfill but balked at the two-million-dollar price tag to do so. Now the discussion is about how high the trash can go. "Who builds a landfill in a place like that," Steve asks rhetorically, describing this as a case of dug-in-heels that attracts sometimes embarrassing national media attention.

Other issues trouble his city and also the small panhandle communities alike. "There is a gap between the skill level of people and the jobs that are available. Kids who go to college move away, and it is hard to lure them back, so we have to lure people who've never been here. To them it sounds like the end of the world. It really is not. It is a hardworking community with a good work ethic and a good school system," he says of Scottsbluff. "At the same time, there is a transient population, with high school dropouts, a high teen birth rate, and people who don't get educated well enough to do the jobs that are really needed."

True, life in Scottsbluff and in the smaller communities of the panhandle has its bumps. I wondered during our conversation if Steve maintains his contentment with small-town life because he takes frequent breaks from it, maybe heading a few hours away to Denver for an urban fix. Not so.

"I'm a small town guy at heart. I like to fish and write about fishing. I like to get in the car and explore. I can be out of cell phone range in half an hour." He told me about a recent trip to Seattle to visit a friend there. He noted that because of the way the mountains and the water are situated, it is almost impossible to go anywhere there without getting funneled onto a twelve-lane freeway. Everything they do there is dictated by traffic. "There are really cool things there. But here I can get to work in six minutes."

He senses that other people are starting to feel the allure of his adopted state. "Nebraska is no longer just a backwater," he says of the changing attitudes of people on both coasts. "The tide can't go out forever. The population of the planet is doubling, and people have to live somewhere. We have low unemployment, low crime: why wouldn't you want it?"

I could think of several reasons I would want it, and only a few why I would not. Then I realized he meant you in the second-person plural, not you as in me. Yet I'm very familiar with this part of the country, having spent a lot of time here, albeit mostly in my car. On a recent trip from Iowa to Wyoming I saw my chance to escape I-80, and took the cutoff to Highway 26 at Ogallala. You can start to feel a hint of the westernness Steve Frederick noted, at that point along the trail. Maybe that's because the elevation is over 3,200 feet, with only about eighteen inches of precipitation a year, on average. That means less of the color green, and more of the color brown. That means fewer crops watered by clouds, and more irrigated by wells. And it means more use of western fonts on town signage and websites. Ogallala's website features a silhouette of a cowboy on horseback driving a steer. The town's economy and lifestyle is more diverse than what that image conveys, but they are staking the territory many western communities stake: standing firmly on the agricultural traditions they are known for while nervously realizing that at some point they must rebrand.

Driving northwest on Highway 26 past Ogallala means taking in Lake McConaughy. This twenty-two-mile-long reservoir was created by damming the North Platte River. It is a popular recreation destination and the largest reservoir in the state. A few miles west, Highway 26 crosses out of Keith County and into Garden County. The road forks at Bridgeport. One fork continues westerly toward Scottsbluff, then the Wyoming border, another fifty miles away. Along that route are natural sites like Courthouse Rock, Jail Rock, the Chimney Rock Historic Site, and the Scotts Bluff National Monument. The other fork leads to Highway 385 north. Less than forty miles along that route is Alliance. Fifty-file miles beyond Alliance, the town of Chadron is home to the Museum of the Fur Trade. To the southwest of Chadron is the town of Crawford and Ft. Robinson. Fort Robinson is a former US army fort and a present-day state park located in the Pine Ridge region. To stand for any time in the panhandle region with open eyes certainly does invite the question: why wouldn't you want this?

Cue the academics at the state's land-grant university, who developed a useful research project as a way to market this highly rural state. Researchers noticed 2000 US Census figures showing that new residents are moving to the Nebraska Panhandle, in spite of what has been documented about overall rural depopulation. The study alludes to the Buffalo Commons scenario, as developed by New Jersey-based researchers Drs. Frank and Deborah Popper. They felt that large areas of the Great Plains were on track to lose population so quickly that prairie restoration would be the most appropriate use for those deserted ranches, empty farms, and dilapidated towns. As the University of Nebraska-Lincoln (UN-L) study introduction states, "The Poppers saw the rapid decline in rural populations throughout the Great Plains as an 'inevitable disaster' where deaths exceeded births; farms, businesses, and communities were forced to close down, and residents were forced to move on. The proposal to reverse this disaster was to return about 140,000 square miles of the Great Plains to their 'pre-white condition', or the way the Great Plains was found by the settlers in the 19th Century."

One doesn't even have to visit the Great Plains to get their point. Just look at a road map. The farther east, the more crowded the map becomes with all those town names and highways. The farther west, the map reflects the reality of elbow room between towns, and roads that wend around obstacles of landscape. Yet UN-L researchers believe that people will always remain in the Great Plains areas. That's why in 2005 they began an examination of new residents in rural communities. Data from the 2000 Census indicated that 20 percent of people in rural western Nebraska were new residents. Census data did not indicate where these folks came from or why they were there; however, UN-L researchers had anecdotal evidence that communities in the panhandle were attracting new residents from the Denver area. They were hearing that people were finding Denver too full of the problems of poverty, crime, and crowding that tarnished the appeal of the place. Researchers believed that if they understood why those folks chose the panhandle specifically, additional new residents could be recruited to move to the region.

Key findings of this research, published in 2007, were these: new residents rated the high cost of living and urban congestion as the top reasons for leaving their previous community. The top rated reasons newcomers move to their current communities involve quality-of-life amenities. These include a simpler pace of life, a less congested area, and proximity to family. Other reasons for moving to the panhandle included the decreased cost of living, the quality of the natural environment, and the presence of higher-paying jobs. Families cited the better environment in which to raise children and better quality schools as reasons for moving to the panhandle.

The City of Bridgeport is essentially in the center of the panhandle, and also in the epicenter of the region the Poppers suggested would be best used as prairie. In 1990, Bridgeport had 1,592 people. In 1998, there were 1,610 folks. But in 2009 the population dipped to its lowest point, 1,439. In 2012 it had rebounded to 1,511. So yes, people are moving there, on and off. But why don't they all stay? That's one thing the City of Bridgeport wanted to find out when it did its most recent community survey, a follow up on one they did in 1999. The 2011 Bridgeport survey report shows that 196 out of 469 surveys were returned. The majority of those who responded were age sixty-five and over, and had lived in the Bridgeport area for twenty years or more. The lowest respondents were people with children under the age of four and people who have lived in the Bridgeport area for less than five years. One explanation is that people who have lived in the community the longest had formed the strongest opinions and wanted to give voice to those. Another likely and not contradictory explanation is that they believe their voices carried the weight of experience, and had a chance of being heard.

One question not included in the 1999 survey was about economic opportunity. People who have lived in the area between ten and nineteen years had a satisfaction rate of 28 percent in that category. People who have lived in the area for less than five years have a satisfaction rate of just over 56 percent. It cannot be known from the survey, but it is possible the most satisfied people are those who came to the Bridgeport area because they were adequately prepared to take the kind of job that is in demand, as Steve Frederick suggested.

Also seeking to get at the jobs issue, another survey question reads: "If you have children who live outside of Bridgeport, what do you think could motivate them to move to Bridgeport?" Responses can be summarized as jobs, jobs, jobs, nothing, jobs, and jobs. "I encourage them to get out of Bridgeport and go someplace they can succeed," one wrote. "Bridgeport is too overrun by drugs and that's all kids have here" wrote another. "Housing that doesn't eat a paycheck," suggested another. "Jobs that pay from $100,000 to $200,000 and homes ranging from 3,000 to 5,000 square feet. And better weather."

Although the city cannot do much about that final respondent's wishes about the weather, other comments might prompt action. From the returned surveys, we learn that people are highly satisfied with city parks, the library, fire protection, garbage collection, the golf course, electric services, and the ambulance/EMS. They were moderately satisfied with street lighting. The community center was nice but some surveyed felt fees were too high. Poor sidewalks seemed to be an issue, and there could be fewer loose cats. Downtown needed more variety of business and better parking. Besides economic opportunities, some other categories that had less than 50 percent satisfaction, including condition of railroad crossings, the housing market, water service, town appearance, recycling, street maintenance, and storm-water drainage. Availability of recreational opportunities scored just over 58 percent satisfaction. People really liked getting out of town to the Bridgeport State Recreation Area for camping, and fishing at the small lake. The most frequent comment in this category was that most residents would like more entertainment venues such as skating rinks, movies theaters, bowling alleys. By my count, the word "bowling" was written thirty-five times by these 196 citizens.

One of those could have been Bridgeport native Stacey Watts. She and her husband, Shawn, spent the early years of their marriage in Fort Worth, Texas, where he is from. But when they started a family, they came to view Fort Worth not as a big city that could offer enriching opportunities for their family, but as a place where bringing up children was not appealing. So they moved back to Stacey's hometown. She teaches fifth grade, and he works at a local co-op and runs the family's small cattle operation.

Stacey says they are quite happy to be back among her family and that they love the town. However, "There is not much for the youth to do besides driving around." She's grown tired of driving to Scottsbluff in all kinds of weather to do things with their three children. She had enjoyed the town bowling alley as a kid, but it closed down around the time she graduated from high school, in 1997. It sat vacant, enduring roof damage and other issues, but was basically intact. The Watts decided they should purchase the building and restore it to its early glory, giving themselves a business to operate and the kids in town something to do. They bought it in June 2014. "When we turned on the power for the first time we were cheering." All the balls started rolling back down from behind the machines where they'd been since the last ball was hurtled down the lane. "It was a time warp," she said. "The shoes were still behind the counter."

They've named the place Bowldog Lanes, a play on the school's nickname, the Bulldogs. They hope bowling will be part of elementary and high school physical education classes. The alley can also be a site for birthday parties and youth leagues. They intend to make part of the space into a sports bar and install several large televisions and a video arcade. Shawn will work there during the day and Stacey will pitch in once the school day concludes. If there is community support, she figures they'll hire several employees to staff the sports bar.

I'd noticed that bowling alley in my last visit to Bridgeport in summer 2014. I'd seen some of the less appealing areas of town that residents had noted in the survey, with the broken sidewalks and boarded-up storefronts. But I also saw inviting sights, like the Pioneer Trails Museum, restaurants that looked promising, an attractive old train depot, and a sense of the area's history embodied in signage for the old trail crossing that gave the town its name. I spent some time at the lake. At noon on a summer weekday, it was lively with people fishing and picnicking, or just driving up and down, checking out who was there on this warm June afternoon. I could see how this sort of natural beauty was an important amenity to residents of this small town. It would be nice to be able to sit and look at water and pleasant surroundings, enjoy a bit of nature during a hectic day, just a few miles from town. Enjoyment of the outdoors is something that can't be bottled but can be engrained, and in my observation is a key reason many people love small-town life. Being able to see the edge of town from where you live or work gives hope that soon it'll be five o'clock, or the weekend, and you'll have a chance to get out of that office or work place and go play outside.

Very few acres of land are set aside for public access in most midwestern states, so residents make good use of their small local parks. Photograph © Julianne Couch.

That is an impulse that Melody Leisy understands and appreciates not only personally but professionally, as a nurse in the public health system. She is the medical response system coordinator for the Panhandle Public Health District based in Bridgeport. Her husband used to work for the railroad in Alliance, which because of distance and long hours was not great for a family lifestyle. So he took a job for the Nebraska Division of Natural Resources' Bridgeport field office. Then three years ago he purchased a chemical-spraying lawn business, and Melody helps with the business. "He loves it, and we're able to make a living. We have no reason to get discouraged. We have what we need."

Melody was born and raised in Bridgeport, graduated from high school there, attended a community college, and then got her bachelor's degree in nursing. She worked in a variety of medical centers from small hospitals to medical oncology. After four years working in chemotherapy, she was burned out. She and her husband moved to Bridgeport, where she has worked in public and preventative health care for the last ten years.

As a public-health professional, she sees the strengths of her community's health and well-being, as well as areas where it could improve. Bridgeport is a community that doesn't shy away from surveying people. The department was culling the findings from its own community wide survey when Melody and I talked, looking at how they might build on identified community strengths. Positive health behaviors she's noticed in Bridgeport include people getting up and moving much more than they used to. Melody started running for exercise in 2006, and says that as a result she lost weight and became much healthier. At the time she started, she saw very few other runners out hitting the pavement. "Now I see people out all the time, taking part in 5K fundraisers, and so on." Another key to health is that the local grocery stores take part in the NuVal nutritional scoring system, which makes it easier for shoppers to select healthier foods from the shelves.

While these trends are indeed positive, there are also some areas for concern, she says. There was a time when a family physician served the community for decades, and built trust within the community. Those days are mostly gone. Now doctors come to town for just a few years at a time as a way to satisfy requirements of their medical-school loans. Although the Morrill County Hospital is located in Bridgeport, people are willing to drive a little farther to go to a larger town's hospital. Indeed, I had noticed in the 2011 community survey comments voicing dissatisfaction with local health-care and emergency-response services, not so much around quality of care but around perceptions of confidentiality. It made me consider how I would feel if I'd had a car accident or medical incident, and the young man in Bellevue I know best as my plumber was the one who showed up to rescue me. He's a dedicated member of the Volunteer Fire Department, and I'd be grateful for his help, of course, but I would feel less self-conscious bleeding on a stranger than on the guy who replumbed my kitchen a few years ago. But that's small-town life, in a nutshell.

Melody seemed to sense my thoughts as she returned to an assessment of her town's strengths. "When we talk about resources in this rural community, we talk about the people, not the things," she says. That means they talk about the people with the capability and the energy to get things done. It is these movers and shakers who believe in a sense of community, and giving back, and seeing the bigger picture. At the same time, Melody has seen from a quick review of the public-health survey that newcomers relocating to Bridgeport have challenges fitting in. "People who have lived in a big city and come here struggle at first. For example, they complain when the stores aren't open 24/7. Then they realize a deeper meaning behind it: maybe the store isn't open because the family is together. Maybe that isn't the reason at all, but they do think about it for long enough to get that concept." She's also seen from respondents that they like Bridgeport's location at the intersection of a north-south and an east-west highway. It means they have regional offices of many state agencies, such as the Nebraska DNR, the Nebraska Natural Resources district, a Health and Human Services office, and a whole slew of offices as the seat of county government. Cheyenne and Denver aren't too far away. That proximity can also bring problems in, she notes. They do have domestic violence and theft issues in town, which she attributes to drug traffic. Now that marijuana has been legalized in Colorado, she wonders if those pot users are also involved in illegal drugs. Possibly people find Bridgeport an easy location to hide out for a while because it is rural and off the radar. Just a few years after Colorado legalized marijuana use, Wyoming raised the speed limit on I-80 to eighty miles per hour. Now the local joke is "Colorado got the pot, and Wyoming got the speed." That raises the question of what Nebraska got.

A quick look at a national crime statistics comparison shows that Bridgeport's crime rate is low. Looking back to 2001, the total crime index was 8.70, with the national average being 100. This figure earned the town a grade of A+. While "grades" are just one organization's way of making statistics tangible, this site is readily available online and no doubt many people besides me have used it to compare their community with others. If perception is reality, I'd sure choose an A place over a D place.

Melody says she and her husband feel comfortable about their two young sons's safety in Bridgeport. To help keep an extra watchful eye on them, she is very involved with youth in the community, coaching Little League and girls' volleyball. Because Melody knows the local youth well, I wondered if she had noticed an attitude that they couldn't wait until they were old enough to leave Bridgeport and head to someplace like Denver, where jobs and fun and potential mates abound. "As freshmen and sophomores, some have dreams about going away," she told me. "But by the time they are juniors or seniors, they are looking at going away but with a pathway to come back eventually."

That is different than the attitude of her peers when they were that age, she recalls. These days, she says, a few of her friends from high school who've moved away still send her that "why are you still there vibe." But now her friends who have left and are living more urban lives are seeing that people in small towns also have rich lives and fulfilling experiences. "That's because we do get out, travel around the country and the world. The stereotype that people in small towns don't have any 'experiences' is not true," Melody said. She's starting to sense a change in attitude among her friends who've left that maybe it is becoming cool to live in rural America.

For small rural towns that are fighting for survival, a common weapon is the colorful past. History is used to inoculate the community against the ravages of depopulation, aging, poverty, and functional obsolescence. Towns celebrate the stories of their founding, of their ancestors, of their European or Native American culture. And in doing so, they just about wear out their current residents under the burden of volunteerism, the pressure to maintain a place not so much because it is needed, but because it is wanted, at least by some and at least for now. The town may die a death one day, but it won't be on their watch. That's why to succeed communities can't rely only on homage to the past, using western imagery on town signs to entice tourists to yet another agrarian theme park. They must also consider the visible present and the viable future.

Bridgeport is trying to do just that. It hosts three major events annually that appeal to locals and tourists alike, and takes over for what nearby towns cannot do themselves. It plays on its historic trail history and hosts an annual event called Camp Clarke Days, held each spring. The Camp Clarke Bridge Site just outside Bridgeport dates from 1875. This is the location of a toll bridge built in that year by entrepreneur Henry T. Clarke, who provided a crossing over the North Platte River for what became the Sidney-Black Hills Trail. Now the town event includes nineteenth-century-style rendezvous and other activities. Then, each July the town holds its Independence Day celebration, which doubles as a class reunion for past graduates of the high school and as an informal homecoming event for folks who've left town but come back for a visit during the summer. Then each August, Bridgeport is the site of an annual festival for the Assumption Orthodox Church. The church is located sixteen miles away in Bayard, but the festival takes place in

Bridgeport because of the facilities the community center offers. It attracts up to a thousand people for traditional food, music, and other activities related to Greek heritage.

Those are three major events in less than three months that take place in Bridgeport. Pulling it off requires volunteers with energy and devotion. So says Steve Plummer, who has lived in Bridgeport most of his life and is president of the Bridgeport City Council. He is also a Shriner, a board member of the Nebraska Sports Council, a board member for a community college, and more. It goes without saying he contributes time and effort to all three of the town's festivals. "When you are in a small town you wear a lot of hats," he said.

Steve sees the town's placement at the intersection of two highways as an advantage it has over other panhandle communities. He's also glass-half-full cheerful about the fact that the nearest large town is almost forty miles away. "Some here do prefer to go out of town for groceries, dentist, doctor, and prescriptions. But people here bond together more than they might in places that are closer to a big town. That means they can support stronger business here." He ticks off evidence of this claim, and indeed, the list is impressive for a town of this size. There are two pharmacies, two groceries, the hospital, a dentist, a chiropractor, an optometrist, the community center, twelve restaurants, ten churches, a library, a museum, the bowling alley, and four banks. "That's an ATM for every 375 people!" As proof of his theory about how being too close to a larger town can kill off a small town, he points to Bayard. Although the population of Bayard is about 1,200, it has just one bank, one grocery store, and no hospital. And it holds its church festival in the Bridgeport Community Center. Steve cites Bayard's proximity to Scottsbluff—less than twenty-five miles compared to more than thirty-two from Bridgeport—as being too near for local shoppers to resist the allure. Being somewhat remote but at a highway crossroads accounts for Bridgeport surviving and in some ways prospering, he says. In fact, Bridgeport recently passed a $9 million bond issue to build a new school. "The community is vibrant for the size we are."

Steve was born in Scottsbluff, and his family moved to Bridgeport when he was an infant. He went to college in Hastings, Nebraska, in the southeast part of the state. He worked in a variety of occupations, such as selling cars and working for the railroad. Then he bought an insurance agency from a man who was retiring. The man knew the Plummer family, who had been customers of the agency, and the families went back a number of years. "He wanted to leave it to someone who'd take care of it." Now, Steve has a succession plan of his own. His son is preparing to buy the insurance business as Steve himself looks toward retirement. "All three of my kids are entrepreneurs or business owners. All of them want to stay here."

Succession planning is important not just for businesses, but for dealing with agricultural property as older generations pass on and adult children have to decide whether to share the land, develop it themselves, buy out the others, or sell outright. It might seem odd, but in spite of all the 22,000 square miles of the panhandle far from urban areas, there is almost no place one can go anywhere to explore it, other than via the paved or graveled roadways. And that's not true of just the panhandle. That's true of the whole state, which has lots of beautiful places that would be a treasure to explore, if only one could get to them. But almost all of it is in the hands of private property owners.

All states have some public lands. Public owners can include the federal government, the state government, and tribal governments. Most of the states with large swaths of land in public ownership are in the West. They include places like Alaska, Nevada, Utah, Idaho, and Wyoming. Some people argue that having most of the land in public ownership allows a management style that keeps people away from the resources they feel should be available to the public. Sure, people who have the time, funds, and inclinations to vacation in national parks or state forests enjoy their experiences, they allow. But these lands cannot be directly accessed for multiple uses like grazing, or for coal mining, for gas drilling, and so forth, without an extensive permitting process. By contrast, states that produce most of our nation's food are associated with private ownership. According to US Census data, Kansas is number one for private ownership, followed by Iowa, Nebraska, Texas, and Indiana. The people who feel strongly that land belongs in the hands of private property owners are probably very pleased about states like these. But what about public access to hunting, fishing, hiking, and other forms of recreation on lands that are locked up by private owners? Some states have access agreements with landowners that allow hunters to legally enter a property for the purpose of deer hunting and so forth, which wildlife managers deem necessary for ecological balance. But anyone driving through the Nebraska Panhandle who wants to pull over and walk across a pretty stretch of grasslands and photograph a spectacular sunset is mostly likely trespassing the minute they step out of the car.

An organization called Platte River Basin Environments (PRBE) is hoping to make a dent in the public access problem in the panhandle area. This nonprofit corporation was formed by a group of sportsmen of western Nebraska "concerned about deteriorating conditions of important wildlife habitat and the natural areas in the North Platte River basin," according to their website. Their task is to "preserve, conserve, enhance, and restore vital wildlife habitat and natural areas within the North Platte River basin and adjacent drainages with a commitment to applying sound environmental science to determining projects to be undertaken, restoration work to be completed, enhancements to be done, and areas to be conserved and preserved."

Since its inception, PRBE and its partners have acquired more than 33,000 acres in the Wildcat Hills and Pine Ridge areas through ownerships, easements, and management or cooperative agreements. More than 29,000 of those acres have been opened up to the public for educational, scientific, and recreational use. Other projects include developing a trail system that will span the organization's properties and establish a partnership with the US Fish and Wildlife Service to help private landowners restore more than 16,000 acres along the North Platte River.

For me, as an avid user of public lands in spite of my suburban upbringing and current residence in a private property state, this is huge. Steve Frederick, the Scottsbluff newspaper editor, is involved with this organization through his tourism efforts. He told me that the PRBE appeals to ranchers who are nearing retirement and are considering succession plans for their properties. Not everyone has a family who wants to keep land in agriculture. PRBE helps these landowners continue what Steve calls their "landowner ethos" in a slightly different way, assuring that their conservation practices are respected into the future. PRBE currently has thirteen properties in wildlife habitat lands, which means thousands of acres for wild things to flourish. But that's also thousands of acres less heavily invested in agricultural activities.

Steve Frederick addresses concerns about land use changes. "Many of the lands are in the Wildcat Hills or along the North Platte River, and they're not prime farmland. Some of them are grazed or farmed, however. Some of the PRBE lands get converted to Wildlife Management Areas, and others simply provide public easements for allowed activities, such as hunting, fishing, and hiking. In most cases the previous owners wanted the lands preserved and were willing to give them up or grant the easements rather than see them spoiled by the wrong kind of development."

By "wrong kind of development," he means in part the sort of rural acreage and subdivision property that strongly appeals to people who want to live in a beautiful, wide-open environment without being remote from jobs and other conveniences in town. However, there are some people who do not like seeing those choices placed out of reach. Indeed, working lands are an important part of a healthy rural community. Taking lands out of agriculture does mean a change. But Steve Frederick points out two important considerations. First, these lands aren't necessarily taken out of use. There are still ranching operations, with both wildlife and livestock able to use these lands in concert, as they have for many years. Second, other land uses can also be positive for the community, he says. "There is a bit of an impact when land gets taken off the tax rolls. In general, ag land is more productive economically. But that's offset by tourism," he said, "and will be more so in the future as the public gets familiar with the opportunities."

I've started quizzing my friends and acquaintances both from the urban part of my life and from the more rural about their own preferences and expectations. If you were starting out now and raising a family, I ask them, would you rather do so in a big city or in a small town, and why. Obviously I'm creating a false binary—"big city" is a broad descriptor of the urban experience, and towns are "small" as matters of comparison. The people I ask consistently identify urban areas as a good choice because of the cultural amenities, diversity of people their children would encounter, opportunities to participate in sports and other activities not widely available in smaller schools. And living in a town with only a few hundred people that is more than thirty miles from a large town translates into way too much time in the car. That would be just as bad as being in the middle of a large city and driving an hour each day just to get to work. But "small town near bigger city" is usually what my acquaintances reply, possibly not considering that small towns close to large cities might not stay small for long.

A few say they prefer life in the country, on a farm or ranch, where children can learn to work hard. One such friend is Nancy Curtis. She lives near Glendo, Wyoming, a town of just a few hundred people. The town is on Interstate 25 and is about seventy-five miles from the western edge of the Nebraska Panhandle, as the crow flies. But crows don't take the highway route, and Nancy doesn't live in town. Rather, she has spent decades living and working on her family's cattle ranch. When she isn't performing one of a hundred ranch chores, she runs her own publishing company, High Plains Press. Nancy told me about a recent conversation with her nine-year-old granddaughter. The young girl had told Nancy that she likes living in the country because it gives her a chance to help. Nancy explained that her granddaughter helps garden, move, sort, and work cattle on horseback, and care for chickens. "She does things that make her feel like she is an asset to the family, not just someone to be cared for."

Nancy points out that a child can and should be raised to feel like an asset to the family, regardless of where that family lives. But her granddaughter's perspective made Nancy think about the difference between what it is to be a helper and what it is to be truly responsible for something. "Plenty of kids have a chore chart: make your bed, pick up the towels, take out the garbage." But on the ranch, the whole family is involved in work that requires cooperation from a lot of people, each with a job.

"When we move the cattle home for the winter, it takes someone to lead the way with the pickup and open gates—usually an older person, maybe with some little kids secured in the pickup; several horsemen to gather the cattle and move them along—experienced people, including kids, who know what they are doing; someone to guard a known weak spot in the fence where calves sneak through—a non-horseman adult, maybe a novice; someone to make a warm meal for when the work is done—grandma, babies," she said. "A kid can see that everyone is truly needed to do work that is important. It's different than a chore."

So work, such as ranching, makes a child feel needed and respected. I asked Nancy how that might translate into a young person's future choices of where and how to live. "I think it might make a difference in the long term for a kid to see that they contribute something of value to the family, that they aren't just someone that needs to be taken to soccer practice and piano lessons." The hope is, a young person who feels not superfluous, but actually needed, might realize that the smaller the town, the more important each set of willing hands. That might give that young person incentive to find what Melody Leisy called the path back home, after graduating from high school and spending some time away.

Just as it is important to have a succession plan for a family, it is important to have a succession plan for a community. Will a business simply close, or will it find a new owner to keep it going for another generation? Will land be divided within a family, or placed into public hands, sold to develop housing, or zoned for commercial use by a small town that badly needs both in order to grow? Just like a family, the legacy of a town is something that can, and should, be thoughtfully managed. Bridgeport has its problems like everyplace else, but if self-awareness is a trait of resilience, the town should continue to be the anchor community for a large swath of the Nebraska Panhandle.

NORTON, KANSAS

3

ON THE CUSP OF THRIVING

Paradoxically, the more I contemplate small-town culture, the more I find myself considering Kansas City, both the part in Missouri and the part in Kansas. That's where I was born and raised, but I took a very different path in my life and now I know almost no one there, outside of my family. Some of my acquaintances have simply faded into the past, as happens with most lives of any duration. It is also because of Kansas City's increasing population that the pool of people I do know has become diluted in the ocean of those I do not.

I also mention Kansas City frequently because it is an important metropolitan hub in this region from the Mississippi River to the Rocky Mountains. In far western Kansas, the lights of Kansas City are dimmer than those of Denver. People go to Denver for the mountains, not to Kansas City for the barbeque. Football fans are more likely to root for the Broncos than for the Chiefs. Norton's location on the high plains near the 100th meridian puts it at the spot where it is said the West begins. One term of that premise has to do with climate. With average annual rainfall of about twenty-one inches, crops are usually irrigated with groundwater, not watered from abundant rainfall. The 100th meridian marks the shift from the "humid continental" to the "semi-arid" climate and resulting environments. When I get this far west, I can feel the High Plains in the loft of my tires and in the broadening of the view from my windshield as I crest each hill. Eventually, the hills soften and flatten, and the view isn't so much about distance as it is circumference.

Norton County is in the northern tier of counties on the Kansas/Nebraska border. It is four counties over from the Kansas/Colorado border. They grow wheat here, graze cattle, pump a little gas and oil from the ground. The area is heavily Republican, Christian, and white. That makes it very different from Kansas City or Denver but gives it much in common with eastern Colorado. In fact, eleven counties in eastern Colorado voted in 2013 on whether to secede from their state and form a new one. They didn't like where Colorado was headed, with its marijuana legalization and other mani-

55

festations of liberal politics. Eastern Colorado folks looked for a model and found conservative western Kansas, where the central premise is farming, family, and being left alone. Of those eleven counties given the opportunity to vote on the question, six voted no, but five voted yes. This so-called 51st State Initiative has not died down in spite of its defeat and will continue to make its case in various public forums around Colorado.

Ad astra per aspera—"to the stars through difficulties." The Kansas state seal uses those words, printed in all caps on a banner hung above thirty-four stars, representing each state in the union at the time Kansas joined. I've come to interpret the reference to stars not to mean turning to heavenly bodies in times of need, but to turn to each other.

––––––––––––

Aaron Hale is a typical small-town guy who left home after high school graduation and thought he'd never look back. A native of Norton, he attended community college in Great Bend, Kansas, then a vocational-technical school in Goodland, Kansas, to study telecommunications. He joined the Kansas National Guard and served as part of Operation Iraqi Freedom. He worked in the broadband technology field in Lawrence, which is just outside Kansas City and home to the University of Kansas. He worked for one company, then for another company, then for a third company that bought out the second one. Such is the way of corporate life.

"I didn't want to go through this again," he said of the last buyout. "My job wasn't in jeopardy, but I was just getting tired of the corporate feel and seeing the reduction of more than half of the staff. That was a little bit more reason for me to start thinking about possibilities." He said he struggled between sticking with a company that was treating him well, and listening to his nagging urge to get out. He and his wife of six years had started their family and were thinking about the future. She is from Council Grove, Kansas, much closer to Lawrence than Norton. They made frequent trips to visit his extended family, especially during holidays and harvest to help on his father's farm. Together they started asking, "What if we moved to Norton?"

On the one hand, after twelve years in Lawrence, they had put down "pretty good roots." They were part of a gardening group, a beer-brewing group, and a charcuterie club. "Ultimately in our hearts we felt like this is something we can't ignore—the feeling, the draw to be near family, to raise our kids in a rural community, to help out with the family farm. Those factors outweighed the earnings potential and the interesting unique groups, the friendships, the church family. Our desire to live in a small community prevailed."

Aaron estimates that Lawrence is the most liberal town in Kansas, so coming from Norton to Lawrence and back again gives him a unique perspective, "My views have always been conservative in some areas, so being in a college-town environment was interesting to see." For example, Douglas County, where Lawrence is located, sells alcohol on Sundays, although that is not available in Norton County. "That is not a big deal, but I can see there are some political items and policies where we may be a little bit behind and that maybe people are starting to question." Loosening some of those policies might make Norton a more attractive place to outsiders. He calls the Norton community "pretty conservative" partially because of the farming culture that "breeds that alignment." That, and the strong Christian faith.

There are twelve churches in Norton. Although Christian churchgoers have a choice when it comes to houses of worship, it wouldn't be convenient for people of other faiths. For those choosing to worship in a synagogue, Wichita would be the closest community in Kansas to do so. There are synagogues in Nebraska, but Lincoln, near the Iowa border, is the closest. These choices would all be several hours away. Same with traveling west into Colorado, where one would have to travel at least five hours. If one were seeking a mosque, again, Wichita would be the closest choice.

Norton is also far from large shopping areas, large airports, and interstate highways. Aaron Hale, thinking about his former town of Lawrence, said, "There are things I miss on a temporal level, shallow stuff, like I love the Home Depot." In Lawrence it was five minutes away. Now it is ninety minutes away. "It's the little things that get to me," he admits. But he has a two-minute commute from home to his office where he sells agribusiness, crop, and commercial insurance.

When Aaron set about planning how to make the transition back home, he found himself looking at a western Kansas jobs website. The site is sponsored by the Western Kansas Rural Economic Development Alliance (WKREDA). In addition to providing job listings, the organization promotes western Kansas as a good place to retire, to start a business, or to return after time away, such as Aaron ultimately did. In its brochure, WKREDA focuses on the "Western Kansas alum" who already knows what the region offers. In fine sales promotion copywriting style, what some might see as a negative is turned to its best advantage. People from urban areas might look at a map of western Kansas and see the thirty-mile gaps between towns of 2,000 and think, "There's nobody out here." But the brochure celebrates this reality as wide-open spaces, star-filled skies, personal safety, small class sizes, and freedom to thrive. There are plentiful job opportunities in both agriculture and new technology, and the "workplace needs you and appreciates you": these are simply more positive ways of saying, that's right, there's nobody out here, but still it's pretty awesome.

That's the selling of the arid West; the same way it was sold to settlers who were assured that rain follows the plow. Although droughts and dust bowls taught hard lessons, some people stuck to this landscape. Aaron knows if the community is going to continue to thrive in spite of the odds, those who do choose to live there need to do more than simply show up. They need to make an investment in the community. That's why he gathered his strengths in sales and technology and his background in agriculture and put them to use on the Norton City/County Economic Development board (NC/CED). "There are some really strong things Norton has going for it and other areas that need some attention."

For example, housing, which he says is a "real challenge out here." There is very little housing to rent or buy. He notes that the cost of materials and labor to build housing is the same whether you are in a big city or small city. "You have to spend $150,000 or more to build a decent property for yourself, but it is really hard to sell a house like that. From a builder's perspective it doesn't make a whole lot of sense. They can't get out what they put in, so there is not a lot of incentive in new construction."

Aaron is bullish on the positive things, especially with jobs. Low unemployment and the presence of a strong manufacturing base is a positive thing. In April 2014, the unemployment rate in Norton County was 2.8 percent. There are skilled positions at a wide range of manufacturing plants. There is a very fast, stable Internet, he says, some of the best in the state, with fiberoptic to the home, even in rural areas. "That is a huge resource because telecommuting can potentially thrive here, as can businesses that sell technology."

Although he's been back in the community a short time he senses a growing interest in people his age group who want to return, make a contribution, and be near their families. He was not in town yet when the economic development board developed its strategic plan for 2011–2016, but he is in the thick of things now. The group reports that its top goal is business retention and expansion. This means expanding existing business, helping small businesses obtain capital investment, and workforce development through post-secondary institutions. It includes developing entrepreneurship. Another goal is developing a marketing plan to promote business in the county, as well as the quality of life here. The plan also addresses housing. Finally, a goal that could color the town's sustainability is youth retention. According to the strategic plan document, "Youth cite lack of jobs, negative public relations, better opportunities for quick advancement, and the sort of higher education or vocational training they cannot get in Norton" as reasons for leaving. The plan suggests there are ways to be sure there are enough good jobs that pay well so that young people can make a living if they do choose to stay. And as for those who leave, the board wants to keep in touch. Regardless of a young person's choices, the board wants to work with them to develop youth business programs and focus on business succession planning to help develop the next generation of leaders. "Current business owners can groom them to assume ownership of a business they are passionate about. This will assure survival of individual businesses and stability of our county."

This list is almost identical in spirit to the strategic development plan put in place in Bridgeport, Nebraska. Who wouldn't want better jobs, affordable housing, and ways for young people who wish to stay in the area to be able to do so. And who wouldn't want to see a succession plan in place for businesses and agricultural operations. A thousand small towns in this region can say the same thing. The question is whether they can all succeed, or if this is a zero-sum game.

One individual who was part of the NC/CED board's strategic plan has her hands in most parts of it. Carolyn Applegate grew up in Denver, but both sides of her family have deep roots in Norton County. Her father's family were pioneers in northwestern Kansas after the Civil War. During

World War II, her family left Kansas for Colorado. Her father couldn't serve in the war because of his health, she says, so they went to airplane-manufacturing center Wichita so he could get a "war job." They eventually settled in Denver. She had talent in the dramatic arts so she moved to California to work in the movie industry. "I had a different view of the world from living in Hollywood," she said. Her children were born there, but she frequently traveled to Kansas to visit relatives.

That's how she met and fell in love with a rancher, and returned to Kansas for good. Her kids were grown and gone. The year her daughter finished her master's degree, 1999, Carolyn and Stan were married. She's been busy since she moved to Norton, to say the least. Besides serving on the economic development board she ran a retail store, and then was the director of the chamber of commerce. One day she and the economic development director came across a magazine published by a small town in Nebraska. Although there is already a newspaper in the community, they were confident there were enough advertisers and readers to support both. Starting a Norton magazine could accomplish two things, Carolyn said. First, it would show people of the community how much they had to be grateful for, such as its businesses, clubs, and organizations. Second, "It would give us a calling card for the community that we could present in Topeka, to show those in the capital what we are doing, and be a voice for rural communities separated by so many miles." *Norton County Magazine* is published quarterly by the nonprofit Frontier Community Foundation. Profits from magazine ads, after production expenses are paid, go to fund grants available to local clubs and organizations. When we spoke in the spring of 2014, Carolyn was already planning content for the fall of 2017. "That shows you how much there is in this wonderful community and county."

Like Aaron Hale, there are certain aspects of her past life that Carolyn misses. For her, live theater was the big thing, and the beautiful weather. "Sometimes in the winter I miss that you can't go out and pick an avocado off the tree in your yard." Naturally, she doesn't miss the traffic. But she misses the diversity. "When my children were in high school, their communications home to parents came out in ten different languages." In spite of those experiences that border on the global, she remembers the day she decided to leave Los Angeles. "I'd just paid the premium for an insurance rider that would cover me for snipers and kidnapping. That's when I figured I needed to leave."

Leaving her life in California was just a transition for her to the next thing. "You don't retire when you have livestock and land and run a magazine," she said. "I just say I've retired from California."

Carolyn notes that farming in western Kansas has been tough in recent years, especially during this period of severe drought. That means tough times for wheat farmers, livestock producers, and anyone who depends economically on their success, which is just about everyone. "Today I prayed for rain, and we got six inches in two hours," she told me. "It ran across the road and straight down the river." In spite of that episode of runoff, she says farming is generally good. I would come to find out during my time in Norton and in speaking to other residents before and after my trip that they sing from the same songbook praising this town. And why shouldn't they? They really do have low unemployment, industry that hires skilled workers, a downtown that is slowly but steadily revitalizing, a movie theater that citizens came together to purchase and restore, a new swimming pool, a bowling alley in the planning stages, and a new motel that was part of an effort by a local businessman. And they have the Norton Correctional Facility (NCF), a medium-security prison where several hundred people are employed. That's where Carolyn's husband has an off-farm job, balanced with growing organic wheat and hay. "That job has medical—lots of people have a spouse who works off the farm for the benefits," she explained.

In some communities, leaders fight to have new prisons built in their towns, hoping for an economic development boost. But then they find that guards and other staff are brought in from the outside and are not really "of" the community. In the case of Norton, however, the facility itself has long been present, in one form or another. Dating back to 1913, the building was a tuberculosis sanatorium, and then in 1963, it housed adults with profound developmental disabilities. That facility closed in 1984. In 1988, the Kansas Department of Corrections converted the facility to a prison.

Most Kansas state prisons are in the eastern part of the state, in the areas of denser population. The Norton Correctional Facility is the most remotely located prison in the state.

Just over 700 men can be housed in this combination medium- and minimum-security prison. That is a lot of wives and children, parents and siblings, who might converge on Norton to visit, especially during three-day weekends when families make the long drive from their homes all over Kansas. Those who cannot find lodging, or cannot afford to do so, face a major obstacle.

"If you can keep a man near his family, he is much more likely to be successful when he gets out." That's the belief of Carolyn Plotts, who lives in nearby Norcatur, Kansas, population 151. She and her husband Jim are part of a group involved with the prison, leading Bible studies and similar activities. Through this work they've come to see the inmates at NCF as individuals with families, just like themselves. They realized they could provide a useful service if they could help inmate families with an affordable and safe alternative when they visit town.

That's when the Haven was born. The volunteer group purchased a three-story home through the previous owner's generous financial terms. After some remodeling, the house now has a communal kitchen, living and dining areas, thirteen bedrooms, four bathrooms, and can accommodate thirty overnight guests. The volunteer group formed a nonprofit organization called Northwest Kansas Inmate Resource Council, Inc. That board is not big on creating arbitrary rules that stand in the way of meeting real needs. That's why their guests are not just prison families. Sometimes they are people seeking shelter from winter storms, or battered or homeless women requiring shelter.

Carolyn says when they took possession of the house in 2005, it lacked furnishings and essentials. She went on a local radio program and got the word out into the community about what they needed and how people could help. Within two weeks, the house was fully furnished. Even though they've been operating for eight years, they still continue to receive generous donations of items like furnishings, dishware, and linens.

The remodeling of the house was done by volunteers Jim Plotts, Jim Rowe, and Bob Virgil, with Carolyn in the role of coordinator and curtain-maker. Work crews from the prison were dispatched to help in the yard. A prison crew does laundry for the house in its commercial-scale facility, which would be a formidable task for a residential-sized washer and dryer. The prison administration gives referrals to families needing lodging during visits to Norton. But as far as managing that human flow, the Haven is on its own.

Enter Lori Shields. She is a fast-talking ball of fire from Lawrence, Kansas, whose Kentucky accent betrays the origins of her earlier life. She moved to Lawrence at age twenty-one, because that was her husband Damian's town. He later got into what she calls a "bad situation" involving drugs. "He got arrested and that led him to Norton Correctional Facility, three years ago."

The couple had two small children when he was incarcerated. For them, making the five-hour trip from Lawrence to Norton was expensive. That's until she found the Haven and became a regular guest. "At that time, no volunteers actually stayed in the house," she recalled. "It was on the honor system when you came in to find your room. There was no one to really greet people and help them. I offered to take that on myself. It became my ministry."

Lori started out informally running things during her stays, making sure she was present when families arrived, even when they came in late at night. Soon, she decided to move to Norton permanently and live with her children in a small room in the Haven. She took a job as a paraprofessional at the local elementary school. Now promoted to school secretary, she spends days organizing children, teachers, and parents. At 4:00 p.m. she gets to the Haven and starts returning phone calls, scheduling people into the bedrooms for visits and writing their names on a diagram of the house drawn on a white board. Lori says she sometimes has moments when things don't run exactly right, like if a guest does not strip the bed upon departure, as requested. She might think to herself, *Oh, these people!* "Then I realize, I am these people," she says.

Lori is now a paid employee of the Haven, although Carolyn refers to her salary as more of a "stipend." Watching the two women work together in the house, caring for Lori's young daughter, and planning a Memorial Day picnic for the large group they are expecting, is to see two people who function together like the best of friends, or even like family. "She calls me Grandma," Carolyn said, nodding at Lori's young daughter.

Lori's husband is expected to be released from prison soon, and she has located a residence for her family to move into. They will be one of the few African American families in the community. She notes that it is unusual for prisoners to remain in Norton upon their release. But her husband, who is a certified welder, already has a local job in the works. Their children are accepted in school and are making friends. "I have met wonderful people here, and never felt more like I belong to something," she said. "I love this town. It has been a blessing to me."

I have asked at least a dozen Norton residents about the prison, wondering how it factors in to the way they see their town. I had thought the proximity of a prison might make residents worry about possible criminal activity by people who would be coming to their town to visit inmates, and very possibly it does. But without exception, they have framed their explanation in terms of the good jobs it provides and the extra business it brings to motels, restaurants, and other businesses. Naturally, they are careful to present their community in a positive light. Yet crime in Norton is not substantial. Take for example, a week in July 2012, during the Norton County Fair, which brings hundreds of extra people in town for rodeos, dirt-track races, concerts, and carnivals. During fair week, the *Norton Telegram* newspaper reported incidents such as stolen storm windows, kids sitting in the street, a dead deer in a convenience store parking lot, several incidents of keys accidentally locked in cars, and kids pushing a lawn mower through a mud hole. To be fair, there was also a fight, and someone finally got around to reporting that goods had been stolen, two years previous.

In the 2010 Census, there were 2,928 people in the city of Norton. That translates to 1,290 households containing 763 families. According to US Census American Community Survey data, in 2010, just under 11 percent of Norton County residents lived in poverty, in a state where the poverty rate was just over 13 percent. Compare that to almost 19 percent living in poverty in Douglas County, where Damian Shields got into trouble with drugs. That county, which is also where the University of Kansas is located, is seventh on the state-poverty-ranking list. Norton County's ranking is sixty-four. Just to compare the rural with the urban, the two counties that make up the bulk of the metropolitan area of Kansas City that lies on the Kansas side of the border are Johnson and Wyandotte, just a few miles north. Johnson County's poverty ranking is ranked at 101, where only 6.4 percent of people live in poverty. Wyandotte County comes in at number one, with the highest poverty rate in the state, at over 23 percent. It seems a popular trope to conflate crime with dense population, and safety with low population. These statistics seem to show it isn't necessarily the number of people; it is the number of people in poverty that translates into higher crime.

When I was planning my trip to Norton, I knew I would be traveling by myself. I gave serious thought to tent camping at Prairie Dog State Park, located a few miles west of Norton. I mentioned this possibility to Tara Vance, director of the Norton Chamber of Commerce, to see if I heard any hesitation in her voice about a woman camping alone in the 1,150-acre park on the shores of Lake Sebelius. Maybe it is the confidence of a young woman, but in her voice I heard no such hesitation. I went so far as to pack my camping gear and some easy-to-prepare food. I had a backup plan, and I'm glad I did. When I got to the state park I found that all the tent sites were taken. Plus it was hot, windy, and I didn't like the look of those afternoon thunderheads filling that wide-open sky. So it was that I found myself lodging at a mom-and-pop motel operated by an East Indian couple, paying $50 a night. My motel parking lot companions were single men from area work crews, their stereo playing music featuring accordions, the lyrics sung in Spanish. I enjoyed listening to their music and conversation from behind the curtains of my loudly air conditioned, Wi-Fi–ready room. In spite of the fact I didn't feel comfortable pulling a motel room chair out onto the sidewalk in front of the door and drinking an evening beer of my own with the guys, when I considered pulling up stakes for my second night in town and heading back to Prairie Dog State Park, the motel still seemed preferable. At least there, I could charge my cell phone and get some work done on my computer.

Probably because I slept on a bed and not on a bedroll, I got an early start on my first full day in town. The chamber was my destination. Tara Vance told me a great deal about Norton, from the perspective of someone who grew up in a community about an hour away. She went to college at Fort Hayes State and then lived other places for another ten years. "I was not opposed to staying in the area, but I did realize there was life beyond northwest Kansas." She studied organizational leadership in college, with a minor in business. Her husband is a high school math teacher who coaches the forensics team and the debate team.

As chamber director, Tara notes that the city of Norton is fortunate to be "very healthy compared to our peers." She indicates that hard times in agriculture are challenging, but there are other legs of the stool to rely on. There are the industrial employers, the state prison, and the Valley Hope Drug & Alcohol treatment center, which has its headquarters in Norton and employs highly educated and skilled workers including individuals with doctoral degrees. The local hospital is not technically a regional one, Tara says. "We have a litmus test in rural America: can you have babies here? And the answer is yes!"

She sees the community as very progressive where small businesses are thriving and services and contractors are doing well. "Our goal is to be a hub in the area. We are an hour from a Walmart, which we love, because it encourages people to shop in town." Smaller towns around Norton might not be faring as well. Tara says that within a thirty-mile radius, Norton is the only one that can say they're growing, thanks to various local employers. "We've sustained population loss in northwest Kansas. But in Norton we're on the cusp of thriving, not dying."

During my chamber stop, staff there loaded me with brochures and information about the community. I took a copy of *Norton County Magazine* and used it to find information about restaurants and attractions. But it was the ad for Kowpoke Supply that summed up what it is to live in a small rural town where people do what it takes to stay in business and make a living. Located on the town's main drag, Kowpoke Supply sells lumber, hardware, appliances, tools, paint, gardening supplies, boots, and outerwear. And oh yes, jewelry.

I didn't make it to that store but, brochures in hand, I started my trek around town. I stopped into the old courthouse, in the center of the town square. There were displays of historic photographs, and racks of county extension literature. There was even material about agricultural archaeology, encouraging farmers and landowners to think about "historic farmhouses, prehistoric cornfields, isolated soddies, and large villages that have left their mark upon the land." From there I stopped at the new public library, with its lawn decorated with three full-sized sculptures by western artist Frederic Remington. Several more pieces of western sculpture stood inside the library. There was also an exhibition of two-dimensional art created by prison inmates, to whom the interpretive signage refers to as NCF residents.

I stopped at Las Canteras for a good lunch of Mexican fare, which is slowly becoming easier to find in small towns in the Midwest and Great Plains, as Latino immigration and entrepreneurship emerges. In so many small towns, if it weren't for the Latino entrepreneur, many more Main Street storefronts would be empty. Norton's Las Canteras was full of the gaudily colored furnishing and decorations I'd come to expect in Mexican restaurants that cater to a broad clientele. What I wasn't expecting was to see such a bustling place. Sure, it was a Thursday at about 1:00 p.m., but there had been almost no one on the streets as I wandered about. It was a nice day, not too hot, yet Norton seemed almost a ghost town. As it turns out, this is where at least some of them

Mexican restaurants are a common site in most urban areas.
In small rural communities, they can indicate a Main Street, and
a community, on the upswing. Photograph © Julianne Couch.

were: a diverse crowd of business people, travelers, farmers, and families eating the so-named Speedy Gonzales lunch special or one of the other items from the menu, some sipping iced tea and others, margaritas, spending a bit of time out of the midday sun.

In order to work off my overly ambitious lunch, I visited more places in town, stopping into the county historical museum, housed in the building that once was the public library. There I met Ruth Lofgreen, her husband, Denzel Lofgreen, and their fellow volunteer, Joe E. Ballinger. Ruth said she couldn't be considered a Norton native because she'd only lived in the area sixty-eight years. She and her husband live on a farm that straddles the Nebraska/Kansas line. They used to live on the Nebraska side, she said. But one year a blizzard snowed them in for two weeks before the highway department dug them out. They were so mad they decided to put their house in Kansas. All three volunteers are retired—Joe, from a military career that took him around the world. But he settled back in Norton, now spending time at the museum sorting through the old photos, old files, and collection of prized personal items that locals want to make available for public viewing for generations to come. Items range from farm equipment to pencils to fossils to meteorites to furniture. Joe cleared out some space in the building to paint one room in bright colors and put in items that would appeal to children. And sometimes children do come to visit, assigned some task or another by a schoolteacher. The visitation there is slim compared to the traffic in the They Also Ran gallery.

This portrait gallery honors men who ran for president of the United States, and lost. It is housed in the First Interstate Bank in Norton because the man who had the idea for it, William Walter Rouse, was the founder and owner of the bank. The year was 1965, and Rouse had been inspired by a book called *They Also Ran* by Irving Stone. Today, the sixty images of losers from Thomas Jefferson to Mitt Romney fill the walls of an upstairs wing of the bank.

Lee Ann Shearer is the de facto museum curator. She works in the bank doing bookkeeping, money transfers, and the like. In between, she gives tours to groups of kids, international tourists, people on the Wheat Tour from Kansas State University, and drop-ins like me. Most of the visitors are not locals, she tells me. It seems to be the case that most cultural offerings in a community are enjoyed by outsiders, and that small-town residents think first of the metro area an hour or two away if they consider visits to museums, galleries, or live performances.

Lee Ann grew up east of here in Smith County and attended Kansas State University. "City life was not for me," she said. Instead of remaining in Manhattan, where K-State is located, she came to Norton driving a truck on a harvest crew. "I planned to meet and marry a farmer and travel. I did meet and marry a farmer, but now I'm too busy to travel." That's because not only does she continue working on seasonal custom harvest crews, she raises her young children, sings in a band, participates in 4-H, and volunteers with numerous organizations in town.

Lee Ann has a special place in her heart for the photo gallery. She has a few favorites among the losers, which she points out as she guides me around the room. One is Horace Greeley, the newspaper man famous for the slogan "Go West, young man," defeated in 1872 by Ulysses S. Grant. So that no one feels too badly for the losers, in 2009, Lee Ann started organizing an Inauguration Day open house just a bit ahead of the presidential inauguration. When Barack Obama was inaugurated as president on January 20 of that year, he was thirty minutes behind John McCain's inauguration into the They Also Ran gallery.

Being a generalist who can pick up specialized skills quickly is an essential trait when occupational options are limited in a small town. Being adaptable and able to regroup when something doesn't work out is an essential trait for the presidential candidate, for the settler, for the farmer, for the entrepreneur, and for communities as a whole. Lee Ann Shearer is one example of a person who started out doing one thing, and then before she knew it, was doing something else. Another is Dana Paxton, editor of the *Norton Telegram*. Dressed in high-heeled sandals as she headed out on foot to run ad-sales errands, Dana paused to talk to me when I dropped in unexpectedly. She says she did not think she'd start working for a newspaper at this middle stage in her career. In fact, she went into the building that houses the *Telegram* a few years ago simply to pick up a copy of the paper. She wanted to peruse the classifieds to find a job after the in-home day care operation she'd planned didn't work out. She didn't see anything suitable in the listings, but she was told there were two openings at the *Telegram*: reporting and ad sales. She had no background in journalism but interviewed for the reporter position. She got the ad sales job instead. A few years later the editor left and she was selected for that position. Now she handles both jobs.

The *Telegram* is part of a consortium of northwest Kansas papers. Norton is the smallest community in the group. Dana praises her staff as "the best" but admits it is hard to hire reporters on the paper here. "They think they are going to come here and really do something," she says. "But it really isn't like that. Plus, if you are single, the dating pool is zilch. The whole town revolves around agriculture and high school sports. Everyone is at the games. If those things don't appeal to you, Norton does not have a lot to offer."

Although Norton may be on the cusp of thriving, attaining that goal has been slowed partly because of something it really can't control: drought. As Dana says, "There have been no crops to speak of the last three years, and this year hasn't started much better." That means nothing about the economy is stable. "We are so dependent on agriculture. When ag is down, the whole economy suffers. When customers aren't in the stores, the first thing those stores do is cut back on ad sales with the paper. Eventually everyone is affected." Norton used to have three grocery stores, now there is one and it has raised its prices. On the positive side, "The town is working on historic preservation and economic development. Two years ago this was a ghost town."

Things are different in recent years. The Prairie Dog State Park campground is full on weekends, with locals and nearby residents filling everything from primitive tent sites all the way up to electric sites set up for motor homes, as I'd discovered. There is also the county fair, which takes place mostly at Elmwood Park, in town. A disc golf course has been set up there, with help from a work crew at the NCF. Although this fair doesn't feature a full-scale rodeo, there is mutton bustin', in which young children don helmets and attempt to ride upon the back of a sheep. There's a dirt-bike-racing track, but after a rider was killed in a racing accident they stopped that event. Now they are trying to attract stock-car racing instead.

They have a hometown carnival, which means it is operated by residents of the town. There had been safety issues with these in Norton and elsewhere around the state, and the authorities considered shutting them down, but that did not happen. One time in Norton, Dana recalls, a ride was improperly assembled. However, the error was recognized before anyone was hurt. In spite of safety issues, Dana says she feels more comfortable with people she knows being in charge of the rides. She trusts that they have the ability to do it properly; after all, it is their friends and family taking those rides.

Some Norton residents have had many years and opportunities to get to know local youngsters and watch them grow up. One such, Charlene Weskamp, was born and raised near McCook in southwest Nebraska, about an hour's drive from Norton. Because she was one of seven siblings and was the oldest girl, she told me that meant while the boys did farm work, the "indoor jobs" fell on her. She did the cooking, cleaning, laundry, cared for the four younger kids, helped with the garden. She lived in town her senior year of high school and when she graduated in 1959, her father told her she was on her own. A year later she married her high school sweetheart, Andy Weskamp. He was in the navy, which took them to California for three years before they returned to McCook. She said because she married and started a family, she had no opportunity to go to college. Had she done so, she might have become a teacher or social worker. But she eventually landed a job with the USDA in the Norton County farm-service agency, where she worked almost thirty-four years. She retired at age seventy. "I loved the challenge of working on the different programs and keeping up with how the government changes its mind on a daily basis. I was blessed with a good job and got to retire with a good salary." Her children went on to professional careers in the medical field and do not live in Norton. Her husband, who got his training as a lab technician, eventually oversaw the lab at Norton hospital before his retirement.

With this long history in town and working with farm families and government policies, Charlene has observed some changes in modern culture that trouble her. She is not alone in her assessment of how civic life in Norton has changed over the years. She and her husband have rental property, so they get to meet a lot of people who come to town needing housing. She wonders how newcomers with no children in schools or any church affiliation would get acquainted in the community, which she describes as "welcoming." Charlene was favorably impressed by a potential renter from Kenya who had been a home-economics teacher, then went to school to become a nursing-home administrator and had a job nearby. "She was a widow with four kids, a nice sweet lady," Charlene said.

However, because of her rental property, Charlene has firsthand experience with people who use drugs, including some of her recent renters who were arrested for selling methamphetamine. "Young people smoke and drink before they pay the rent. It is not like the culture where we were raised, where you pay your bills first. If they had any idea how we struggled as a young family to pay our bills. If we couldn't afford it we didn't buy it." She's also concerned about the number of people having children without being married, and the effect of that choice on the children. "It has become more acceptable, which is good in a way because it doesn't harm the child, but it hurts the family. If they had a little bit more training in morals and religion they'd know what they are doing is not good for them."

These views about the state of the family and the potential loss of the younger generation to directionless drifting are easy to understand, especially when voiced by someone who came from nothing and who has worked as hard as Charlene and her husband over the years. They are bolstered by their strong Christian faith, and like seemingly everyone else in rural Kansas, their Republican politics. The GOP has dominated Kansas politics since the party was established in 1859. Its association with concepts like individual rights and low taxes appeal to landowners, like ranchers and farmers in the West. Under Republican Governor Sam Brownback, in 2012 Kansas cut state taxes on top earners and on some businesses, in a move they thought would draw business and industry to the state. The result, they thought, would be unprecedented prosperity. Instead, the state budget has been cut to the point where Republicans worry about how Kansas will pay for even the most basic jobs of government.

As I anticipated, I had to do quite a bit of digging to find a Democrat in this part of the state. I checked the Kansas Democratic Party website and found that although all 105 counties in Kansas have a Republican Party organization, only sixty have a Democratic Party organization. Most of the forty-five have-nots are small rural counties in western Kansas. This geographic distribution made me think of Democrats like a species with finite ranges, like the eastern bluebird or western rattlesnake. I decided to speed up my quest by asking Carolyn Applegate, who, as editor of *Norton County Magazine*, knows everyone. In fact, she said she thought maybe she knew two Democrats, but that Jake Durham would be best for me to talk to. He's what she called an "equal opportunity Democrat," whom she had just recently seen being photographed with former US Senator Bob Dole, a Republican, at a local meet and greet.

Jake has a long list of accomplishments that are well-known and respected in the community. He entered military service as a private in 1951, during the Korean War, attended officer training school, and became platoon leader of the 25th Infantry Division in 1953. Then he entered the US Army Reserve and finished his career in the National Guard, and retired as a lieutenant colonel. He started teaching school in Norton in 1955 and was a 1990 entrant into the Kansas Wrestling Coaches Hall of Fame. He coached six state-championship wrestling squads. Now he can go to any town within eighty miles of Norton, step out of his car, and people say "Hi, Jake."

That's what he told me when we visited by phone. He was expecting my call and was ready with his best one-liners about his friends and neighbors, the Republicans. He calls himself a Kansas transplant although he's lived in the state about sixty years. But he comes by his Democratic inclinations honestly, inheriting them from his father, a tradesman in Granite City, Illinois. He once asked his dad about the difference between Democrats and Republicans. His answer was that when Republicans are in office, the rich get richer and the poor get poorer. "Dad was a steel worker in a steel town. As working-class people, you go with that group," Jake said.

It might seem that Jake would feel politically isolated or alienated in this town. But it is his belief that there are other Democrats out there, they just don't advertise themselves as such when running for office. "If you are a civic minded Democrat at all, half the time you are registered Republican. Even the good Democrats don't get elected. Even their mothers wouldn't vote for them."

Jake acknowledges that Republicans are well organized and well established with county committees, and that by contrast there is little Democratic political organization in rural western Kansas. "There are two or three people who have been able to win seats in the Kansas legislature as Democrats. One was a lifelong doctor who'd delivered most of the babies in the community."

In spite of what might seem to be a recipe for conservative factionalism, Jake says that rural western Kansas is not a stronghold of Tea Party politics. He believes that movement is centered a few hundred miles away in eastern Kansas in the area around Topeka, the state capital.

As someone who lived almost twenty years in the largely one-party state of Wyoming, I wondered if Jake ever felt like leaving western Kansas and living someplace that aligned better with his politics. But Jake says he has no desire to find birds of his own political feather.

"It's a good place to live," he says of Norton. He has lots of friends, has taken three turns as commander of the American Legion, and knows nearly everyone in town. He also knows all the relevant economic development data. "Norton has industry, like the aluminum product plant that hires more than a hundred people, another plant that makes micro-parts for airplanes that hires seventy-five people, the state highway shops that employ forty to fifty people, the alcoholism treatment center and the hospital that employ seventy-five people each, the school system that employs a hundred people. We have things going for us that other small towns don't have: the opportunity to have a job. Also, we have the prison."

He knows most kids do leave for college, thereby "educating themselves out of town." In fact, an outreach program through Colby County Community College offers a nursing program in Norton. "That is an opportunity for young kids to get plugged into and have schooling locally, though that's not typical. Most try to get out and go to college somewhere like K-State to study agriculture." Yet, there is a nucleus that stays here and runs the town, he said. Others might leave and then return if the town can offer employment and an appealing way of life.

Neal Willmeth is an example of this species of Norton native. He left town after high school and eventually returned to Norton, where his family still lives. Unlike Aaron Hale, though, Neal did not return because he wanted his children raised near their grandparents. In fact, he is single and has no children, but came home because it better suited the operation of the family business, which had been housed in Houston. Plus, he just likes it.

Neal graduated from high school in 1992 and went to college for a year in Fort Hayes, Kansas. He moved to Houston to work for Compaq Computers. After five years, the company moved production to Mexico, and nearly everyone in his division was laid off, himself included. Being adaptable, his next career move was to enlist in the army. He served for nearly five years. By the time he got out of the service, his father's temporary holiday store business was taking off. It had started in 1989 in shopping malls in various locations around the country. In 1999, Joe Willmeth began supplementing his temporary stores with Internet sales. By the time Neal got out of the army in 2003, Joe decided to try running the website full time. He realized he could do more business online than with the stores. By then, Neal and Joe started working together. They acquired a 2,500-square-foot warehouse in Houston, and then added to it. Business boomed and warehouse space became tight, but building more warehouse space was cost prohibitive. "Even in the boondocks, the average price was $250,000 per acre of land," Neal told me. "The warehouse we needed would be another $250,000, so we were looking at half a million to build a warehouse if we wanted to be close to the roads we needed to be on."

Neal consulted the Norton grapevine. A man who'd once been his school bus driver had two acres of land to sell for a lot less money than they wanted in Houston. Between the obvious financial incentives and the fact the Neal was starting to miss small-town life, the choice was made to move Christmas Decorations & Gifts to Norton.

"When we started building the warehouse, we had a few problems with the wind," he recalls. "It is hard to set up a steel building in thirty-mile-per-hour gusts, so that was a slight delay." By the fall of 2012 they had everything in good enough shape that they could transition out of their Houston location and work entirely from the facility in Norton.

The family business employed three full-time workers when they were in Houston, plus himself, his father, and a woman who still works for the company but is based out of her home in Houston. During the height of the season, they would hire five or six temporary employees to package merchandise and fill orders. Now that they are in Norton, so far the help consists of Neal and his mother, with his father in charge of the website. They also sell their goods directly through Amazon and eBay. Every year in January or February, Neal goes to trade shows in Dallas to visit vendors and select the items to order. It is usually July when those orders are filled. Most of what they purchase comes from vendors in China, but a few items come from Europe. I wondered if trading a shipping center like Houston and moving to the intersection of two-lane highways proved a disadvantage for a company dealing in global trade. Turns out, it is an advantage. "Being in Norton cuts distance off because goods can come from Chicago. Or if they come in from the East or West Coasts, the mileage didn't change much whether it was going to Norton or Houston," Neal told me.

Neal is in early middle age, and working on a family business he figures is set up to last his lifetime. The business climate in Norton is good for him and the technology infrastructure is excellent. But what does a single man like him used to big city life do for fun?

"Houston has a lot of great stuff and a lot to do, but I didn't have many friends to do it with," he says. It turns out he had a hard time meeting people in Houston. He lived in an apartment complex where people either stuck to themselves or did not stay in the complex long.

But in Norton, even though many of the people he knows are older, he still finds people he knows to chat with. He is busy with the Lions Club and its projects around the Norton community. "For instance, we just put in a new concession stand and announcer booth for the local ball field." Norton also has a movie theater that shows two movies. "I don't need much more than that. I watch summer baseball and softball games. When school is in session, I see football, basketball, wrestling, and track." And he can buy a season sports pass for $35 or $40, which in Houston was about the price of one game.

The only obvious thing missing from his life is in the romance department, and he is working on that. He has met a woman in China through his business associations in that country, and had just returned from visiting her when we chatted by phone. Their relationship is far enough along that he considers her his girlfriend. They visit frequently online. He has told her all about his life in Norton, and shown her pictures of the area. It is quite a contrast to her city of three or four million people. For one thing, in Norton you can breathe clean air and see the stars, he said.

Neal believes it is difficult for a single woman in China to visit the United States because their government worries that she might not come back. I considered the Northwestern Kansas Travel Council's tourism slogan, encouraging everyone to visit the high plains of northwestern Kansas and "discover the history, scenic beauty, and friendly people that puts us on a higher plain." I suggested maybe he needs to get on a different kind of high plane, go get his girlfriend, and bring her back himself. And in that deliberate, no-nonsense voice that is the hallmark of the western Kansas man, he replied, "I'm thinking I might have to do just that."

Now that's being on the cusp of thriving.

SEDAN, KANSAS
PLEASE, SOMEBODY HAVE A JOB

4

I've always thought of myself as a Kansan by birth. Which is odd, because I was born to a pair of Missouri natives, in a hospital on the Missouri side of Kansas City. My parents had moved several times with my older siblings—my father transferred to Oklahoma, Arkansas, and Florida. Each time my mother was ready to give birth, she traveled "home" to St. Louis to deliver. When the transfer came in for Kansas City, they selected a neighborhood on the Kansas side of the line in which to buy a home.

It probably didn't enter my parents' heads that they were staking a claim as Kansans when they moved into a postwar cracker box on a dead-end street full of big families like ours. Their choice of state seems arbitrary to me now. They probably just wanted a Catholic school within walking distance and an easy trip to my dad's downtown office. All their years of moving around must have detached them from their identity as Missourians, if they ever had it.

If you know the Kansas City area, you know that the divide between Kansas and Missouri is affected by the thinnest of barriers: the eponymously named two-lane State Line Road. In other parts of town, the Missouri River makes a much more evident barrier. But for about half the city and suburbs, the border is really just a residential street. Though I grew up only a few blocks from the Show Me State, it was as a Kansan that I got my first driver's license, that I first voted, and that I selected an in-state college. It was as a Kansan that I learned there existed such stuff as "landscape." It was when I started regularly making the drive a hundred miles southwest to my college town of Emporia that I noticed rural lands—some crop country, sure—but mostly grass, cattle, and low hills rising up into flat plateaus. As it turns out, I'd stumbled into selecting a college situated in the little bluestem grasslands of the northern Flint Hills.

This was the first time I'd really thought about my relationship to grass, or rocks, or topography. Much of the Flint Hills area is privately owned, which limited me to windshield tourism. I obeyed the rules about trespassing, unlike most of my college friends, and didn't crawl under barbed-wire fences for beer drinking or star-gazing in somebody's pasture. But I loved to take road trips through the area, visiting wildlife refuges and state parks. The more I thought about prairie, the less I thought about Kansas City.

Fast forward thirty-five years, finding me in Iowa. Although I've visited the Flint Hills on occasion, I've seldom traveled US Highway 160 and the bottom tier of counties along the Oklahoma border. That road cuts through several physiographic regions, from the Red Hills to the Flint Hills, the Chautauqua Hills, the Osage Cuestas, and finally the Ozark Plateau.

That there is a distinction between these regions says something about Kansas of which most people are unaware: parts of the state are prodigiously hilly.

I had discovered through talking to folks in the Sedan area that many of them had left city life behind in order to move somewhere less crowded. I could relate to that. In 1960, Johnson County, Kansas, where I was raised, had a population just under 143,000. But that was a 129 percent increase over the population in 1950. From 1960 to 1970 the jump was a more modest 53 percent, and it has slowed since then as most of the rural farmland was chewed up and spit out by development, regurgitated as strip malls and subdivisions. Still, its population density of 1,160 persons per square mile is nothing compared to other areas of the country, and of the globe. On the other hand, there are seven people per square mile in Chautauqua County.

The essence of a place can disappear through overcrowding, as it did for me in Johnson County. Or, it can disappear because so many people leave. I wanted to know why anybody would want to live in what is left of Sedan, in Chautauqua County, a place in danger of losing its essence as unarguably as Johnson County has. Like a slow-motion tornado, rural depopulation is a disaster that one can prepare for when one sees it coming. But what form does that preparation take? Trying to get people to stake a claim as loyalist to a place, sticking it out no matter what? Trying to excite people about entrepreneurship? Developing fun and quirky roadside attractions for tourists? Exploiting natural resources like wildgame hunting, and drilling for gas and oil? Or settling down quietly, calibrating the new sparseness from a comfortable rocker on the front porch, watching dust rise from the gravel road and wondering if the traffic is coming or going, and what difference that might make.

You can live here if you want. But you'd better know how to do something.

This sentiment could have been expressed in the late nineteenth century, when people were snapping up public lands in Kansas either through the homesteading process or by purchasing it from the railroads. If you were going to acquire land in the nineteenth-century countryside, you'd better know how to farm, and tend livestock, get along with your neighbors, and maintain a household for your family.

The same is true today, with a skill set only slightly different. These days the sentiment of knowing how to do something might also go like this: "If you want to live here, you have to be an entrepreneur." That's what Dick Jones, a realtor in the Chautauqua County region, told me about how one can live a good life in this county when few employers are hiring. In spite of job shortages, contrary advice also seems sound: "If you want to move to a small town, please, somebody have a job." So says Rudy Taylor, publisher and editor of three small community newspapers in a three-county area in southeast Kansas.

So which is it? Be self-sufficient? Be a job creator? Be employable? How about all of the above, shape shifting as necessary to fill as many roles as required to make rural southeast Kansas active, bustling, and competent, not simply ceasing to bleed, but sustainable and resilient.

Rudy Taylor, now in his sixties, has seen and reported on events in this region of Kansas for most of his life. He lives in the small town of Caney, in Montgomery County, part of his three-county coverage area. He knows what happens when money leaves a region. He's seen employers close shop, working people lose their jobs, and small-town residents forced to pick up stakes and move to the cities. He's seen the ones left behind face real poverty for the first time in their lives. He's written about the ways desperation can lead to drug abuse, domestic difficulties, and the general downhill spiral of people living without hope. Some might say those who stay behind lack gumption, imagination, or brains. Others find hope in what those who remain behind can contribute. Indeed, they encourage the youth, in particular, to do just that.

In the last half-century, farming and ranching became a money sink, oil and gas development began its tip into slow decline, and reasons to remain in a small town became fewer. As Rudy notes, Chautauqua County has lost 1,100 residents since the year 2000, and there is a steady leakage of population every year. "I visit with local merchants often, and we discuss this trend which we believe is mostly due to deaths. In our newspaper, it is not uncommon to see three to six deaths per week. Speaking generally, I can say that a good percent of them were subscribers to our newspaper. They also were loyal customers at the local grocery store, at the local bank, in local restaurants, and other businesses."

So, aging and dying are happening in his area of the country. Rudy would like to feel optimistic about this grim fact. "I would like to report that a balance exists; that for every older person who dies, there is a young adult who rushes to our office to say, 'Hi, I'm new in town and I want to subscribe to the local newspaper!'" But that just doesn't happen, he says. Times change. He says that even many teachers in the school system are out-of-town residents, which was never allowed a few years ago. "But as society has become more equal in our thinking, we realize that spouses live and work elsewhere, and one of them must commute."

Rudy can't think of any specific event that dealt a blow to his region. In fact, he says, the local oil business, ranching, hunting-guide services, and wind-farm technology have combined to create some pretty darn good opportunities. "But unless young people have a good reason to come back home, it just doesn't happen. Rural Kansas simply is not a good draw for younger people when they seek occupations. In truth, there are still some good jobs and business ventures in rural Kansas, but they're better in Wichita, Kansas City, Dallas, or Tulsa."

Rudy knows there are reasons why most people aren't too interested in moving or retiring to these low-income communities that are located 100 miles from a larger city. He says the only way to stop the tide and reverse the damage is for people to be willing to invest in their communities, rather than abandon them. He cites the example of a local family who sold their oil business for a sizable profit. With that money, they invested in a town recreation center, a convenience store, and a restaurant. The oil family got individuals involved in part ownership of these businesses, mentored them in daily operations for a time, until eventually the family was bought out by the new entrepreneurs. In this way, local money was reinvested locally, creating business services the community wanted, and helping some people become business owners while others were hired for jobs that could lead them to careers.

Conundrums of sustaining rural populations and viability are not confined to southeast Kansas, but occur in most areas of the state where increasingly, all roads lead to urban areas. Going back through the years, one can see a trend, with Chautauqua County as a good example. When that county was created in 1875, its population was about 7,400. Then in 1880, the population spiked to 11,072, spurred by the arrival of the railroad. By 1890 it had grown another 11 percent. Only two more times in the county's history did a decennial census show population growth. The other two were in 1920 and in 1980. As a result of double-digit population loss for many decades, the county's population stood at 3,669 in 2010. Sedan, the county seat, reflects this trend. Between 2000 and 2010, the town lost more than 16 percent of its population. As of 2010, 1,124 citizens do their best to keep the place going.

The state of Kansas has shown concern for the rapid shrinkage of many of its rural counties, like this one. Seventy-seven of the 105 counties are losing population fast enough that, in spite of budget woes, the state is offering financial incentives to get people to move to them. "There is something special about life in rural Kansas," goes the pitch. "Something authentic and wholesome. Something that makes it the ideal place to live, work, and raise a family. And thanks to the new Rural Opportunity Zones program, there's never been a better time than now to make rural Kansas your new home." New, full-time residents can receive Kansas income-tax waivers for up to five years and student loan repayments. Although specifics vary by county, to be eligible for Kansas income-tax waivers, individuals must have established residency in a ROZ county on or after the date the county became part of the program; have lived outside Kansas for five or more years immediately prior to establishing residency in a ROZ county; and earned less than $10,000 in Kansas Source Income in each of the five years immediately prior to establishing residency in a ROZ county. To be eligible for student loan repayment, individuals must have graduated from an accredited post-secondary institution in Kansas and move to a ROZ county.

One might think with these sorts of incentives that Chautauqua and other similar counties would be burgeoning with young college graduates burdened by debt but eager to launch a technology company slash cattle ranch or maybe open a funky clothing boutique slash coffee shop on Main Street. And in fact, as I've attempted to track down state-incentivized individuals, I have found evidence of their existence. But rather like Bigfoot, they are elusive, at least in Chautauqua County. That doesn't mean some people aren't moving in to the area. In spite of the evidence of what might turn out to be a debilitating loss of population, city leaders have learned to measure success by whether one new family comes to town, or when a Main Street business has a good week, or if a rancher who opened her property to white-tailed-deer hunters has a lodge full of guests.

People tend to gravitate to where the jobs are within driving distance. Towns like Independence or Coffeyville are both less than forty miles away, in Montgomery County. These towns are the shopping and employment hubs for the small communities around them. Better jobs are often farther away, like in Bartlesville, a little more than an hour's drive, or Tulsa, a bit farther than that. Some people work as far away as Wichita, which can take close to two hours to reach depending on where in the city one's job is located. And spending that much time behind the wheel gives one a lot of time to ponder which needs to go: the job or the rural lifestyle.

Chautauqua County's Jack Newcomb once measured many miles between home and work, although it was during a time when he lived and worked in the Kansas City area, commuting from the suburbs to the city. He didn't start out as a city boy. He grew up in Coffeyville and earned a degree in finance from the University of Tulsa. Then he worked in urban corporate America and owned his own business for many years before feeling the urge to return home. "There is always that tug in your heart to go back to the rural way of life," he explains.

He and his wife, Elizabeth, now own a peaceful, tranquil cattle ranch in Chautauqua County. But when they first started considering the move, they took pause. "I was appalled at the difference, how far things had fallen, from where they were when I grew up here," he says. "The decline of population through aging, outmigration of young people, jobs and business going away, forcing a greater number of people to out migrate for jobs, education, shopping: that struck a chord with me. That drove home the fact that if we didn't proactively attack issues, they'd get worse."

In addition to raising cattle, Jack coaches entrepreneurs in starting, maintaining, or growing their businesses in southeast Kansas. He also teaches and mentors other business coaches. He is interested not only in entrepreneurship, but in community development. He is the facilitator of the Quad County Enterprise program, which includes Chautauqua, and neighboring Elk, Greenwood, and Woodson counties. These represent four of the five poorest counties in the state. Facilitators like Jack are hired to work with clients, but they don't recruit businesses, unlike traditional economic development efforts that "chase smokestacks" in hopes of bringing more jobs to communities.

"We focus on one-on-one business coaching to entrepreneurs. The coaches embed themselves as a local resource to provide that assistance, creating a trust factor that doesn't typically occur when federal or state help is available." His approach is to help local people who are already in the region—or who want to be there—become more successful. As those individual businesses start up and grow, ideally they create opportunities that would help the community to grow.

With all the ebb and flow of the national economy and the ripple effect on farm, ranch, and oil country like southeast Kansas, it is hard to gauge whom to credit, or blame, for successes and failures. "Lots of people in the area have microbusinesses, but there are also businesses earning $10 million a year. It is not up to me to measure an entrepreneur's success, because they all have a different definition of what they want and what success means to them," Jack said.

Of the 20,000 people in the area, he has worked with more than 600 of them to help determine if their business idea has a chance of success. "Rural people are hesitant to ask for help, but if someone like me is there, and becomes a friend of a friend, then confidence is built up, and people are more likely to approach me."

Jack realizes that success has to be measured more broadly than at the individual level. "One thing that was eye-opening was that we were helping lots of businesses to start, that could then sustain themselves, with a 90 percent success ratio in startups. But what we weren't seeing was correlation between new successful startups and community growth and development." His program started in 2002. By 2005, he said it became apparent they weren't having far-reaching effects on sustaining the community. Now he's working more toward community development on the regional level rather than only the county level. At present, Jack is a partner at Advancing Rural Prosperities, Inc., with a mission to "breathe life back into rural America and enhance the stability of its communities."

Not everyone is comfortable operating at the state-initiative level, and Jack understands there are multiple roads to success. However, "There is a contingent, and not a small one, of the population in the county who do not want change, specifically, do not want what we might consider 'progress.' They like it the way it is, they say they don't want to make too much change because then people will move in and we won't have the same style of life we have currently." This is an understandable response of individuals who love their way of life and want to protect it, whether they live in large cities, suburbs, small towns, or the country-side. Yet if they do not try to achieve at least slow but steady progress, they are in danger of losing what they have, and not on their terms.

As Rudy Taylor puts it, "This is a town that seldom looks to government for answers," and that might be an understatement. Countywide governance is through the county commission, and local governance is through local city councils. In a county this small, it can be difficult to find people willing to invest the time to serve in these offices. But Jack has an idea of the sort of leader who could move this area forward. "A good county commissioner is not only a successful farmer and rancher, but someone who understands the budgeting process, how taxation works, how investment in the future is just as important as putting gravel on the roads, understands that you can't take the approach that maintaining the status quo is satisfactory. We need someone with a vision."

One logical way to cultivate people with vision is to turn to a community's youth. Sedan has a nearly 100 percent high school graduation rate, and about 75 percent of those students say they want to go to college. So in the Sedan area, the outmigration of eighteen- to twenty-five-year-olds is almost 100 percent. They leave because they want to go to work or school, or to see some new places and experience nightlife and fun they can't access in Sedan. Staying home and doing nothing can be read as failure among not just peer groups, but among parents who would like to turn that bedroom into a sewing room, after all these years. But once people hit their thirties and start having children, some decide they want their kids to have the upbringing and educational system they experienced. That's when people look at returning to their hometowns.

Jack is a believer in good education and that college should be a choice for people to pursue, to a degree. "Convincing kids and their parents that success means college is one thing. But success meaning college followed by a job in a city: that is where I break ranks." They don't need a job with a company to be successful, he argues. "We can help local people create good sustainable businesses that create jobs where people can work. We can embrace that as a success, not a sign of failure that they've returned home. That's a huge culture shift."

Getting young people to reinvest in their communities through civic engagement can only happen if those individuals feel invited into the fold. "Small communities are often led by the same group for a long time, not necessarily elected officials," Jack said. "The younger people see that, and so they don't view leadership as an avenue for them to participate in their community's future. We need to reach out to young people, to help them have a voice at the table. They have good ideas, a willingness to work." He notes that teaching youth about leadership only goes so far without willingness among the established leaders to listen to them. "Young people need to voice and showcase their talents so the general public knows how bright they are."

There is a certain independent nature that is a common thread among people who want this lifestyle, Jack notes. He includes himself in that group, along with several early retirees who've moved into the area from careers elsewhere, some of whom are native to the area, some of whom have no real connection. Yet they find the lifestyle and remote beauty of the place appealing. "Sedan is just a few hours' drive from millions of people. Surely some of them will continue to settle there, just like they did in the early days of the town's incorporation as a cattle and oil community."

Dick Jones and his wife, Nita, are an entry point for many of those potential newcomers. Jones Realty in Sedan offers residential, commercial, and agricultural property in this area of Kansas and Oklahoma. When I was seeking people to interview before arriving in town, Nita's was the first name most people gave me. Indeed, when Nita and I first spoke on the phone, I had the sense I was speaking to a colorful individual used to being the town's publicity spokesperson. With charm, sweetness, and a practiced delivery, Nita related the high points, and downturns, of Sedan's history. She did it all in a twang I never realized people in my native state had in their speech. Note to self: just like other aspects of culture, dialects don't stop at the state border.

When I let Nita know I'd be coming to town, she connected me with Mary and Jack Warren, who operate Grandma's House and Grandpa's House, two fully furnished residences available by the day or week. Both places are furnished with Victorian furniture and homey artwork. I stopped there first to get settled before meeting with Nita. The refrigerator at Grandma's House was stocked with various goodies, which were a welcome sight. I didn't think about it until I arrived, but stopped in my tracks when I saw the Warren's NO CREDIT CARD policy taped to the kitchen wall. I didn't think to carry a checkbook, stupidly forgetting that many small businesses in small towns don't accept credit cards. I spent twenty-four hours panicking, not knowing my credit card PIN number for use at the ATM, or really if that was even a *thing*. I had cash, but not nearly enough. I felt trapped like a fly between the window and the screen of somebody else's kitchen. Until I flagged down Jack Warren on one of his many passes down my block in his truck, and explained my predicament. No problem, he said. Just put the check in the mail. You can believe that's just what I did, as soon as I returned home.

To keep my appointment at the Jones Real Estate office was a matter of walking just a few blocks from Grandma's House. Nita is not herself a real estate agent; rather, she runs the business end of the office. But that doesn't mean she doesn't present herself as though she was about to show a wealthy house hunter into some of the best-appointed residential spaces in the two-state area. Bright yellow pants, gold knit top, black strappy sandals, statement jewelry, beautifully arranged dark hair: I don't look half as good as seventy-something Nita did on this Saturday at noon, not even on my very best days.

She greeted me with a hug and showed me around the office. The converted bank was as vibrant as Nita herself, with lots of beautiful bright artwork on the walls. Dick immediately made my heart flutter with his western boots and shirt and southern gentleman courtesy, removing his black cowboy hat as he shook my hand and greeted me with a "How do you do, ma'am?"

They introduced me to their daughter Melodi Jones, who moved back to Sedan after more than twenty years in Tulsa because she got tired of big city life. She'd been working as a legal secretary for eight years, developing experience in oil and gas, real estate, wills, and trusts. Melodi told me she wanted to be near family. She found a home not far from her parents' place, so now her children are near their grandparents. And now that she's obtained her broker's license, she works side by side with her parents.

Nita told me about the 1980s, when thirteen businesses went out of business, including the Sedan State Bank, where her real estate office is housed. "That's the death of a town when you lose that many businesses, in a downtown area of four blocks. That's when you know you're in trouble." At the time, Nita was in the clothing business with a partner. She saw four other clothing stores go out of business during that period, until hers was the only one left. "It is not good to have no competition; the more businesses you have, the more that will come, offering people more variety."

To demonstrate that variety, Nita pointed me out the door to start the tour of the various resources in Sedan and Chautauqua County. She drove me around in her brand-new red Cadillac, occasionally tapping the dashboard screen to answer a phone call or note the outside temperature. She pointed out some of the highlights, like the Emmet Kelly Museum housed in the old opera house, Buck's BBQ, the Dollar General, the high school, the rodeo grounds, the courthouse, the airport with its turf runway. She pointed out the school and said pragmatically: "If you lose the school, you've lost the town." There were several new enterprises in Sedan and she made sure I thought about those as much as I did the things that were gone. That's what natural-born salespeople and community leaders do when they see their town shrinking in front of their eyes. Nita understood why some people gave up and left for Bartlesville after the economy got rough. But the Joneses and a few others didn't give up. "Dreamers and doers need to work together rather than apart, whether they like each other or not."

This group formed SOS (for Save Our Sedan committee) in the late 1980s. Their focus was tourism. When one thinks Kansas, for better or worse, one eventually gets to *The Wizard of Oz*. Never mind that L. Frank Baum never stated exactly where in Kansas Dorothy Gale and her family lived. Never mind that the town of Liberal, 300 miles to the west, had already decided the Gales were from Seward County, and in the late 1980s opened their own Dorothy's House tourist attraction. Never mind the spare high plains around Liberal seem a much better geographical fit for the story. The SOS group decided they'd capitalize on the concept and build a yellow brick road, by golly. They took their idea to the local government and learned there was no funding for such a thing. No matter. Zero funding was no obstacle for this group. Surely celebrities would want their name on a yellow brick that would join others on a road— really a sidewalk—through the downtown business district of Sedan.

Nita learned something new about city officials when the project began. "They take offense if you start digging up sidewalks, even if the

Playing on the *Wizard of Oz* theme, the Yellow Brick Road attraction lures tourists off the highway and into town, into the heart of Sedan's businesses and restaurant district. Photograph © Julianne Couch.

sidewalks need replacing after fifty or seventy-five years." So they agreed the local street crew would dig out the existing sidewalk and haul off the material. Then the money earned from brick-buyers would go to replace the sidewalk, this time with bricks. They started out charging ten dollars, then fifteen, then twenty-five, for an inscribed brick, which isn't so much gold as it is dusty beige.

Between 1989 and 2013, they've sold 11,556 bricks. The SOS crew worked hard to let people know about the Yellow Brick Road, which brought in tourists, some of whom bought bricks of their own. The word then spread to celebrities such as Bob Hope, Liz Taylor, and Whoopi Goldberg, all of whom have bricks with their names inscribed running through downtown Sedan.

"That got us rolling on this thing called tourism," Nita said. "The cattle and oil people looked at us like we were crazy. Every town has assets—you just gotta find them."

To demonstrate this truth, Nita drove me past a section of a creek in town that had long been an unofficial dumping ground. She told me how the SOS group arranged to dispose of the accumulating car bodies and trash, dumped there over many decades. "Everybody got on that bandwagon, we cleaned it up, and had a naming contest. It was just known as the gulch, now it is the Hollow." She showed me a beautiful flower garden with a boardwalk along the creek, and little spots visitors can sit and watch birds. I never would have guessed it had once been an environmental disaster.

"The work was all done by volunteers," she said. "If you don't have volunteers, you have problems. You have to have somebody with a passion, not somebody who wants to do something and get credit for it." It was a shame when, not long after my visit, vandals trashed the gazebo in the Hollow. The disappointment among both the volunteers who'd worked on the area and the visitors who'd spent time there is hard to measure.

That made me think about something else Rudy Taylor had told me about the appearance of small towns in rural America. "They look terrible when compared to urban or suburban communities. We're dirty, unkempt, and downright shabby. Our curb appeal sucks."

I wasn't sure I'd go that far but I knew what he meant about some small towns in the rural middle of America. The kind with one main drag through town that is the only thing most travelers see. Where they are welcomed by billboards for Christian churches and native-son military heroes. Where matching decorative banners hang from antique streetlights for a few blocks, complementing cute storefronts and large flower pots. One or two tri-colored Victorian homes stand high on hills. A grain silo and railroad track spur signal the edge of town is coming, and the modest homes on the edges lack paint and the lawns lack grass. This signals that someone is too busy, too old, or just too broke to keep the property up the way they'd like. And travelers through this wide spot in the road hit the gas pedal and wonder how a town like that stays on the map, with no sign of large employers or shopping centers. Everybody here must be on disability or welfare, the traveler concludes. And unfortunately in small rural America, that conclusion isn't always wrong. Nita's tour was designed to show me that, in spite of Sedan's steadily shrinking population, there were some individuals left who were getting by, making a living, loving the slow-paced lifestyle their town offered.

Walking from shop to shop, along the Yellow Brick Road, Nita showed me the town's best sites and introduced me to its strongest boosters. In my small town travels I'd gotten rather used to bumping around alone, sidling up to friendly looking people, edging my way into their conversations. That was not the case here. "You mean they don't all come out to meet you?" Nita asked, incredulous. Before I could come up with an answer, we were joined by Sue Kill, economic development mover and shaker of Chautauqua County. We picked up others along the way. Sue was attired in a bright yellow jacket, adorned with diamond and ruby Oz-themed pins, to underscore the concept. I felt like Dorothy Gale, picking up a new friend at each stop, but without the terrifying witches and flying monkeys.

Sue is a self-described country girl who has spent most of her life in Chautauqua County. She is an important part of the nonprofit Sedan Area Economic Development Committee. She is a retired clerk and treasurer for the school district. At the time of our conversation, she was on the board of the cemetery district, the rural water district, and a long list of other professional civic organizations. She has spent enough time in larger cities like Wichita and Tulsa and Joplin, Missouri, to know that she hasn't "lost anything" by not living in one of them. She knows she can visit these places whenever she wants to get her city fix. But she doesn't relish the crowds or the traffic.

She sees most of Sedan's economic difficulties as a maddeningly simple but connected set of problems. "We need more families. We need improvements in housing here, and we need more jobs for people."

What population would be comfortable? "Fifteen hundred. But I'm not sure if that would be obtainable with school enrollment going down. We're trying to get families here by promoting our small school, safer community," she said. She regrets that the number of kids around the nation who grew up on farms and learned to work and develop a work ethic, such as she developed in 4-H and scouting, is shrinking. She senses that rural kids who have that background have an advantage over their city peers.

Sue agrees with Jack Newcomb, that trying to get kids to stay in town after graduation is an important goal, especially since she believes a good percentage would like to do so. Encouraging entrepreneurship among those who have that bent is important, as is attending community college for some education and experience. "They should go into the world and get some training, and then come home if they want.

Not everybody needs a college education, especially because of the high debt they'll incur. They may graduate but not find the job with pay they were looking for. Then they'll have the education but not the work skill or job experience."

Later during my visit, Sue loaded me up in her little red pickup truck and drove me a mile or two into the outskirts of town, south along US Highway 160. She pointed out the facilities of a local success, Sedan Floral, a third-generation company founded in 1948 by Jim and Eileen Cudé. In 1975, their son Gary joined the family business as general manager. Gary was nineteen, proving Jack Newcomb's rule about giving young people a chance to show they are bright. Gary worked his way up, learning the business and expanding the plant-growing area about 20,000 square feet every year. In 1989, Gary purchased the business and built a second growing range in nearby Independence. In 2007, Gary's son, Jonathan, returned home after graduating from Oklahoma State University to become the third generation to join the family business. In 2009, another of Gary's sons, Jeremy, returned home after graduating from Kansas State University and is the company's operations manager. This family business is an example of the kind of entrepreneurship both Jack Newcomb and Sue Kill hope to see more of, especially since it has created a business that has kept younger members of the family home and is a strong contributor to the civic vitality of the area.

One ongoing discussion is whether Sedan's future lies with attracting tourists, who only require entertainment and lodging, or recruiting new residents, who need employment and housing. Nita thinks tourism is simpler and quicker to pay off. The town doesn't really have the infrastructure, such as employment and housing, needed to bring in a large number of new residents. So it is easier to have tourist attractions that appeal to people, provide lots of positive news coverage, and encourage visitors to part with a bit of cash.

What really stands in the way of tourism is the scarcity of lodging, Nita says. With more overnight accommodations, people could make Sedan a destination rather than a place to simply stop for an hour or two. Sedan is a few miles off US 160, part of the Tallgrass Prairie Parkway. Sedan is reached by turning off that road onto US 166. But that highway bypassed the town a few years ago. This was a blow to the town, but the energetic volunteers found a way to swing back. While crews were removing rocks for the construction, one especially large hunk of sandstone proved stubborn. Nita and others talked the highway department into making a monument of it, and it stands as a marker outside Sedan. "It is just like Chautauqua County, too tough to break," she said.

In addition to tourist attractions, the area has a stable of other resources. These include oil and gas deposits, fertile farmland with plenty of rainfall, and game animals. Game-bird and white-tailed-deer hunting are popular, and a few local landowners have gotten into the outfitting business, bringing hunters to town, lodging them in their farm or ranch houses, and making sure they have food and other supplies. Hunting season can be lucrative for not just the outfitters, but for other businesses, like the grocery store, the hardware store, and even shops that sell gifts a hunter may want to bring back home.

One of these outfitter/ranchers is Reta Pipher, who operates Stagecoach Ranch. She raises red Angus cattle, Arabian horses, Shetland sheep, and offers ranch stays and hunting on her property. She says that although she makes thousands of dollars by opening her ranch to hunters, she believes their presence has taken a toll on the wildlife. "All the biggest deer, genetically, are gone now because hunters want trophy animals," she explained. Another concern: "There are some bad eggs among the hunting parties who climb fences they shouldn't, leave gates open, and so on." These she doesn't allow back. In addition to maintaining the ranch, Reta has a shop in town. That's where she has a loom and weaves scarves and other items. Although her husband has passed away, she told me she originally set up the shop in town because he had so much clutter in the house there was little space for her work. Now she's in good company with other business owners up and down Main.

I had a chance to meet a few of these business owners on my town tour with Nita and Sue. There was Charles Meadows, president of Ackarman Hardware & Lumber, which has been in business since 1879. Charlie had lived away from town over the years but moved back to the area a dozen years ago. He took us into his office, where he'd hung historical photos of Sedan showing the hardware store and the street scenes of the period. Back when transportation was arduous, it was essential that materials could be obtained efficiently, so it helped having things close by. But now people think nothing of driving thirty miles to a larger town for perceived better variety or prices. "It is only natural to go out of town to shop: that's what people enjoy doing," Charlie said. "Then they go to restaurants or do various things to get away for the day." That's why he focuses on offering what local customers need and having it there when they need it.

After saying so long to Charlie, we stopped down the street to see Kimberly Morton, owner of SwankyDudz. Kim has dark hair and an olive complexion, like Nita's. They could pass as mother and daughter in their looks and manner. Their outgoing personalities bounced over each other like diamonds on denim as they buzzed about jewelry and clothing for a few minutes as I eyed a pair of cowboy boots I wanted but did not need. Kim told me she moved to Sedan from Wichita a few years ago, where she ran a retail shop. "I was sick of the traffic and the crime. I wanted out." When she opened the store in Sedan she quickly realized she'd have to "change her inventory a hundred percent to appeal to shoppers here." She and her retired pharmacist husband bought a building across the street from their shop and thought they'd put in an eatery of some sort. Then Kim's mother, who makes and sells crafts, decided to join Kim and family in Sedan. Now the plan is to sell her crafts in the other store, along with light pastries, and "whatever will go."

Nita and Sue took me next to meet Leota Casement at Leota's Gifts & More. "Gifts" refer to clothing, jewelry, handbags, and an assortment of anything fun you can think of. "More" refers to ice cream. She sells enough that she can hire high school kids in the summer. She favors those who are going off to college that fall because "they need the extra money more than the younger ones." Then, if they come home for Christmas break, they can easily work in the store because they are already trained, she says. Leota admits that as the sole proprietor of the business, she sometimes feels trapped inside the store. But she's on the main street of a small town. She can simply put a note in the window that says *Back in Five*, and go visit with another shopkeeper. Customers will either wait, or come find her if they are in a rush.

After our brief visit, we walked a block to a newly opened restaurant, where Nita and Sue had arranged for various individuals to meet me. The restaurant Nita chose happened to belong to her son and daughter-in-law. Her son is known locally as "Safari" Mark for his numerous hunting trips to Africa. He's got the mounted trophies to show for it, and these liberally festoon the walls of the restaurant and attached bar area. This building was once the town's elegant hotel. Mark and his wife, Amanda, hope to reopen the hotel rooms one day as a partial solution to the town's lodging problem. They're looking forward to the zebra-print awning with "Safari Mark's" inscribed on it, which was on order and expected to arrive soon. "Then people will see where we are," he said.

Judy Tolbert, a former director of the Sedan Chamber of Commerce, was also in the group. She'd had a career in the insurance business and was living in Bartlesville until it became clear her parents in Sedan needed her help. She met a man in Sedan, fell in love, and married. "Before I knew it, I was chamber president." Now she's spearheading an ambitious plan for a new library to serve as a center for learning, communication, and community activities. At present, the library shares space with a commercial building, and conditions are crowded.

Currently, Sedan has about as many library books as it has yellow bricks. It isn't enough to have books in the library, Judy said. Instead, the library will have multiple uses. "There will be a community safe room so that the next time the tornado siren blows, residents won't have to shelter in church basements hoping the steeples don't collapse on their heads." It will have two meeting rooms and twenty computers. These can be used by library patrons, adults studying for high school equivalency exams, and nursing-home residents who can visit the library in small groups to use computers. There will be a full kitchen where area experts can teach classes about canning and preserving food grown in the community garden that will be located on library grounds.

Sedan has had a leg up that many small towns in the region have not had, and that came in the form of a patron. Bill Kurtis is a television journalist, producer, and news anchor, best known as host of *Investigative Reports*, *American Justice*, and *Cold Case Files*. He was also raised in nearby Independence, Kansas. Throughout the 1990s Kurtis worked to help bring Sedan from the brink of deterioration by making numerous investments. He bought 10,000 acres of ranch land and started Red Buffalo Ranch, just a few miles from town. He purchased and renovated eleven downtown buildings. Then, he rented them to businesses at free or reduced rent for a time. Although he has sold some portions of the ranch, he has left a large footprint on the town, one that separates it from the standard crumbling brick and broken glass of other communities in decline.

His daughter Mary Kurtis operates the Red Buffalo Ranch, where she lives. She also spends part of her days at the Red Buffalo Gift Shop and Coffee House on Main Street, in one of the buildings her father renovated. She moved to Sedan from San Francisco in 2007, in order to help her father with the business. We visited for a bit while I was in town and then later by phone. She really made me wish I could live in two places at once. I could have spent a great more time in her company. "I was taken by the architecture, the Flint Hills, how different it is from the rest of Kansas, so I came for family and to take care of our investments," she told me. Her father spends much of his time in Chicago, and realizes he can't be an out-of-town landlord of a ranch. "Even with a manager in place, nobody cares about your land like you do," she said. Overseeing the ranch is a big responsibility for Mary, as are some of the other projects her father started, such as the downtown gift store bearing the Red Buffalo name.

"I thought business was slow before the recession came, and then I found out what slow really is," she tells me. "But hope springs eternal, and you find out what works. I decided to go to people wherever they are, so we've amped up Internet sales."

Access to technology is adequate in Sedan but not perfect. For instance, she'd like to have a wireless hotspot in the coffee shop but the solid rock walls of her building don't allow for that. She believes the city leaders are not quite as excited about state-of-the-art Internet connectivity as she is, to say the least. That's not the only way Mary perceives her differences here. Although the gap is closing now, there was a fairly wide social and cultural moat to bridge when she first moved to town. "My partner and I weren't married when we moved here, and that was a big deal. We should have gotten married first. Who knew!" Another difference is that they don't have children. "That is not a big deal in San Francisco, as far as belonging. Here, that mattered." And Mary presented yet another difference. "We also don't go to church. That's all of the hot buttons."

Mary realized she'd need to make a personal attempt to get to know people one on one, rather than through traditional institutions. "I realized if they like you, they'll forgive you" for being a little different. "It was nice, actually, to be nice. I learned not to talk politics at all." Mary has sensed less tolerance for difference in a small town like Sedan, at least compared to the big city. "The fewer people a city has, the more everyone wants people to be the same," she observes. "It doesn't matter. After a while, one by one, they're gonna like me."

Mary has put in the shoe leather to be liked, or at least to be known. She's active in the business and civic life of town. The Red Buffalo store carries locally made items and high school sports team T-shirts. Red Buffalo Ranch is a tourist destination year-round. She used to offer hunting and horseback riding, but found those tourist activities too difficult in terms of insurance liability and property damage and therefore has "scaled back." But the ranch is open for people who want to visit scenic spots such as Butcher Falls, with a visitor center and entry point for hiking trails.

It is unavoidable looking at downtown Sedan to think of Bill Kurtis and the financial contribution he made to stabilize the town. I wondered if that meant residents would have an expectation of that support continuing in an open-ended way. "There are expectations that I will do things because of who I am," Mary acknowledged. "My dad was very generous. I've been more about 'no' because of finances." On one occasion Mary did physical labor on a project rather than writing a check, but she said that form of contribution was not enthusiastically met. "Now I'm picking projects more selectively. For instance, a group of citizens is trying to save the Gregg movie theatre. That's all the culture we have. That's one task I'm trying to help with because it unifies people." The volunteer effort is what gets things done in town, she said, but it gets exhausting. Like everyone else I talked to in Sedan, Mary wishes younger people would remain in the area and bring new energy to civic efforts.

But in order for them to stay, Mary believes the town needs some form of industry that would supply solid jobs that can support "blue-collar families with kids." There needs to be an employer because most young people are not going to purchase land and run a farm or ranch, she believes. "If you aren't inheriting land it is impossible to pull off. Agriculture has such a slim margin. To put a land payment on top of that for a young person is tough."

She sees hope in the "weekenders" who buy houses here and then retire to them. "They know the deal and have chosen to be here. They help the tax base, although they're not putting kids through the schools." She says she sees the weekenders in her store more than a lot of local people. "And because of them, I'm not the newbie anymore."

Spending time in Mary's store made me feel I was in the most thriving town of 1,200 imaginable, and that if one could sell gourmet coffee beans and hand-knit scarves here, all things were possible. I prepared to leave the store with a bag full of such goodies myself, outfitted on the outside but also warmed on the inside with the feeling I really had made longtime connections and friends in Sedan. I had to interrupt a conversation Mary was having with a small group in order to say good-bye. A few middle-aged guys with facial hair and enthusiastic voices were among them. They seemed exactly like the sort of people I hang around with in Bellevue, and once hung around with in Laramie, and in Kansas City, and Emporia. I know my tribe when I see it. I was not at all surprised when one of them, the one with the guitar case and gray watch cap, turned out to be Mark Palmer. I'd spent an hour on the phone with him a few weeks previous, chatting about life and home ground as though I'd known him for years. Before we hung up I had the names and phone numbers of several people in town he thought I should connect with, including Mary Kurtis. I had thanked him with enthusiasm.

"It doesn't cost me anything to be helpful," he'd replied.

Mark is a retired engineer from the Cessna Aircraft Company in Wichita. A native New Englander, he has owned land in Chautauqua County for about twenty years. He built a house on the property and has lived there for a dozen of those twenty years. Though that is a decent amount of time to become known in the area, he says he's still an outsider. Even so, he's made a study of the history and its connection to the economy of this region. "A hundred years ago, there were five times as many people in the county as there are today," he said. Oil and gas development was responsible for both the higher population, and now for the decline. Oil and gas was discovered in the 1920s, prompting a rush that peaked in the 1930s and 1940s. Not only did oil and gas bubble or rise from the earth, it was almost as if it brought dollars with it. A great deal of wealth was generated during that time, and that wealth lasted into the 1950s and 1960s. Most of the wells are now stripper wells. Sometimes called a marginal well, the term refers to an oil or gas well that is nearing the end of its economically useful life. These low-producing wells around Sedan are cost-effective in times of high oil and gas prices, in part because the reservoir in this area is shallow and easier to work. Although these stripper wells are estimated to have years of life in them, the energy economy is nothing compared to what it once was. And that has repercussions, he explains.

"We need energy to run the economy," Mark said. "Liquid hydrocarbon fuels are a crucial part of the economy. That economy is leveling off here, which has a major economic impact and affects the fundamentals of a town." Mark asks me to imagine the economy as a pyramid. The bottom tier is energy extraction. Just on top of it is agriculture. "In the late 1880s this was homesteader country, and it was hard living. It was the development of the fossil fuel resource that made it possible." Now there are fewer ways to enhance economic activity. They are left with ranching, farming, and hunting for white-tailed deer—none of which can replace the flow of money once figuratively pumped out of the ground.

Although traditional energy sources are waning, there is a 200-megawatt wind farm about thirty-five miles northwest of Sedan in Elk County, near the town of Howard. Construction of the Caney River Wind Project began in 2011. The project is believed to be one of the most wind-rich sites of any wind project in development in eastern Kansas. The Caney River Wind Project has entered into a partnership with the National Fish and Wildlife Foundation to manage $8.5 million in funding directed toward the purchase of conservation easements and issuing research and conservation grants within the state.

The site was specially selected due to its proximity to existing power transmission lines, which the company says means no new transmission lines or rights of way will need to be acquired or constructed. In addition, no scenic byways or other threatened or endangered species or habitats are impacted by the project. The project will take approximately 150 acres of farmland out of service, including land for roads, turbine foundations, and maintenance buildings. The rest of the approximately 14,000 acres leased for the project will still be farmed and ranched by the owners already present there.

Developers say the project will provide $3 million annually in rent payment to participating landowners, and payments in lieu of taxes to Elk County. These payments represent a 50 percent increase in annual county revenues for Elk County, which, unfortunately for Chautauqua County, is one county too far north. But they can take solace, perhaps, in knowing the project will offset an estimated 600,000 tons of carbon-dioxide emissions per year, 2,000 tons of nitrogen oxide per year, and 2,800 tons of sulfur dioxide per year. The project will generate enough power to supply the needs of approximately 60,000 households, although those households won't be in Elk County or Chautauqua County. Instead, the electricity will whistle down transmission lines to customers in the southeastern United States, served by the Tennessee Valley Authority.

Mark explained some of these facts of Chautauqua County life to me as we sat on his front porch, looking out onto a beautiful little valley where his farm acreage lay. He'd had a long day driving to Tulsa and back to pick up his Martin guitar, which was there for repairs. He suggested I come out to his place to visit. Mark had already told me his wife had become disaffected with country life and had "punched out" to return to Wichita. I thought for one nanosecond about the wisdom of driving into country I wasn't familiar with to hang out alone with a man I really didn't know from Adam. Most of my thinking turned to pinning down the moment I stopped worrying about such things. It might have been midway through my time in the frontier state of Wyoming. Of course, Mark didn't know me from Eve either. Maybe that's the bigger point.

Mark had given me good directions to get from Grandma's Place to his place, about ten miles distant. While driving, I marveled at the beauty of the scenery and how wrong people are to think of Kansas as flat (not that there's anything wrong with flat). Locals tout the area as the Ozarks of Kansas, and while they lack a really big and overly developed lake resort, they don't lack in beauty. Even the ERS Natural Amenities scale manages to calculate a read of between 0 and 1. That doesn't sound like much until you consider that the scale ranges from below a –2 for low amenities to +3 for high amenities. Of course, while pondering this, I got mixed up by Nita Jones's big granite road marker and found myself driving directly west into the blazing sunset along the wrong road. A quick call to Mark got me righted, and I arrived at his place just before sunset on a late October evening. I was greeted cordially by his two Pyrenees dogs, there to guard his goats but also to present a general look of watchfulness about the place. Those worker dogs, plus the house dog and assorted farm critters, registered me as just another interesting tickle in their day. Mark poured me a rather full glass of a rather robust chilled white wine. Before we got into serious conversation, I had to ask for a demonstration of the Martin. He played James Taylor's "Sweet Baby James," and when I joined in on harmony I knew I'd scored some points for knowing the words. I borrowed the guitar long enough to play "Lodi," by Credence Clearwater Revival.

He'd conjured New England with his song, and I, California. Smack in the middle the two of us sat in Kansas, on the porch of the home he had built by hand as a labor of love, situated to align with the North Star.

He pointed into the darkness toward his organic gardens, where he grows everything from asparagus to okra to watermelons. Between the vegetables, the goats, and the fruit trees, he has plenty for himself and to sell in the Sedan farmers market. He's also a figure in the local bartering economy, trading what he needs for what he has. But he doesn't raise cattle, which might be one reason for his outsider status. He says he doesn't believe that so much land needs to be for grazing, which is its chief purpose for many landowners. To get good quality grass, ranchers use herbicides so the cattle don't ingest harmful vegetation. This is vegetation that goats and sheep could eat, so herbicide would not be required, he says. Another problem with herbicide is that the airborne particles might drift onto his organic produce, endangering his ability to sell them as such.

On the positive side, water is plentiful, with forty inches of rainfall and good wells and aquifers. "Land here is cheap and pretty," he said. "You don't need to be a bazillionaire to live here. Moving here has started to seem like a pretty good idea," he said. After a tiny touch more of the wine—I was driving but now I knew the way—we got into comparing reading lists. I wrote down names he rattled off, like T. Colin Campbell (nutritionist and vegan advocate); Robert Hirsch (energy development expert—notably, fusion); John Michael Greer (blogger on Druid conceptions of nature, culture, and the future of the industrial society); Dmitry Orlov (engineer and writer about the economic, ecological, and political decline and collapse in the United States); and James Howard Kunstler (writer, speaker, podcaster on suburban sprawl, the end of cheap oil, and urban planning). I gave him names of a few writers I thought he'd enjoy, such as John McPhee. He didn't need to write down the name William Least Heat-Moon, who'd written a tome about Chase County, Kansas, titled *PrairyErth*. "That book is this place, too," Mark told me. "He nailed it."

Reflecting on that comparison, we both pulled our jackets tighter against the chilly autumn air. Neither of us wanted to break the spell of this beautiful evening by going inside. Down in the meadow a barred owl called "who cooks for you" and we made silly puns about a "bard" owl reciting Shakespeare. Off in the valley a pack of coyotes started their nightly song. The guest cabin he'd pointed out was starting to look pretty attractive to my suddenly weary self, so before I succumbed I kicked myself in gear and organized myself for my temporary home. Mark fixed me up with a jar of his homemade honey, complete with comb. He invited me to the next Chautauqua Hills Blues Festival, an annual Memorial Day weekend event that benefits the county's children, in part through the local "Blues in the Schools" program. I would have guessed music fans in this area would be in to classic rock, or maybe Christian, or country or even bluegrass. That doesn't mean they aren't, but it was a pleasant surprise to learn there was a pocket of fellow blues lovers in these hills. This place was full of surprises.

As Mark walked me through the Pyrenees guard, he told me about some of his neighbors who'd moved onto nearby farms. "Everybody here is trying to get away from something," he said, stating what was starting to register as a theme. There were two young families he characterized as "new homesteaders." There is a fairly widespread movement of people who are described with that term. Not all live in rural areas like this; some live within the borders of cities or suburbs but still adopt certain practices that seem based in the nineteenth century. For example, they are interested in producing and consuming locally sourced goods, homeschooling their children, and cutting the cord from the grid as much as possible. "These new neighbors have serious concerns about the government," he said, and they are pretty sure they'll need to be able to survive with their own wits and resources as the national economy and other federal structures disappear.

"These young people give me hope. Top-down initiatives don't work. These young people make me feel that if this area, this country, can survive that it will be because of people like them."

I did not get to meet the people Mark told me about because by the time I was ready to reach out to them, they'd already faded back into the Chautauqua Hills or points beyond the reach of a cell-phone conversation with a stranger. But in Mark I'd already met their prototype. He gave me the feeling they gave him. That if this area of southeast Kansas is to sustain its population, it will be because of people like him, and some of the other folks I met on this trip. There just needs to be a whole lot more of them with a feeling for the place. The Yellow Brick Road is a two-way street, after all.

5 KNOX COUNTY, NEBRASKA
TRAVELING IN GOOD COMPANY

There is something somber in the quiet of this place; the distant bugles of sandhill crane above a background note of coyote song; a hologram of the centuries rising and flashing then waning in the sun-bleached landscape. I'd come this way through the Missouri River Valley and experienced this sensation before, but never by myself. Always in the company of spouse and dog and road atlas and unsteady coffee mug, worry about weather speeding us there, or back home. This time, alone in my car on US 20 in far western Iowa, I realize I'm traveling through time. Not toward the future, as one does every second of life. But toward the past. Toward a sense of loss but also of potential. Toward a choice of roads to take, rivers to paddle, shelters in which to moor and drop anchor.

Loss took a front seat on this trip, uninvited. I was not far from Sioux City, Iowa, when traffic was stopped for road construction. It was to be a long delay so I lowered my car window and stopped the engine. I took a quick glance at my phone and saw I'd received a text message from a friend in Bellevue: *Hate to be the bearer of bad news. Have your heard about Curt? He passed away last night. Massive heart attack. Shocking.*

Curt Gothard was a sixty-year-old business entrepreneur and lifelong resident of Bellevue. I'd known him about a year, since we began serving on a board together. Hearing he'd passed away so suddenly jolted me. I thought about his wife and children, whose sense of loss I could not fathom. Then I thought about his many business associates and friends. About how many people in town were temporarily frozen, unable to move forward, without Curt's input or advice. How the smaller the town, the more important each individual in it becomes. How for the first time in my short time as a Bellevue resident, someone I knew personally had died, without warning and way too soon. I felt unanchored, wishing I could swap Curt stories with friends, the way one does after a death, with each telling more assured that we ourselves are still solidly grounded on the solid side of the divide.

I returned my friend's message with a few texted words, devoid of much power to convey feeling: *Wow. Thanks for letting me know.* Then, alerted by the roadside flagger, I started my engine and followed the pilot car. In a long line of cars, I made my way into Sioux City, doglegging onto I-29 north, to pace the Missouri River. Like Lewis and Clark and their Corps of Discovery, I was headed upstream. To my right, I noted the tall obelisk marker on a bluff above the river that commemorates Sgt. Charles Floyd, a member of the Corps who died not far from here on August 20, 1804, on the outward stage of the voyage. He was the only member of the two-year expedition to die on the trip. Farther along, I could see the Argosy Casino, operating aboard a permanently anchored riverboat on the Missouri. Commercial Sioux City has a fanciful Disneyland demeanor to it, coming across in a manufactured yet somehow charming way that feels inviting. But I was headed north into South Dakota. At the intersection of I-29 and Highway 50, the sky stopped being that of the Midwest and became that of the Northern Plains. I took Highway 50 west to the University of South Dakota in Vermillion to be in the company of some wonderful writers and students. Following that event I headed south, crossing back over the Missouri River into Nebraska.

I pulled in at the Lewis and Clark Visitor Center and walked to the top of the observation bluff. I took in scenes of the vastly braided Missouri National Recreational River. Upstream dams control the water, but it still flows comparatively free here. I considered how Lewis and Clark would have seen something like this beautiful sand painting and that's when I felt time go *click*. Not to a time in my past but to a time in *the* past. Two young couples walking just ahead of me stopped to photograph each other in front of the vast view. I wondered if they felt it. I wondered if, like me, they heard the whispered voices of a thousand years, felt the shifting sand beneath their feet that had given ground to a million footsteps before theirs. An ancient place is testimony to resilience. I wondered what I'd find ahead in Knox County, Nebraska, home to a few shrinking but stoic towns and villages, the Santee Sioux Reservation, and the Missouri and Niobrara rivers, both of them wild, scenic, and forthright.

I had trouble choosing my target town in Knox County because hardly anybody wanted to talk to me. That is, they didn't want to respond to an e-mail from a stranger asking to arrange a phone interview or perhaps a meeting in a few weeks, even when that stranger had gotten their name and contact information from a friend of a friend on social media. Go figure. It was then that I developed a new strategy. Reviewing my county map I considered the forty-nine towns, villages, census-designated places, unincorporated communities, and townships. The biggest town in the county is Creighton, with 1,154 residents. I realized all these small towns, and the Santee Sioux Reservation, united into a highly diverse and storied Knox County. I would make Niobrara my headquarters because it is on the Missouri River and has a large state park. From there, I would visit all the communities I could and make contacts as I went.

I started my research with Winnetoon because I'd found someone there willing to speak to me in advance of my trip. Gayle Neuhaus is a little bit famous, already. She contributes to an online genealogy blog titled *A Few Nuts from the Tree*. She was interviewed for the Nebraska Public Television news feature, *Winnetoon Back in Time 1910*. The video, which I found on YouTube, shows a collection of old buildings and memorabilia she has pieced together to represent the Winnetoon of a century ago when she says the town was at its peak. "I love history," she says in the video. "I belong in 1910." I conjectured that if Gayle was going to go public in those forums, she wouldn't mind a phone call from me.

We arranged a time to talk when Gayle wouldn't still be working in her garden but wouldn't yet be behind the counter at the Winnetoon post office. As postmistress, Gayle literally keeps Winnetoon on the map. Without a post office, a place is not only less convenient for residents—it can disappear from the state map. Gayle also operates an antique store. Her grandparents settled in this area in 1872, before there was a town, and owned property where the church is now. The church cemetery was originally her family cemetery. Gayle says she still feels close to her parents because of her work, which includes compiling a history of Winnetoon, which she published in 2006.

"My roots here are very deep," Gayle said. However, she and her daughter are the only members of the family still in the area. Her brother lives in another state, her two children live elsewhere, and her parents are deceased. Gayle started her historical research as a twelve-year-old girl when she became interested in the history of the town. She has no formal training as a historian, but has the passion to take photos, distribute and tally questionnaires, and create the resulting documentation. Her other historical work is as a volunteer with the website Find a Grave. Every week she visits the local libraries to find current newspaper obituaries. She records the obituary information on the website so as to cement the vital statistics of their lives into the public record. Not only does she put information on the site, she photographs gravestones and posts those pictures on the site. In that way, people can learn where their family or friends are buried. Through her efforts, the full population of the Winnetoon cemetery is now online. "I'll put someone on Find a Grave, and then if someone notices an error in the newspaper obituary they contact me," she explains. "When I put people on there, I can almost hear my mother tell me stories about them," she said.

Gayle lives in an ideal location for this sort of quiet life devoted to the comings and goings of flowers, of mail, and of lives. "I'm not a lonely person, but I do like to be alone. Going back in time keeps my family close to me." She enjoys Winnetoon but has noticed some changes in it over the years.

"The Winnetoon of today is quiet and laid back, like it always has been. However, some aspects of the town are not like when I was a kid or when my kids were young. Then, people who lived here took an interest in the town and their property. Now, so many people are moving in without having a feeling for the town. That really bothers me. They move here but I'm not sure why. Some houses that are for rent are not kept up by the owners, and the renters don't keep them up, either."

Mostly, Gayle can overlook these housing issues. She likes that it is quiet, that she can work in her garden and historical boardwalk and not worry about people bothering her. "Sure there is some occasional youthful vandalism, but it isn't like living in the city at all." She knows of what she speaks, having been born in Los Angeles and having spent time there in her younger days. Now she doesn't go back except to visit family. "In Winnetoon I can garden or walk in the dark with no fear of people accosting me."

Although it may sound like Gayle lives a very solitary life, she does have a bit of company. In 2010, there were sixty-eight people in Winnetoon. In 2012, there were sixty-seven. In 2013, there were sixty-six. The median age is 51.5. There are a few employers not far away that bring people to town or keep the ones already there in place. There's a hospital, a nursing home, some farm jobs. Some people work in Springfield, across the river in South Dakota, about thirty miles away, bringing their paycheck back to Knox County. But Gayle says younger people still leave. "There isn't much for them here," Gayle said. "Both of my grandsons have moved away because they can't get a decent job. I think it hurts when they move away because you want people with a feeling for the town to be able to stay. If younger people with families would stay, they would have that feeling."

A few families with children do remain in town. Unfortunately, the Winnetoon school closed in the 1960s, so these children have to go to Verdigre or Creighton. That is good for the lifespan of those two communities, but not for Winnetoon. "Losing the school was a significant event for the town," she said.

Gayle isn't sure what to predict for Winnetoon's future. "When I started there were several small homegrown businesses run by women, now there are only two of us." The other is a bar/café. It had been Gayle's family's business originally, but when the time came for her to take over, she didn't want it. There was a fuel-tank business, she says, but now it is gone. "There's a feed store but the grain elevator is closed. It is sad. When people get older and can't drive they want low rent housing in Creighton, so now Winnetoon not only doesn't have many young people, it doesn't have many old people, either." There also is no grocery store, which Gayle says is one reason she spends so much time gardening, growing her own food.

Thinking about what would help Winnetoon stay on the map, in addition to the post office, she draws a blank. "I can't imagine what type of business might want to move to town that could do well, considering how things are. We're a farm community. It is a bad thing that the village council has not made rules about buildings in town, so now we have grain bins and metal buildings where once there were houses. That is a shame. I don't think anybody would move here who didn't have an attachment to the place. But as long as the bank and post office can keep going, I would hope the town has at least twenty years or more left."

With a population of 563, neighboring Verdigre hopes to have a longer life span. About ten miles northwest of Winnetoon and about twelve miles from the Missouri River, Verdigre can credit some of its success to tourists visiting the area for boating, fishing, and other recreation. It also has the Verdigre River, which ripples through the valley attracting anglers who come in part because the nearby fish hatchery keeps these waters stocked.

Winnetoon does not have a town website or town slogan that I could discover, but Verdigre does. It is the "Kolach Capital of the World!" Kolach, I found out, is a Czech and Slovak pastry filled with such things as prunes, poppy seeds, apricots, cherries, or cottage cheese. The town was founded mostly by Czech people and since 1939 has celebrated Kolach Days, complete with the crowing of a Kolach Queen. To prepare as much kolach as is needed for a festival, one would need a good bakery in town, and Verdigre has that. The bakery owner, Mary Pavlik, told me how she came to move to Verdigre. She had been living the life of an urban professional in places like St. Paul, Minnesota, and Omaha, Nebraska. But her husband, Pete, started to hear the call of the rural and a tug in the heart to return home to Knox County, where his family had lived for generations. It was his idea to have a business on Main Street, and eventually, they became owners of the Verdigre Bakery. The bakery has three employees, although Mary's the only one who works full time. She describes the few years of the business as horrible. Although there'd been a bakery in town, it had been closed for some time. Mary and Pete started from the ground up. "We are finally at the point where we'll quit when we are ready, not because we can't make it."

In her mid-sixties, Mary is a part of that civic machine that keeps Verdigre running. For a time, Mary was on the board of the local community foundation and helped with grant writing. One achievement was an after-school program for young children who would otherwise have had to go to day care after school but whose working parents couldn't afford it. Then there is the Verdigre Improvement Club, which raises money for scholarships to help high school students going to trade school or college. There is a thrift store run by volunteers who take in anything useable and resell it for community projects. There is some sort of fundraiser in the community almost every week, Mary said, from the churches to youth groups, to 4-H. A core group of volunteers hope younger people will take some of the weight off their shoulders. Mary said that in Verdigre, there are some young people who've stayed in town and other young families who've returned, for example, the new school principal. That gives older people hope that their work to keep the town going won't be for naught.

"The problem is for the people who know how to organize and get things done, and have been in that seat before in a former life," Mary says. "There are a handful of them and they get burned out because they are always called upon to do things." Some of the younger ones are starting to pick up the reins, yet it is hard to get younger people involved. "Volunteering and helping takes someone with energy who knows where they are at in their life. Here people have limited resources. This is a whole different world than in the city, with the kind of job opportunities and advancement they could expect there," she said. Even modest opportunities like working in a chain such as McDonald's, Shopco, or Target, where you learn on the job and can be promoted, do not exist here.

There is a good range of public services available, so people who are in need gravitate here, stay awhile, and then when they can, move on, Mary notes. "Transient families outnumber the stayers," she said. One issue is the housing shortage. There isn't a lot of space to build new housing, because the Verdigre Creek forms the town's eastern and southern borders. For those who do manage to find a place to live, there are conveniences like a grocery store, several medical practitioners, a few places to get a haircut and a newspaper, the *Verdigre Eagle*.

When considering the county as a whole, Mary believes each community in the county has something to offer. Center only has ninety-four residents but is the Knox County seat. It is the county seat because it is in the center. Wausa is the "Swedish Capital of Nebraska." Bloomfield is "the Busy City" and offers a golf course and airport. Crofton has those things, too, and is the gateway to Lewis and Clark Lake. Lindy, an unincorporated village on the Santee Sioux Reservation, has thirteen residents and boasts of having the only country club without a golf course. Santee is also on the reservation and is the site of an annual powwow and a branch of a tribal college. Verdel has the distinction of having the only traffic light in the county. Niobrara is both the oldest and newest town in the county due to relocating several times, thanks to Missouri River flooding.

Knox County Development Agency (KCDA) director, Matt Cerny, lives in Crofton but his office is in Center. That is a good spot from which to contemplate what his county needs, what its resources are, and the intrinsic value of hope. Matt grew up in South Dakota but had visited this area long before getting the job. He told me he'd long thought the area had a great deal going for it, especially its natural beauty.

The KCDA was formed in 2001 when local communities decided it was in their best interest to cooperate rather than to compete for economic development. It just completed its first countywide housing study. One wouldn't think in a county of this size with so many small towns that aren't exactly busting at the seams that finding a place for people to live would be that hard. But as Mary Pavlik indicated, adequate housing is one of the biggest obstacles to growth. When Matt and I spoke, he was busy sorting through the findings, developing action plans, and determining which would be the easiest to achieve. Regardless of where they start, Matt said, "planning has gotten the county and communities talking about what is needed, and how we fix it."

Employers may be trying to hire but there is nowhere for their employees to live, but there is hope, Matt believes. "Creating jobs is difficult to do but housing is something tangible. Rental housing exists in the county but is limited. That's because it is difficult to find a property owner who wants to be a landlord." So instead of trying to cultivate landlords, they plan to focus first on building affordable single-family housing that people can purchase.

Matt sees his job as helping communities accomplish whatever it is they think they need. It is possible for a town to get so small it has to consolidate services, such as schools, banks, even grocery stores. But if there is still a drive within a community, they don't have to give up. For example, a community might need a senior-friendly apartment building, and that is an achievable and useful goal. "You try to improve the quality of life with what you have. You do something that is scalable for those 300 people who live in a town they are proud of."

Community pride is one step to attracting tourism, and Knox County has an undeniable asset in the Missouri River. The "39-mile District" of the Missouri National Recreational River flows through Knox County and includes the Niobrara River, which is a tributary of the Missouri. The Missouri is regulated by the Fort Randall dam but is still allowed to meander in a scenic way through the valley. A little farther east is the "59-mile District," which reaches nearly to the Iowa border. Wide, meandering channels, shifting sandbars, and backwaters provide wetlands habitat that are essential for wildlife and nice for recreation. The Lewis and Clark Lake pools between these two stretches of river. Nebraska's second largest lake is about sixteen miles long and three miles wide, with campgrounds and cabins for rent. It also has around 300 recently constructed homes, about half of which are summer or weekend residences. But tourism and part-time residents won't keep Knox County afloat, Matt says. They need families to locate there and stay. "Our biggest thing is to stabilize the population. Then retail services can function. Then a higher level of economic activity can take place."

The agency has even developed its own countywide version of the *come back home* plea undertaken by many rural states. Theirs is called the Knox County Roots program. This networking program connects former residents with opportunities in their hometown. Matt says individuals are identified who would consider moving back if a "certain situation would occur or a job would become available." They create a list of people that they monitor confidentially, and if a situation happens that matches, those individuals are contacted to be made aware of the possibilities.

And of course there is entrepreneurship. Maybe someone desiring to return home works as a manager and would be willing to buy a convenience store. Or maybe five like-minded people who want to move back could team up, and they might recruit someone to open a business where they'd all work. "If two people are interested and passionate about something, I am there to try to help with economic development," Matt said. "It is about quality of life, to recruit for jobs and develop housing. You can get depressed if you look at the population loss. All you can do is focus on your community and the things you can change and keep plugging away at. We'll keep going as long as there is hope."

Some people have made up their mind they want to live in Knox County, and others want to leave it, in part because of its sparseness. Recalling the USDA's Economic Research Service scale of Frontier and Remote, Knox County is a level 4 FAR. Just because people are FAR from things does not have to mean they are isolated. They can bond over enjoyment of beautiful natural areas, such as the state park in Niobrara. They can participate together in fishing, boating, or spending time with friends and family. They can load up in a car and travel together to a larger town for a day of shopping and dining or going to the movies.

They can meet at the local bar and watch sports on TV and share a few beers. They can read their community's newspaper.

True, many small-town residents read the paper from the nearest big city, either on newsprint or by subscribing online. That's where they get national news, read editorials about statewide issues, get a broader picture of the world. But it is the community weekly that gives people a chance to read about themselves. Some people might wave off the paper as being full of fluff or non-news. But they read it anyway. I suspect even they realize their community paper is a center of civic engagement in an increasingly fractured world.

Kevin Henseler has been the publisher and editor of the *Crofton Journal* and *Niobrara Tribune* since 1977. When we spoke, he was just a few weeks away from retiring after thirty-six years of covering public meetings, high school basketball games, house fires, and flu-shot clinics. The paper, normally twelve pages, combines news from both communities into one weekly paper. Kevin lives in Crofton and works from an office in a hotel building he restored. The newspaper's office is on the ground floor; his residence is upstairs. Although he has an editor in Niobrara working on the *Tribune*, he has no other employees, save for some freelance writers. The paper is printed and mailed from a location out of state. He writes and edits stories, lays out the paper, sells the ads, fills the news racks.

"The job of a publisher is hard to nail down," he said. "We are there to report the news, but a lot of times I think that I should call the paper the *Crofton Verifier*. When you have a weekly, news happens, like a major fire at the grain elevator, but it will be a week or ten days before my paper gets in readers' hands. Breaking news is often broken by the time we have a chance to report it. That doesn't mean we shouldn't report it or find a unique angle, but it's a challenge." Kevin said his job is to report the truth of what happened, which is different from the version of the story being told around town. "In a small town somebody can trip and fall, but by the time that information spreads it is totally inaccurate. I can put in what actually happened. I verify the truth."

In addition to presenting accurate news, Kevin feels a community paper has the responsibility to provide leadership. He writes a weekly column, which sometimes includes musings on a local issue, sometimes an opinion about a national story, and sometimes a personal issue. For example, Kevin said that many years ago he was diagnosed with depression and has been on medication for that condition ever since. "It is just something about how my body and brain work, and I just live with it." But that's not quite all he does. He's also written about it for the paper. "For many years the subject of depression was shunned, or just whispered about." But now, he says people working in the mental-health field tell him they appreciate what he writes. His columns may prompt people to come to them for a checkup and receive needed help.

On subjects less personal, he might face some resistance. "My opinion may or may not be the most popular one in town but at least I'm stepping forward and raising ideas and options for issues. You have to do that in order to be the leader and voice in the community."

The *Journal/Tribune* might not have the most current information and may lack colorful charts and graphs, but people want their paper. "There must be fifty people who buy their paper in town on the newsstand even though subscribing would save them money. But that would mean they'd have to wait from Wednesday to Thursday, when it arrives in the mail. Those fifty people want the paper right away."

During Kevin's time as an observer of Knox County life, he's concluded that a shrinking rural population is the biggest problem his county faces. In 2012, Crofton's population was 710 people. It competes with Yankton, South Dakota, population 14,528 and growing. It seems counterintuitive, but being that close to Yankton almost makes things worse for Crofton, Kevin said. "Starting in the 1980s, Crofton has struggled because of losing retail business as older owners retired. Who would want to buy and take over a clothing store in Crofton, fifteen miles from shopping malls and chain stores in Yankton?"

He recalls that Crofton used to have clothing stores, a TV repair shop, a flooring place, and two hardware stores. Those are all gone, he said. The grocery store is still there, having absorbed an existing flower and gift shop. One of the hardware stores became a consignment store and is now closed. There was a butcher shop and it has closed, then it became a restaurant serving steak, then pizza, sitting empty in between. Soon it is going to open showcasing a private individual's collection of pulleys. Yes, a man is moving his pulley collection out of his home by Lewis and Clark Lake and moving it into town, in order to open a pulley museum.

The presence of Yankton is also a lure for reasons other than downtown commerce. "Most folks who work jobs, work there, including guys who farmed for years and couldn't make it. The reality is it is tougher for small farmers to stay alive. The trend is going to bigger but fewer farms than there were twenty years ago. They are farming the same amount of land, but instead of twenty-five farms north of Crofton we maybe have five. Every time a farmer sells, he's got to find a job, and that takes locally earned dollars away from us into South Dakota." So even though that farm family might be paying local bills with a South Dakota paycheck, they are doing most of the family's shopping in South Dakota, as long as they are there anyway.

These changes also have an effect on the newspaper. "Now you've got a generation coming up that gets information from the Internet, not from a newspaper." The *Journal/Tribune* is not online, simply because Kevin hasn't felt the need to keep up with the technology or wanted to spend money on a website. He gets requests for online subscriptions from people who've moved away and want to continue reading about their community. Instead, he sells them mail subscriptions. That has worked, for now.

Change is in the works for the paper, and maybe for those people who want to read it online. Kevin has sold the publication to an individual who owns a few other papers around Nebraska. Although the negotiations and banking paperwork have taken some time, the actual offer to buy the business came within a few months of its being advertised for sale. Newly married, Kevin is leaving the immediate area for Beresford, South Dakota, where his wife lives and works. Now he's trying to decide what to do with the rest of his life. "I feel excited and kind of scared," he said. "I'm 59 years old, and newspaper work is all I've done in my adult life. I'm not sure what I want to do because I'm not sure what is available: freelancing, online writing, I've never paid attention. I thought I'd do this my entire life. I'd been divorced twelve years, and thought it would be nice to find somebody, and then I started to give up on the idea. I was okay living in Crofton being a grandpa, spending time with my family. Now I will only have to go to a girls' basketball game on a Tuesday night if I want to."

I thought about what Kevin told me about Niobrara, which has maintained a population hovering between 350 and 400 for decades. It is about thirty miles west of Crofton, but not far from the base of another route into South Dakota, over the Missouri River on the Chief Standing

Bear Memorial Bridge. Kevin observed that the forty miles that separate Niobrara from Yankton is just enough that people tend to do their shopping in Niobrara as much as possible. I wanted to find out what shopping in a town of fewer than 400 people would look like, so I made my way there. I found a room at the Hilltop Lodge, my little SUV sharing the parking lot with several duck-hunting groups. I identified them as such by the fact that they towed duck-blind boats behind their pickup trucks. Across the highway from the lodge was a Ford dealership, and then the land sloped down into the river valley. Across the side road from my lodge was the downtown district of Niobrara. There, in a small concrete block building that also housed a beauty salon, was the office of the *Niobrara Tribune*, and its editor, Valorie Zach.

Valorie told me she grew up in this area and has worked at the paper for more than thirty-five years. Her tenure was interrupted by a move to Montana, where she also worked on a newspaper. But her family is in Niobrara, she said, and her husband's, too. They wanted the grandparents and grandchildren to be together under the skies of one town. "They enrich the life of kids so much. We are where we're meant to be."

Valorie recounted a series of mishaps that have made life in Niobrara challenging, to say the least. It started with the first relocation of the town due to flooding, in 1881. The town faced another big hurdle in the mid-1970s when the water table was up and peoples' basements flooded, Valorie said. So the whole town moved south, away from the low area I could see from the Hilltop Lodge. Now that area is a golf course. There are no historic buildings left in town, except the old high school and the old library/church, which isn't usable unless they receive a major grant to repair it. "You can't go back home because the old town is gone. We lost nearly half of it when the town moved in the 1970s," she said.

In 2011, another major flood came through, affecting much of the Missouri River, with Niobrara's proximity to the river making it especially vulnerable. Then in 2012 came a serious drought. As a result of the hardship drought takes on wildlife, the area white-tailed-deer population was devastated by Epizootic Hemorrhagic Disease. "This is a hunting town and tourism town, surrounded by agriculture. These things really hurt us," Valorie said.

After the 2011 flood, a large number of state tourism people came to help salvage the season, Valorie said. "They came during the summer with suggestions, but we got overwhelmed and put the information on the back burner. People suffered those three months of business loss, had to struggle to keep open. By 2013 it became clear we needed to boost our economy."

So the newspaper did what Kevin Henseler refers to as taking a leadership role. They held a contest to pick Niobrara's "word of the year." A high school student suggested "expand" as the motivational word. That was the winner. Next, the newspaper developed a list of ten priorities to pull the town ahead, selected from the suggestions of the state tourism people who came after the flood. Readers voted on their top ten priorities from the list. One: work with Niobrara State Park to figure out a way to enable the rivers to be part of the Niobrara Experience. Two: erect a billboard advertising all of the area attractions. Three: make a new Niobrara brochure. Four: do something with the tremendous amount of history. Five: promote the entire area, not just Niobrara. Six: do more social networking. Seven: work on bringing in more innovative businesses, something to give people jobs. Eight: continue the Old West theme. Nine: make improvements at the boat dock. Ten: add more things for teens and kids to do.

"We are working on getting these done," Valorie said. "Then maybe we can move to the next ten." She explained that there was no FEMA or other funds after the flooding. Instead, the community is helping themselves. "We didn't need low interest loans, we needed money. We voted for a bond issue to move forward with a school improvement project, which was $9 million to replace the old high school. We developed a new town festival to draw people back, called Desperado Days, which trades on the town's outlaw history. It includes a scarecrow contest to bring people to town."

"We need both increased tourism and people to move here," she adds. "There aren't a lot of jobs but we have good kids here. Tourism is what brings people, and hunting, outfitters, buffalo and elk hunts, pheasant hunts, deer and geese and turkey hunting."

I was a tourist in town and decided it was time to act like it, even though I wasn't hunting. The weather was seasonally cool on this second day of November, but even so, I was surprised to see no one out on the streets. I drove around town, located the high school, and cruised through a few neighborhoods on the hill south of my motel. Nobody. Maybe they were all out hunting or fishing on this Saturday afternoon. It was eerie to be in a town where almost all the buildings were constructed in the 1970s. As I drove around a few more blocks, I noticed a large structure with signage for a restaurant and a few businesses. At first I thought it was a strip mall. Then I noticed it was actually a mall, in the sense that businesses had outside entrances and signage but also opened up into the interior of the building. Into the Niobrara Mall I went. Nobody.

I could see the post office, and the small grocery store. I gazed at a few photos on the wall depicting a powwow at the Santee Sioux Reservation, and other scenes of local life. As I wandered, I started to hear voices. Not coming from inside my head, the result of loneliness, but coming from a business about thirty yards away, at the other end of the mall. I could see a sign for the Sportmens Bar but I couldn't see through any of the windows. From the sounds of it, though, I'd figured out where residents of this village hung out on a Saturday afternoon.

I pushed open the door only to be engulfed in waves of cheers, and hooting, and high-fiving. No, they weren't glad to see me. They were glad to see their Nebraska Cornhuskers on the receiving end of a Hail Mary, clinching victory with a last-second reception. It took a few minutes for everyone to settle down and get back to their tables and their drinks and notice a stranger in their midst. Chris, the bartender who wore her waist-length hair in a single braid down her back, was the first to come out of her victory-induced reverie and speak to me. I ordered what everyone else seemed to be drinking—a Busch Lite—and insinuated myself into the bar conversation.

Upon Chris's inquiry, I explained who I was and where I was from. I explained I was a writer and thought Niobrara was a pretty cool place. I pledged my love for Nebraska Cornhusker football. I said if they knew anybody who'd want to talk to me about their community, I'd be grateful. Niobrara isn't built to receive tourists or journalists in the way I'd found Sedan, Kansas, to be. Yet, these folks sized me up pretty quickly as harmless and told me all about the previous night's Halloween party, which seemed to have given a few townsfolk a late start today. Two of the folks who chatted with me the longest were Diane and Calvin Krupicka. All decked out in red Cornhuskers gear, they were among the few fans who stuck around for a while after the game.

Diane and Calvin operate an outfitting business called Niobrara Adventures. They offer adventures by boat, by air, and by land. Their water adventures take people on the lower Verdigre Creek and Niobrara River—part of the wider Missouri National Recreational River—by canoe, kayak, tubes, or floating island rentals. Their "air" adventures are also by boat, but an air boat. They cruise the Missouri River east of the Chief Standing Bear Bridge by Niobrara. Their land adventures are composed of trips on a Sport RZR, also called a Sport UTV, which is like a four-wheel ATV but faster. They guide groups through the "rugged scenic hills overlooking the Verdigre Valley, through beautiful unspoiled cedar, oak, and walnut forests rich with beauty and history."

Not only could they give me a scenic experience of the valley, they could also guide me through the social culture of Niobrara. After our visit at the bar we arranged to speak on the phone once I got back to Bellevue. Diane wrote down her phone number and I called at the appointed time, but I misdialed by one digit. When the phone rang, a man answered. "Calvin?" I asked. "No, I'm his cousin. Calvin lives next door. Do you want me to get him?"

"Oh no, thanks, that's ok, I'll try again," I said, first smiling at the coincidence, then realizing in a village this size, it was really not a coincidence, after all.

Calvin and Diane started Niobrara Adventures because they'd already been operating an airboat, taking float trips, and riding an ATV for their own pleasure on their land near the river. They realized they could turn their recreation into a business that could help them but also bring tourism to help the local economy. They confine their adventures to small groups so everyone feels they are having the sort of fun, private trip they'd have if they were one of the couple's friends or family.

The business has been operating a few years, but because it's seasonal that is not all they do to make ends meet. Diane has retired from nursing due to her health and now spends the off-season working on the business. But Calvin also works as a lumberjack, cutting walnut and making mantels or wood flooring for homes, or building log homes, or cutting cottonwood for pallets, or helping farmers clear timber to allow for more corn planting. In addition, since the emerald ash borer infestation has begun to affect trees in this area, Calvin will be prepared to clear those trees, as well.

Although Diane worries about the dangers involved in logging, Calvin enjoys what he does. Their nephew works with him, who Calvin says may take over the business one day. That would be one younger person with enough work to keep him from leaving the area, but others aren't so lucky. "If they're not born into the farming community, kids take off and go to college. They don't come back here because there's nothing to do," Calvin said. He himself left for fourteen years. He went away to do "construction, electrical, different stuff" in Arizona, California, and Oregon. Then he returned and found that little back home had changed. "I never got situated with life in those other places. I'm glad I came back. I like the remote life."

Diane has lived in Niobrara since 2003, after she met Calvin, and has noticed something very important about the community. "It is hard to be single around here. There are a lot more single guys than single women. Guys are here because they are farmers or ranchers. Guys stay, girls leave," she said.

It might be a truism that guys tend to follow the girls, or maybe the other way around. It might also be true that residents tend to follow the tourists, or at least, it is a wish for most people in small rural communities. That is, if the tourism economy is strong, some of those tourists might decide to become permanent. Calvin said that people from places like Ohio and Illinois come to the area in the fall for deer hunting. "But for the most part, they come with money to spend, and then leave."

Diane sounds more hopeful. "If we get people coming for recreation, they'll attract more people." She points to several new hunting lodges in the area that are already booking next season's hunting visitors. "This is a source of income for the whole community, when people stay in lodges and eat in restaurants." The only drawback to this scheme for re-populating Knox County is the midwestern weather. "Some people don't come here because of winters. It keeps them to the south," she said.

Winter wasn't far from my mind as I drove around Knox County, noticing farmers finishing up their corn harvest. Here in the Verdigris-Bazile watershed, crops and restored grasses grow. Yet the Nebraska Game and Parks Commission warns that many of the native prairies are degraded from lack of fire and from livestock grazing practices that reduce native plant species diversity and promote exotic plants. This is a popular place for fishing, though, with the numerous spring-fed cold-water streams. The Missouri River bluffs and breaks are home to northern loess and shale-bluff prairie, tall-grass prairie, and deciduous woodlands. I found every acre quite beautiful.

I thought back to the Department of Agriculture's scale that determines how FAR places are from services and the companion Natural

Amenities scale. This is "a measure of the physical characteristics of a county area that enhance the location as a place to live." Measurements include things that people seem to prefer: warm winters, winter sun, temperate summers, low summer humidity, topographic variation, and water.

They make a rather compelling argument that natural amenities drive rural population change. People visit, and then decide to move to or retire, to places with high natural amenities. Some of these people are young families with children, but more often than not they are middle-aged or older people with flexibility in how they make a living, including retirement savings. Looking at the natural amenities scale map, I see that most of the areas that are positively correlated with appealing places to live are coded by some shade of green. This includes many regions in the mountainous West, and much of Florida. Predictably, brown is the color reserved for places less appealing to most people. Although I consider the unglaciated limestone bluffs and blue waters of the Upper Mississippi River Valley beautiful, the area where I live is ranked as neutral, or even slightly lacking in natural amenities. Likely because of its proximity to the Missouri River, the area around Niobrara is valued the same as the area around Bellevue. But as you move farther south into Knox County, you move into less appealing areas, according to this scale. Even though regions I tend to love for their solitude make a poor showing on this map, I can't dispute the logic. People do like sunny skies, moderate temperatures, dynamic topography, and water. Yet, the appeal of those traits can be the very reason those sites are overcrowded with both tourists and residents, creating the type of city many people like me love to visit but would hate to live in.

This area of northeast Nebraska does its best to appeal to tourists, not just those who enjoy outdoor recreation, but those interested in history. When I crossed the Missouri River on Highway 15, which connects Vermillion with Highway 12 in Nebraska, I was on a tourist trail. The so-called Nebraska Outlaw Trail Scenic Byway is a 231-mile stretch of "adventures waiting to be discovered over and over again. What took pioneers, outlaws, cowboys, and Indians days and weeks to traverse, now becomes a fun-filled day-cation packed with captivating stories, breathtaking scenery, and activities for a wide variety of interests."

I'd taken that route and other local roads to pass through the villages of Obert, Wynot, Bow Valley, and Fordyce. These are in Cedar County.

When I crossed the Knox County line I was in Crofton. A few miles later I found the town of Lindy just inside the border of the Santee Sioux Reservation.

During its heyday, Lindy had a number of businesses, including a hardware store, a barbershop, an ice-cream parlor, a blacksmith shop, and an electrical-appliances shop. In later years, Lindy's population declined and its businesses closed. In 1978, it had a population of thirty-eight. In the late 1980s and early 1990s, the town's feed store, general store, and gas pumps were shut down or moved away. By 2002, there were thirteen residents.

It was in Lindy that I learned I was at a stop along the Private Shannon Trail. In 2001, Lindy and fifteen other northeastern Nebraska communities formed Shannon Trail Promoters, with the goal of increasing tourism in the forthcoming bicentennial year of the Lewis and Clark Expedition. George Shannon was a member of the Corps of Discovery. Traveling along the Missouri River they stopped to camp at its intersection with the Niobrara. This was the area about which Clark commented in his journal: "Musquitors very troublesom last night."

The group landed on a point on the west side of the Niobrara River. According to their journals, the men found a tall, sturdy red cedar and used wood from its trunk to replace a broken mast. At some point during the stop here, Shannon was sent to what would become the Wynot area to round up two of the expedition's pack horses. That was August 26, 1804. No one saw him again until September 11. It is said that he went mostly without food for twelve days and nearly starved to death. He spent part of this time thinking he had to hurry to catch up with the party, and part of the time thinking he'd gotten too far ahead of it. Eventually, party member John Colter was able to find him. Now visitors can find Shannon again and again, thanks to this tourism effort.

I couldn't help but reflect on how Native Americans in the area lived with the complicated history of their forced movement at the hands of the nineteenth-century government expansion. I know the Lewis and Clark Expedition triggered government decisions to rearrange peoples as though they were pieces on a chessboard. And yet, I try to think about their explorations in terms of their time. Thomas Jefferson's decision to explore the area of the Louisiana Purchase was not the only time our government's actions have caused a complicated blend of triumph and tragedy.

While not actually on the reservation lands, Niobrara is the headquarters of Santee Sioux Reservation that is shared by the Santee Sioux and the Ponca tribe. According to tribal information, the Santee Sioux Nation ranges from Minnesota to the northern Rocky Mountains in Montana and south through the northwestern part of Nebraska. The Santee division of the Sioux Nation was called the Dakota. Today, the Santee Sioux Reservation encompasses an area approximately seventeen miles long and thirteen miles wide. As of the 2000 US Census, the reservation's population was 878, of which about 64 percent were Native American and the rest white. The major center of population on the reservation is the village of Santee. That village is approximately the same size as Niobrara, but it has something Niobrara doesn't: the Santee branch of the Nebraska Indian Community College (NICC). Its other two campuses are in South Sioux City and Macy, Nebraska.

NICC's role is to provide unique and culturally relevant educational experiences on its three campuses. The school says it is "open to all who are willing to enhance and improve their lives." Within five semesters, a full-time student could earn an associate's degree in one of seven areas. Its stated goals include preparing individuals for their roles as "effective tribal members and citizens in a changing and complex environment and integrating, revitalizing, and preserving Umonhon and Isanti culture throughout the college environment."

Fifty-five-year-old Jim Hallum is a NICC graduate who has worked for the college for twelve years. As extension project director, his position is funded by a USDA grant. He focuses on the health, wellness, and culture of the students and community as a whole. He has helped develop vegetable gardens at the school to help people maintain healthier eating habits. He's set up buffalo kills, in which a buffalo is killed and butchered by traditional methods. He uses his extension program to "bring things back, keep the culture alive," he told me.

One of the primary tools in Jim's arsenal is the radio station KZYK, established at the Santee campus in 2012. The station started in a FEMA trailer, the kind that could be pulled behind a pickup truck, he explained. "That thing was rough. It got hot in summer, cold in winter time. Then there was the wind. Once it actually moved it over about two feet. We could see the trailer's tire tracks in the snow." But now the station operates inside a regular building with an office. Jim himself is behind the microphone much of the time. He likes playing old country music from the 1960s and 1970s. Other deejays feature tributes to the veterans, which involves playing Vietnam War–era classic rock, like Credence Clearwater Revival and the Animals. There is also a blues hour. There are educational programs and national programming such as Native American News and the Voice of Turtle Mountain. There is also *Indian Hour*, which airs twice daily and features all-native music.

Starting a station was Jim's goal since hearing one with similar programs in Sioux City. People at the college thought the goal was unachievable, but here they are. "I don't think there is anybody else doing what we are doing," he said. The station's mission is not simply to entertain and inform. It is also to persuade.

Jim's persuasive energies are focused on the pervasive use of methamphetamine that is wrecking so many lives and destroying families, not just on the reservation but all around the Midwest, he said. He airs two-minute public-service testimonials from the Montana Meth Project. Stories include personal accounts of a fifteen-year-old girl who nearly died from meth use, and the story of a group of young parents who locked their children in another room while they got high and didn't remember they'd done so for two days. "The kids were okay but they are scarred for life," he said. Although these are Montana stories, he says he often hears from people who listen to the station and want to record their own anti-meth testimonials, which he's working on doing. He also runs an anti-texting-and-driving PSA, and promotions for GED completion.

Students of the NICC are mostly not typical high school graduates who go straight to community college. Instead, they are more like Jim. He didn't finish high school but earned a GED. He's a recovering alcoholic who hasn't had a drink for twenty-six years. He decided at age thirty-eight to get his degree. "You kind of wake up after a while and decide to do something different," he said. Most of his old friends are gone; he's the last one of his group he ran with. Most of them have died, but because he got healthy he's managed to last, he says. Now he is trying to reach the younger people through his station.

Jim's radio station isn't only available locally; it streams over the Internet. He said one of the biggest groups of listeners is in the prison in Springfield, South Dakota. "Probably 75 percent of the people there are in for drugs and alcohol, but they like to hear what we are doing," even the anti-meth PSAs. Jim likes to repeat the phrase: "Never be ashamed of your story because you'll inspire others."

When we spoke, Jim was busy preparing for a "community sweetheart" dance featuring a deejay offering both traditional and modern music. He wasn't quite sure how it would turn out. "We've never had one of these before, and people are shy." There are no dorms at NICC in Santee but most students commute in from nearby towns like Verdigre. Santee benefits a bit from that traffic because students will stop and buy cheap gas or eat at a restaurant. But mostly, Jim says, there isn't much to do in the area, or at least people don't think there is. There are two youth centers with computers people can use, and a wellness center where people can go to exercise. Jim wishes more people would decide to get healthy and go use the workout equipment. "It is hard to change your life that way," he realizes. But cancer and diabetes sicken and kill many Native people, he says, and the diet and exercise choices they make do not do them any good. There used to be a chance for outdoor recreation, like swimming in the Missouri River. "But when they made the dam it reversed the river, it is all silted in, you have to go to Yankton to find a place to swim in the river."

And there is the cross-cultural problem of kids who say they are bored. "When we were kids, we went and did things," he says. "Now they have to have computers and phones." There is still basketball, an interest that has spanned generations. And now there's an outdoor swimming pool, which, when we spoke in the dead of winter, was sitting filled with water, frozen and full of leaves. He speculated on what would happen when the spring thaw came. "Won't the concrete crack?" he wonders aloud.

I did not visit the college on my trip to Knox County because I hadn't taken a side trip into Santee to discover it was there. Instead, I spent extra time lingering around the parks and other access points to the Missouri. I'm one of the few visitors who would be disappointed by missing a side trip to a branch of a community college. An enterprise much more visible and appealing to the general traveling public is the Ohiya Casino & Resort. It is hard to miss this 14,000-square-foot facility, located on Nebraska Highway 12, which, though not a major thoroughfare, is the route I and many others take through the area while traveling the Outlaw or Shannon trails. The casino's name is pronounced "Oh-

Hee-Ya," which in the Dakota language means "win," according to their website. Owned and operated by the Santee Sioux Nation, it is one of four Indian-owned casinos in Nebraska. The casino bills itself as "the ideal entertainment destination for excitement seekers" in northeast Nebraska, southwest Minnesota, southeast South Dakota, northwest Iowa, and across the upper Midwest. It offers "every entertainment and relaxation need with the hottest casino filled with the most modern machines, highest payouts, and bingo; several dining options offering a delicious variety of menu items and full buffet; soothing hotel rooms, and the best in events and entertainment . . . every day!"

There is no information available to the public about the payoff of casinos in Nebraska, so I couldn't tell how much the place contributes to the economy of the state or the reservation. I made up my mind to stop there and check out the vibe, at the very least. I finally got it done on a Sunday morning at about 11:00 a.m. It is very hard to walk into a casino at that hour and pretend to be there for non-gambling reasons. There were few cars in the lot, and seeing only Nebraska plates, I took the other people in the casino to be locals rather than out-of-state tourists. They were dazedly staring at gaming machines and I wandered around to see if there was one I could figure out how to play.

I made a few turns around the casino, sizing up the 140 gaming machines and 100 bingo seats. I selected the Spirit of the West gaming machine. I was attracted to it because of the Native American flute music emanating from it, punctuated by occasional buffalo snorts. I felt that if I could just step through the glass wall of the video display, I could ride a bison bareback while dressed in scanty buckskins, knee-high moccasins, my hair perfectly braided, just like the maiden the game's graphics showed to me. In spite of its allure, I didn't want to feed this thing an entire $20, so I draped my jacket across the stool to ward off interlopers and found my way to the cashier's desk. Two lovely and pleasant young Indian women gave me indulgent smiles along with the $5 bills I could feed into the beast and never see again. Eagles, war bonnets, mountain lions, lizards, and other symbols of what an idiot I am spun past my view whenever I hit the play button. I should have asked the nice cashiers what it means when one wins "credit" or what it means to "cash out." I didn't unlock the code of this puzzle until after I'd fed the machine $15. Once I caught on to the rules, I could have walked away with .35 cents in my pocket as proof of my big day. Instead I decided to

The success of the casino, stocked mostly with modest machines like this, has allowed the Santee Sioux tribe to add an eighteen-hole golf course to the facility grounds. Photograph © Julianne Couch.

keep the ticket, which I finally figured out how to print as a souvenir, to what I'm not sure.

I walked outside clutching my jacket against a blasting November wind that had come up while I was inside. The casino is situated on a high hill that overlooks the valley's bluff and bleak landscape. I felt like I could see down the hill clear into Niobrara to the west, although it was about ten miles away. Maybe vision was the wrong sense to describe this moment. It was more like feeling across time. I could hear the fellows of the Corps of Discovery pushing their boats and gear up the low Missouri, on their way to their first winter at the Mandan Village in present-day North Dakota. I could hear George Shannon's calls for help—first hearty, then sheepish, then panicked. I could imagine Chief Standing Bear, generations later, a Ponca man who successfully argued that Native Americans are "persons within the meaning of the law" and have the right of habeas corpus. Then later the residents of Niobrara moving their town to get out of the way of the Mighty Missouri, which didn't intend to flood them out, no not really. Then to the formation of the Niobrara State Park and the arrival of tourists, taking in, as I did, the beauty of this area, both stark and verdant. Then to the arrival of my new acquaintances, such as Kevin Henseler and Valorie Zach, who've documented the daily trials and joys of this place. Then to folks like Diane and Calvin Krupicka, hoping to make a living by helping others enjoy the pleasures of the remote life. Then to Matt Cerny, a young man working earnestly to nibble around the edges, taking bites out of hardships such as inadequate housing, sparse employment, and social injustice between the wealthy newcomers and struggling old-timers who were here in this place's heyday. And like Gayle Neuhaus in Winnetoon, preserving her town like a precious rose between pages of a book, hoping the place holds out for another season.

While warming up in my car and deciding upon my next destination, I clicked on my radio and found KZYK. A voice was speaking phrases in English and repeating them again in Dakota. In English, they were: *I am going to buy groceries. Tammy's going to faint. I'll telephone you later. Someone is flirting with me. I like coffee in the morning. Where are you at? Wipe your nose. I'm tired of being somewhere, so I want to take a trip and be someplace. Where did you go?* Then there was a public service announcement warning listeners of the one-way trip that is methamphetamine use. Then the deejay played songs from a Plains Indian drum circle. I listened to ancient stories being told by an ancient people, delivered through radio waves while sitting in the parking lot of a gaming casino, my car rocking in the wind. The passion in their tones and pounding drum rhythms suggested choice, movement, resolve. I pulled back onto Nebraska 12, down the Shannon Trail, traveling in good company.

6 TARKIO, MISSOURI
RISK AND REWARDS

I am an entrepreneur. That fact hadn't occurred to me until recently. I thought I was a freelance writer, an adjunct instructor, an online editor, not an actual business person. I hadn't considered the fact that I'm responsible for drumming up every penny I earn, and entering into contracts, documenting expenses, deprecating office equipment. It turns out I am that type of independently motivated business person I've always associated with franchisees or inventors.

Although I am self-motivated and disciplined, I am delighted that what I do, I can do from home. At this moment there are six inches of snow on the ground, and snowplows are trawling the street. I can stay out of their way and let them have at it because I'm already at work, in my office, on my laptop, connected with my super-fast Internet, at a desk with a rolltop that I can slide down whenever I wish to forget about it all.

I'm not wearing pajamas right now but I might as well be. I consider jeans and a sweatshirt my dress-up clothes. Jewelry beyond my wedding ring is an extravagance reserved for royal visits. I didn't used to be this way when I had a regular job, coming into contact with people face-to-face on a daily basis. I could be in this dilapidated state I find myself in just about anywhere with a reasonable Internet connection. Norton or Centennial, Sedan or Niobrara. And while I chose Bellevue, feeling confident I could make this type of occupation work, many others struggle to find meaningful employment in the towns where they find themselves living, perhaps because of personal or family circumstances. Few fifty-year-olds with decades of professional experience want to settle for a minimum-wage service job. Few fifty-year-olds with no formal education beyond high school are qualified for the skilled light industry or medical field jobs available in Middle America.

Then there are the people who have business and lifestyle ideas and go to great pains to find the best spot to wed the two. I once knew a nontraditional college student who falls in this latter camp.

He and his wife were both midlife retirees from Microsoft, ready for new adventures. They developed a list of the things that were important to them as far as location, amenities, and so on. Then they wrote a piece of software to determine where they would live after they retired. They wound up in Powell, Wyoming. They'd never been to Powell before, and the only place they'd been in Wyoming was Yellowstone National Park. They had no relatives or friends when they moved there. With their computer expertise, they were able to write an algorithm that measured the things that meant the most to them. This man told me that the hardest part was finding the data to evaluate. In the end, only eleven cities in the western United States met their criteria and Powell, Wyoming, population 6,300, was on top.

As an entrepreneur with no algorithm-writing skills, I can't predict how long it will take me to figure out how long the trajectory my life is now on might last. But I bet it'll be years before I reconcile my competing needs for success and solitude, being recognized and being anonymous.

Sometimes this sort of soul searching happens on a community level. Entire towns wonder about their identities and the future and come to think of it, what the heck happened to the town they used to be. I picture Tarkio like that. It's a place where its older people look back to the good-old days of the meat-packing plant, and its middle-aged people remember life before the college closed down. For its younger people, those ghosts no longer flit in the shadows. They've faded into the corn and soybean fields and timber of northwestern Missouri. Some members of the new generation don't seem to understand metropolitan areas as the only sites of success, and the small town as just an unwanted relic. Instead, they exist in a binary world, where the rural is home but the urban is accessible, and even necessary, in ways that are unlimited and welcome. This is the new normal.

I think about the meaning of the term *entrepreneur*, besides the part about starting a business to make money. I like the phrase Webster's tucks into the middle of their definition: "willing to risk loss." Making a small rural community the focus of one's energy is to be willing to risk loss. Keeping places like Tarkio in business means taking risks, hoping for success, but being willing to deal with rising waters, or drought, or whatever comes in between.

The 547 square miles of Atchison County fill the extreme northwest tip of Missouri. To the north is Iowa. To the west across the Missouri River is Nebraska. Its main communities of Rock Port, Tarkio, and Fairfax, plus assorted folks in the country, add up to fewer than 6,000 people. Most of them can probably hear the semitrucks tearing along Interstate 29, which runs north out of Kansas City, leaves Missouri at Atchison County, heads through Nebraska to Omaha, and on into North Dakota, terminating near the Canadian border. People here like to say they aren't far from things. By USDA Economic Research Service standards, Atchison County counts as "not FAR" because it meets criteria of being about fifteen minutes or more from urban areas of 2,500–9,999 people; half an hour or so from urban areas of 10,000–24,999 people; forty-five minutes or so from urban areas of 25,000–49,999 people, and an hour from urban areas of 50,000 or more people.

The county has proximity, but not adjacency, to mid-sized metro areas. It is close enough for residents to access various types of skilled and unskilled employment. It is also close enough to get out, and move to a city without leaving family and friends too far away. That's one reason the population of this highly agricultural county has been steadily shrinking, projected to lose between 15 and 25 percent of its population between 2000 and 2030. In people terms, that's between one and two thousand construction workers, teachers, farmers, grade-school students, hairdressers, car salesmen, and doctors who, according to the Missouri Economic Research and Information Center, won't be living among these rolling farm fields along the eastern bluffs of the Missouri River. Instead, the data suggests if they decide to remain in Missouri they might head for Christian County near the scenic Lake of the Ozarks, or Lincoln County near St. Louis, two counties projected to more than double in population between 2000 and 2030. Or they might join the fray in the Kansas City area, in one of several growing counties on Missouri's western border with Kansas. These urban counties, and those in the next ring of counties circling these large urban areas, are the magnets for a mobile statewide population.

Atchison County is shrinking in a way that is both predictable and so far unprecedented among other rural Missouri counties. In the last census, it was ranked number one for population loss, a dubious distinction. In 1970, it had about 9,300 residents. Those 547 square miles have become increasingly roomy over the decades. The population in 1980 was 8,605, in 1990 it was 7,401, in 2000 it was down to 6,405, and in 2010 it became an elbow-room lover's paradise at 5,646 residents. Not only can county residents hear the interstate, they can probably see the lights at night from residents of distant metropolitan areas. Little local light pollution blocks the skies of St. Joseph, Missouri, 65 miles away, or Kansas City, 115 miles away, or Lincoln, Nebraska, 90 miles away, or Omaha, 80 miles away.

Atchison County boosters like to say they have easy access to those cities, where jobs are plentiful. The county had a 5.7 percent unemployment rate in 2013, so that access has proven itself valuable. But is it a sustainable choice to live in Tarkio, say, and be employed in Omaha, commuting 160 miles each work day round-trip? Local boosters like to argue that a simple hop onto I-29 and one chapter of an audiobook later, and you'll be to work. On the individual level, that might be a tolerable exchange, but is it the wise choice? The Natural Resources Defense Council (NRDC) suggests that while individual choices of this sort mean a paycheck for a family it is not the socially responsible thing to do. In their 2013 report, *Driving Commuter Choice in America*, NRDC experts estimate that individuals can reduce their total annual vehicle miles traveled (VMT) by nearly 10 to 50 percent if they adopt certain strategies.

NRDC divvies up the commuter population into segments: city, suburban, rural, and town. Regardless of distance from work, NRDC suggests commuters can at least make "some small changes in emissions by increasing transit use, carpooling, telecommuning or trip-chaining." Some of these changes might be possible among the Tarkio–Omaha workforce, for example. But the final suggestion on their list gets to the heart of the issue.

"Living closer to where one works reduces the distance of commute trips, which makes up the largest component of daily vehicle miles traveled. Moving closer to work also makes biking and walking to work more viable options, both of which are low-cost, low-polluting options." They acknowledge this is challenging for some because of other costs of moving closer to work, such as paying higher rent. To get past that problem, they suggest people simply move closer to employment centers. "A suggestion: Move 25 percent closer to work. Moving 25 percent closer to work locations would reduce daily VMT by about 20 percent."

Moving 25 percent closer to work might put many Atchison County residents in the middle of some farmer's soybean field. So let's look at why residents of northwest Missouri are facing these choices to begin with. What happened to the occupations that supported almost twice as many people in the county as there are today?

I've learned from my travels so far that a good place to get an initial answer to these sorts of questions is from folks who focus on business and industry. So my first step was to visit with Monica Bailey, director of the Atchison County Development Corporation. Her organization's website touts Atchison County's location near Omaha and Kansas City and the abundance of jobs in those metropolitan areas. It notes the county not only continues its historic relationship with agriculture, it embraces new business and industry. "Life here moves with the ebbs and flows of farming, but because county leaders recognize the necessity of diversifying our economy, there is more to us than meets the eye." They praise Atchison County's business-friendly environment that encourages alternative energy development such as wind and biofuels. They list accomplishments of progressive local leadership, including county-wide broadband access. They note that pleasures such as shopping and dining are not too far away. They show pride in the locals and the landscape. "Our citizens' deep commitment to bettering our county is evidenced by the limitless donation of both time and resources to make things happen. Atchison County is a quiet and beautiful area where living, playing, and working with your neighbors is just what we do."

Monica promotes her county not just because it is her job, but because it is her home. Now in her mid-thirties, Monica grew up in Tarkio, went away to college at the University of Missouri, and then went on to start her professional life. She returned to the county in 2010 to start work with ACDC. She says it makes her smile to answer the office phone by invoking the name of that 1980s rock band.

Monica reminds me about an event that took place in Tarkio I had been aware of growing up in Kansas City: the closing of Tarkio College. This liberal arts college established in 1883 by the United Presbyterian Church closed in 1992. Then from 1995 to 2004, the campus housed a private educational/treatment facility for adjudicated, at-risk youth. I admit I was aware of Tarkio College mainly because of an album called *Tarkio* by the Missouri-based folk-rock duo Brewer & Shipley. A hit song from the album, "One Toke over the Line," was quite popular among my friends when I was in high school, so Tarkio has stuck in my memory.

Monica, too, was relatively young when the college closed. "It's certainly devastating when you lose an economic and cultural engine as significant as a college, especially in a community the size of Tarkio, and in a county this size," she said.

Monica explained to me the history of the county that led to where we are today. "A hundred years ago there were multiple communities with unique identities. As population shifted, three primary communities remained: Fairfax had the hospital, Rock Port had the county government, and Tarkio had the college." The hospital and the county government are still economic engines, but even with those entities intact, the county is struggling. The reason Atchison County was first in the state for loss of population in the last census, she said, was partly that the college closed and subsequent organizations on campus were not sustainable.

"The loss of the college is important not just from a jobs angle," Monica said. "The county took a big hit culturally with the loss of the college drama department that brought people to town from miles around. That sort of thing contributes to the vibrancy of a small town and drives the community."

People in Monica's age range have different expectations for what is important in a rural community, compared to older generations, she says. "There are some quality leaders in this generation among people who went away and then came back, and in some who chose to stay here. They are motivated to make it better." She doesn't think they are simply trying to recreate their youth or force something to be what it no longer is. "There is a different kind of awareness among people in their thirties and forties that we have to create opportunities, that we have to act as a county, not as individual communities, and that football team rivalries don't matter in the way they once did." But there are things that thrive. She describes the college recreation center as "going like gangbusters, with a volleyball league that has county-wide participation" as an example.

As far as the county's future, Monica notes that it isn't an easy sell to convince city dwellers who've "never left Kansas City" to decide to come to Tarkio or elsewhere in the county. But young people who've left and have made the choice to return? "They're all about this place."

I wanted to know more about the aftershock of Tarkio College closing, not only the devastation to the town, but the resilient attitude with which many residents greeted it. Ed Salmond, a local business-man, is one such resident. In its heyday, he told me, Tarkio College was the biggest employer in town, providing jobs for up to 300 people. Since its closure, the town has suffered. "There are more than 200 vacant houses in town. The biggest employer here now might be somebody who has eight or nine employees," Ed said. "When the college was open, we had a county with close to 10,000 people living in it. Losing 300 jobs has had an economic impact."

Ed is on the board of the nonprofit Heartland Educational Institute. It exists only for the purpose of owning Tarkio College and getting it sold to the right buyer. He was there for the lawsuit against the school for adjudicated youth. When that school closed, the lawsuit arose to ad-dress damages to the facility during that period. Now he wants nothing more than for the school to be in someone else's hands. "We have no reason to own buildings. We only own it now so the banker who had the lien on wouldn't sell it to just anybody."

Although mostly long vacant, Tarkio College is still a lovely and ap-pealing place. A pleasant and snug array of buildings are arranged in a neighborhood of stately homes which, if you don't look too closely, all seem ready to inhabit tomorrow. The property description details the school's attributes: "Some of the building uses include a library, dor-mitories, administrative offices, lecture halls, classrooms and a chapel. The property is served by municipal water and sewer as well as natural gas, electric, telephone and fiber optic lines. An extensive maintenance program has kept the facilities in good condition."

There have been nibbles of interest from at least ten trade schools and two-year colleges over the years, but Ed said those plans have fallen short because of what he calls a perception problem. "Everybody loves the campus when they look at it. But most students have to have jobs when they are in college. Our biggest problem is that there is no employ-ment in our town for their students. The closest place where they can find employment now is in Maryville, thirty-five miles away," Ed said. There are factories and other employers in Maryville, but representa-tives of interested colleges think that is too far for their students to drive for work. That town also happens to be the location of Northwest Mis-souri State University. College jobs are at a premium.

"I try to make the comparison to a place like Kansas City, and how far you can expect to drive to get to your job in a place that size. But they can't get past it," Ed said. "The reality is, as far as I'm concerned, if we had a good prospect, we'd give them the campus. If someone would provide a good business plan and prove to us they have the financial wherewithal, we could make it happen." The board has seen to keeping the grass cut and the walks shoveled. But facility upkeep is expensive. Ed said the roof blew off the science building about six years ago, so now the inside is a disaster. Tearing buildings down is not an option either, because of the expense involved. "We're a nonprofit without a lot of funds. It is an issue; how do you use your money?"

In one positive development, Rankin Hall, the college's central building, has been adopted by a resurgent Tarkio College Alumni Association. I saw evidence of the board's efforts as I walked the campus in early October, the Sunday of the high school's annual homecoming event. The wide downtown streets were decorated with scarecrows, most sporting jack-o'-lantern heads. They gave color and whimsy to a main street that was way too wide for the traffic. A beauty parlor, a martial arts studio, and other mom-and-pops contributed to the town's available services, such as a grocery store, a dollar store, an auto shop, a gas station, a motel. From a high hill near Tarkio College, I could see a wind farm sporting dozens of tall turbines twirling against the sky.

I had just missed the monthly meeting of the Tarkio College Alumni Association, which gathers to work on the college's future, both the mental kind of work and physical labors, too. They give a frequent update on their progress in a newsletter aptly titled *The Phoenix*.

Linda Brunk Smith, who now lives in Kansas City, is a 1965 graduate of Tarkio College, where she majored in history and political science. Training in those subjects prepared her well for the challenge of salvaging at least part of Tarkio College. She is the president of the Tarkio College Board of Directors, and past president of the Tarkio College Alumni Association. Linda, with a crew of other alumni volunteers, is renovating the main campus building, their "beloved" Rankin Hall. The goal is to open as a training center, providing continuing education for professionals in various fields that require certification or licensure. But before they can start offering classes or provide a site for webinars, they have to have a functioning building.

One side of Rankin Hall contains Tarkio College memorabilia displays and alumni association offices. The other side houses the Training Center classrooms and administrative offices for the continuing edu-

This harvest tableau for the Tarkio Homecoming weekend captures the sense of humor one needs to live an agricultural-based life in this region of the country. Photograph © Julianne Couch.

cation program. Three fields are in the pipeline: public service, public safety, and health care. Public service is the first one that will be ready, Linda said. It is a joint venture between Tarkio College and the League of Cities. Students will come to Tarkio for some of their classes and can also accomplish some portions of their training online.

Although the alumni association only began leasing Rankin Hall in 2012, they've accomplished an extensive list of repairs. Highlights include upgrades to the guts of the building such as new air conditioners, furnaces, and plumbing; refinished floors; repainted rooms; maintained landscape; functioning downspouts; repairing the flat section of the roof; and restoration and repair of windows. Frequent work weekends bring volunteers to campus from hundreds of miles away to saw, hammer, paint, landscape, and polish.

Recently, the volunteers have zeroed in on the chapel. Linda said they've spent about $35,000 repairing eight large hail-damaged stained-glass windows. When I spoke to her on the telephone, the sound of sanders buzzed across our conversation. But that sound represented progress. They've been able to hold two weddings in the renovated chapel so far, and hope more couples will use the space.

The biggest challenge now is replacing the main roof of Rankin Hall, a $400,000 job. This project and others are being funded by donations, mostly from alumni and friends of the school. The alumni association is offering sponsorships for various items, such as chapel doors, pews, and windows, display cases, and even the chapel stage. A contribution toward a sponsorship gets that donor's name attached to the item forever.

"I can't tell you how much this institution means to me," Linda said. "It means more to me than anything else in my life. I waited almost twenty years to get to work on the school. It has been a long twenty years."

Richard Oswald has seen the college come and go, and many other changes in this county where he's lived more than sixty years. I discovered Richard in 2008 through his writing for the Daily Yonder, a website published by the Center for Rural Strategies. I was researching energy development, and I was planning a nine-stop trip around the country to see a variety of commercial energy sources. One of my first destinations was the nuclear power plant at Brownville, Nebraska, which is a stone's throw across the Missouri River from Rock Port, Missouri, if one had a very strong arm or artificially propelled stone. Having seen a few of Richard's columns, I knew he farmed just outside of Rock Port. I used our mutual writing connection as a calling card, and dropped him a line before my trip. I asked him what he knew about the Cooper Nuclear Station and how he felt about having a nuclear power plant so close by. "It's one of the best employers we have," he said. "Everyone I know who works there seems to do well, moneywise. I guess being two miles away, if they ever have a serious problem, I'll be one of the first to know."

He also reminded me that Rock Port had just been heralded as "the first 100 percent renewable energy powered town in the nation" which had been featured by the Weather Channel on an Earth Day program. When I made my first visit to the area in 2009 I did not have a chance to visit Richard in person, but I did see the wind towers. I learned that the wind farm did not actually power the town. That power simply went out onto the electrical grid, the same as power from other sources, nuclear included. However, the wind farm produced the equivalent of Rock Port's electrical energy consumption.

Now, in 2014, the Atchison County area has seen a significant increase in wind development. On the day we spoke by telephone, I could imagine those blades spinning mightily on a cold, blustery February morning with new snow and the thermometer seemingly stuck at ten degrees. It was a good thing for me the weather was poor, or I wouldn't have caught Richard indoors.

Richard is part of the sixth generation of his family to work the same farmland in Atchison County. His mother's family came from Tarkio. Her grandfather built a big stone mansion that still stands next to the cemetery on the south edge of town. "He was a state rep and owned the Citizens Bank in Rock Port. He also was on the St Joseph Livestock Commission. And a farmer," Richard told me.

Richard has personal connections with the three towns of any size in the county. He has a Fairfax mailing address and went to school in Rock Port. His family started in Tarkio. He is not sentimental; he can assess all three with an objective eye. "There's not much to do in any of the towns. There's a hospital in Fairfax, which keeps it going. Rock Port has struggled and they try to find ways to keep the storefronts from looking empty."

He recalls the closing of Tarkio College and puts that event into context with other blows the place has suffered. "No one has had much luck attracting industry since the packing plant closed up west of Rock Port." Richard's father had been involved in bringing a producer-owned plant to northwest Missouri. That was in the mid-1960s. Eventually the plant went public and the stock did well. "But not long after the first Missouri Beef Packers plant was built, the High Plains region began to dominate beef markets by becoming an economic center of activity for cattle feeding and corn production. Before long, uniform live cattle from Texas or New Mexico were being hauled to Missouri for slaughter. That's when management at MBP decided it would be cheaper to build slaughter plants there rather than to ship fat cattle to northwest Missouri," he said.

Eventually, Cargill took over the plant as a processing site. After a series of management decisions, the workers threatened to strike, then made good on that promise. As a result, Richard said, "Cargill closed the plant permanently, gutting the buildings of all machinery, electrical wiring, and plumbing."

Although Cargill is still one of North America's largest beef-processing companies, it is no longer part of life in Atchison County. Richard explained to me the difference between the closing of the plant and the closing of the college. "The plant had been great for the area, and it made a lot of people a lot better off. But when Cargill closed the plant, people moved away or found something else to do. The closing of Tarkio College had a great impact on Tarkio, but the closing of the plant had greater impact on the whole county," he said.

Richard notes the role of Monica Bailey's organization to encourage economic development, like a restaurant, a truck-repair shop, anything that will stabilize the county's population. Richard tries to put his finger on why his county is struggling. "I look at what we have at home, and then I drive across Missouri. The closer I get to the center of the state the better things get. Although there are towns that are similar in size, those towns have some industry going on." That means they have at least one large, steady employer that hires people of various skill levels. "But they don't have the agricultural land we have in Atchison. Atchison County has good water, interstates, railroads, the Missouri River, recreation, major cities within an hour, and a low, low crime rate. I don't know why a place like this can't attract more attention."

Instead, Richard describes the steady population decline. "We are maybe 40 percent of what we were in 1950. The family names from my childhood, they aren't there anymore. You can see their names in the cemetery, but there are no living survivors of those people in town today." He says that when the packing plant first started some people in Rock Port were concerned about new people coming in. "This was eighteen- to twenty-year-old farm boys coming to work there, not a completely new culture, but they thought there'd be shoplifters. But when they saw Main Street booming, a lot of them changed their tune," he said. He listed off what stands today in Rock Port: one grocery store, one pharmacy, a couple of beauty shops, two banks, and seven insurance agencies. The proportion of businesses devoted to dealing with disaster seemed telling, to me. "The citizens of Rock Port are thinking of things to keep buildings from falling down. Rock Port is the county seat, which means everybody has to go there for certain things. But for most everything else, people go to Nebraska City or Sioux City." Which means they take their money not just out of town or out of the county, but out of Missouri. Which is the downside to porous borders.

Because of geography, some things are welcomed at home, like the wind towers outside Rock Port. "The wind farms have been accepted," he said. "No one is really critical since you get something like a $5,000 annual payment for having a wind tower on your property. It makes this kind of a green place," Richard said. Now there are between seventy-five and a hundred towers in the county, installed and operated by several different companies.

Richard's farm on the Missouri River bottoms is not good for wind. However, he does have plenty of water and has been victim to Missouri River floods frequently over the years. The home where he and his wife, Linda, lived for decades was destroyed by the flood of 2011. That's the same one that hit Niobrara, and other communities upstream. The Oswalds moved to higher ground, living in, then purchasing, and finally renovating a home higher on a hill, still near the fertile ground of the sort that was stripped away in flooding on the plain.

The Oswalds weren't the only ones with flood trouble at that time, nor was Atchison County alone in its misery. All the talk about how convenient it is to live near Interstate 29 and how quickly one could get to work in Nebraska or Iowa went down the drain when bridges spanning the Missouri River closed. No one could cross for a hundred-mile stretch because of high waters. The bridges remained closed for months because of the damage the high waters caused. Things are back to normal now, until the next big flood, depending on whether or not the US Army Corps of Engineers decides to again break up levees and let flood water flow onto the fields, protecting population centers over farmland.

A dyed-in-the-wool Missouri farmer, Richard has given a great deal of thought to the business aspects of agriculture, as well as the societal interweaving it brings to a community. Yet to succeed now, most people have to operate larger farms, not the mom-and-pop farmsteads of his youth. He wonders how young people today will ever be able to make it in agriculture.

"Young people beginning to farm need loans from the USDA to establish themselves. When those programs were first established it was enough money to buy something worthwhile. Then the land values went up but the size of loans didn't keep up. There was a lot of demand but never enough money put into it to service the people who had demand for it," he told me.

Richard and his son farm and raise cattle together. His daughter and her husband also farm, and raise crops and livestock. "For my daughter and her husband, the pull is so strong they'd do anything to be involved with the farm. A lot of kids like them just don't have the opportunity. Anytime we lose knowledge passed on from generations that pertains to raising food, the sort of common sense that farmers know, it is a loss."

One bright side of modern farming practices is that they allow agricultural families to live in two very demanding worlds at once. They can run a farm, but they don't have to live on it if they don't want to. Ann Schlueter is an example of this split lifestyle. She is finding a way to balance a life and career in town while still working in agricultural production. She grew up in Tarkio, a descendant of great-great-grandparents who came there in the 1930s to farm. In turn, her grandparents stayed in the area to farm and to raise their three children. All but one of the resulting ten grandchildren, Ann's generation, live in or near Tarkio, and most of her generation's children still call the Atchison County area their home. Ann and her husband live in town in a Victorian home they are restoring as they can. Her sister and brother-in-law live on the family farm. All this family means this generation of children is not only being raised by the extended family, they are being "loved by the whole community," Ann said.

Ann graduated from Tarkio High School in 1998. She went to college at the University of Missouri, where she studied political science. She lived in Kansas City for a time, then in 2010 moved back to Tarkio. She works as the director of strategic planning at the Community Hospital-Fairfax. As such, she is involved in development, organizing community health events, and external relations.

Although this full-time job keeps her busy, it is far from all that fills her days. An offshoot of the family farm is a wholesale greenhouse business, which she helps her parents operate. Ann and her husband have three children, and so the whole family is involved in 4-H, youth sports, and numerous activities at the church where her husband is a deacon. Ann's skills as a strategist would appear to be useful ones as she organizes youth programs, creates Christmas productions, coaches sports teams, and coordinates the youth softball program in Tarkio.

In addition, Ann is a member of Tarkio Renewal, an organization started in 2005 to raise funds and tear down houses that blight the community. "After the college closed we lost so much of our population so fast that properties became dilapidated quickly," she said. The organization has removed more than thirty such structures since 2005, both residences and buildings on Main Street. This year they plan to construct a building on one of the lots.

All these activities seem like they'd make for a stressful life, but Ann says it is nothing unusual. "I don't do anything different than a million other people do in small towns. I'm in the middle of the pack as far as involvement goes. Others are even more involved in making community involvement their passion. Living in a small town means you can't sit back and delegate your community. If you don't do the work, your kids can't participate in it."

Giving kids what she calls a "fantastic childhood" is part of a strategy, although maybe not one consciously developed, to stabilize Tarkio's population. Ann doesn't think major population growth in Tarkio is realistic, because "that flies in the face of all that's happening in rural America." But it can be sustainable. "We need to keep our school system and the services that we have, such as the grocery and retail stores, the restaurants. Those are quality of life things which, if lost, would make it much more difficult to live here."

Rather than thinking about that sort of loss, Ann would rather consider what would encourage people who grew up here to return. She believes that going away to college is a good choice for many people, if they have that opportunity. "They had such a fantastic childhood, and now they can recreate that for their kids," she said. "In order to sustain our population, we'll need entrepreneurs to create jobs, and the skills it takes to do that are usually gained elsewhere and brought back."

For an example of how a well-run business can stabilize the whole community, Ann need look no further than her family's wholesale business. "We have two acres of bedding plants. We wholesale 98 percent of that outside of our county borders. Whenever that truck leaves, we bring dollars back from outside the community. Others need to think that way, too. We can make this a place people want to live." In this example, having cross-border commerce is not a losing prospect, but can actually put a business ahead.

In addition to the presence of extended family and the sort of freedom that access to farm life provides children, many people base their decisions about where to live on practical needs: decent jobs, affordable housing, convenient shopping. But access to health care is also important, whether one is a young family with typical active children or an older person needing reliable access to the health-care system. The hospital in Fairfax where Ann works is a twenty-five-bed Critical Access Hospital. This is a designation for rural hospitals that are a defined distance from larger towns and hospitals.

With shifting trends in population and changes in Medicare billing for various services, the conversation among experts in rural health care is focused on how long hospitals such as these can survive. People often simply prefer to go to a hospital in a larger nearby community, perceiving the quality of care to be better there. Meanwhile, in Fairfax, the hospital is moving forward. A new hospital building was constructed in 2010 and the old one torn down in 2014. It employs between 100 and 110 people. Ann says they have excellent medical staff, including nurse practitioners, nurses, and technicians, but that it can be difficult to retain primary-care physicians. "We've been challenged by that," she said. "Rural practice is different from urban. You are isolated, not backed up by specialists. That takes a special kind of physician, to be on call all the time. This is not an 8 to 5 job. It takes a whole other level of dedication."

If I were a trained medical person I'd be quite happy to work at the hospital in Fairfax, not bothered at all by the isolation. I'm the sort of person who would be very happy to work in my own small community if the job was satisfying and paid a living wage. I would sooner eat glass than commute to work, especially on an interstate like I-29. I'd had almost enough of it on my trip to Tarkio, when I was only on that road briefly. One thirty-mile stint on that highway to Tarkio, busy with semi-trucks swaying in the winds and the sheeting rain of an October day, was enough for me. I sought peace and quiet among the winding roads through cornfields along Highway 59 north through Fairfax, and up to Tarkio. Later I would read in the local paper that along the stretch of the interstate I'd avoided, someone had hit not a deer, as is common, but an elk. That unfortunate creature must have felt as out of place in his final moments of life as I did on that highway. I, for one, could not imagine being part of the daily chase from Tarkio to Omaha to get to work.

Joshua Wright agrees with my assessment, although he himself has lived that commuter life. He was born in Fairfax and was raised in

Tarkio, where he attended high school. He went to a community college in Nebraska, then to another one in Johnson County, Kansas. Then he attended Columbia College in Missouri. He was a communications major and although he did not graduate, he got started on his professional career in Kansas City and in the Lake of the Ozarks area, one of the fastest growing areas of Missouri. He worked in research and development for Kawasaki, which operates plants in Missouri and Nebraska.

Eventually after getting into some trouble, Josh said he realized there "is no place like this place, and it drew me back." His family farms in the area, and that connection to the land is a strong anchor for Josh and figures into how he sees his life progress. He doesn't farm full time, though. He is the marketing director and events coordinator for the Heartland Recreation Center and Events, which operates out of the former Tarkio College gymnasium. "I'm the 'and events,'" he said. This was the place Monica Bailey had mentioned was going gangbusters and helping sustain the community's vibrancy. Josh plans comedy nights, talent shows, and music festivals that bring hundreds of people in from outside the area. "One hundred percent of the community backs what we're doing," he told me. He's learned from this work that it is the small things that make people feel special, "down to how the napkins are folded."

Josh says the job is a perfect fit for him. It is just across the street from where he lives, so he doesn't have to face a long commute for work, which is good because work starts at 5:00 a.m. It took Josh some time to realize this job would be perfect for him when he first learned about it. "The salary was comparable to what I had been making, they gave me a lot of chance to advance, and it was something that I would really enjoy. God has to hit me three or four times before I notice. I went to church, and heard about it there. I prayed about it and am glad I did it."

Josh is settled in to small-town life with his wife, ten-month-old triplets, and a nine-year-old child, and with his parents and grandparents nearby. He still maintains friendships with some of the young people he grew up with. Of the main "six or seven that ran around together," about half are still in the area. One works at an ethanol plant outside of Atchison County, one is a farmer, one is a banker. Another is in Phoenix and another in Kansas City. Josh prefers Tarkio, however.

"It is a great place to raise your family, to be outside, to have your kids in small classes. The teachers here care about kids. You can't get that in a city." That might be an overstatement: there are plenty of teachers in urban areas who care about their students, and some in rural areas who would be better off in another profession. But that's how Josh perceives his town and he is not alone in that perception. However, he admits he does miss certain things about city life. Now, when he goes with his family to Kansas City or Omaha, the visit is more special, he said. "It makes it more exciting to go there. City people miss out on that feeling, because they are already there."

That doesn't mean he doesn't have dreams that Tarkio could be exciting, too. That's one of the reasons he works hard at promoting events that appeal to locals but also bring in outside tourists. "I would love to see Tarkio grow. The college being closed has hurt us." He'd like to see the state government involved in helping with the alumni association's plans to reopen it, either on the small scale underway or with a larger effort. "It is a beautiful campus but the state government focuses more on metropolitan areas. There is not much political support to help out here. So, it continues to go downhill."

Wind energy and ethanol have helped provide jobs and he hopes that will encourage younger people from the area to come back. "Some people don't take into consideration the low cost of living." He gets a laugh from watching television programs such as *House Hunters*, which show people trying to decide which half-a-million-dollar home to purchase as a starter place for their family. "Why do people work so hard to have a house the size of my living room? They wouldn't do it if they could see what they could get here for that money."

Craig Martin would like to have something to say about that, also. He's a Tarkio native who has sold insurance for thirty years, and real estate for fifteen. "I would like to say I've been farming all this time, because it has been really good," he said with a laugh. Both of his parents grew up on farms but did not continue in that way of life. "It was tough back in the 1950s. You had to have someplace to start. The families that had been there longest were more able to make it work."

He's now one of the last of his family still in Tarkio. His parents have passed away; one sibling is in Omaha, another in Arizona. He'd like to see the county population rebound, which can't happen without jobs. "Not manufacturing, but small businesses would be great."

Craig considers what population numbers would be comfortable for the county to attain, in order to be sustainable. Tarkio would be better at 3,000, he estimates. Rock Port could sustain about 2,500. And Fairfax could sustain more, too. Craig sees limitations on how Rock Port could grow, simply because of geography. It is right on the river, which means bluffs on one edge, the river on the other. The hilly landscape is beautiful but not easy to build on, and the river bottoms are subject to flooding, "some natural, some not," he said referring to US Army Corps of Engineers practices. But Tarkio is flatter by comparison, and not hemmed in by rivers or interstates. Craig supports the work done by Ann Schlueter and the Tarkio Renewal organization in their efforts to remove blighted housing left over from Tarkio College closing. Some of the older housing stock is attractive to certain buyers, but he says newer housing on small acreage is harder to come by. Because the farmland there is so rich, most individuals cannot afford to buy a ten-acre lot, for example, at the price a farmer would ask. That farmer could earn more money keeping land in corn and soybeans than selling it as the site for one house. The exception, Craig said, would be if a larger developer came in to put in a subdivision. That would mean building and selling numerous houses on converted farmland, which would be a moneymaker.

There is a shortage of senior housing, but other types of housing are available. Craig said home sales are typically slow in rural areas and have been especially so during the recession. Yet, he's noticed an uptick in the last few months. He has homes that are "really, really, really nice," that if they were in the city would sell for half a million or more. "But here, unless someone comes from the outside to buy it, the seller will only get what the market will bear."

As of March 2012, the cost-of-living index in Atchison County was considered low at 77, with 100 being the national average. That sounds encouraging, and underscores Josh Wright's observation that people can buy large homes for little money, compared to other locations. The downside is that those low prices reflect a shrinking economy and low wages. Both Craig and Josh stand firm on the desirability of this area of Missouri. As Craig said: "This is a nice, quiet area of the country. It is a conservative area. We don't have to worry about getting mugged or shot if we walk outside at night. It would be great if people came here."

Again, pride in community overlooks that the odds of being mugged or shot in Tarkio are remote, but still possible. Just like people in Kansas City could live a long full life and never fall victim to muggings or shootings. And yet, it is the perception of these qualities of small-town life that seems to me just as important as the reality. In the back of your mind you realize you never know what life might hand you. But the feeling that you've done all you can to take control of things you can reasonably control gives confidence and influences choices. Josh thinks Americans in general should be proud of its rural areas and more educated about economics there. For example, it does pretty well in its goal to feed America. For another thing, it is key to American energy policies, including development of alternative forms of energy. "Something our county has to stand on is our rural areas," he said. "The attitude that big oil and big corn is bad amazes me. Ethanol development has been good for our area. The ethanol plants have a positive impact on small cities, but people in big cities are against it. Ethanol has helped rural communities in the Midwest. Nobody wants to hear about trickle-down effects, but farmers are doing better because they have another market for their corn."

When Josh told me about his support for ethanol production, I wondered how I'd missed knowing about a plant in the county. It turns out, there isn't one. Yet they aren't far. The closest are Green Plains, thirty minutes north in Shenandoah, Iowa, and Golden Triangle, twenty-five minutes south in Craig, Missouri. These employers, while not in Atchison County, not only provide jobs that are an easy commute, they source corn from local farmers. As long as there is a source for these products, which has boomed since EPA regulations became friendlier to non-petroleum fuel sources. Yet these fuel standards, and ways to reach them, have proved a moving target. Like wind development in the county, and the nuclear power plant across the river, their relevance, and capacity to help people earn a living wage, are subject to change.

At the end of the day, there is plenty to do around Atchison County, and most of the time the lines to do it are pretty short. You can go to the recreation center. You can attend Blackout Fighting Championships. You can take part in a mud run or attend Walnutstock, camping out if you choose at a three-day music event that features country, blues, Christian alternative, and classic rock, an air show, a barbecue competition, bikes and bikers, and sometimes, performances by Brewer & Shipley, both of whom still live in the state.

There was a lot going on in town on my recent visit, as I could see from the Heartland Center's website and the local newspaper. However, the streets seemed very quiet as I moved around. During my few days there, I stayed at the only motel in town, where I had to press a buzzer to be admitted into the lobby. I popped across the street for morning coffee and when I asked the young clerk what was happening in Tarkio, he replied glumly: "Not much." I walked the grounds of the college and saw not another soul. I meandered through the neighborhood of the former college part of town and saw nobody around. I drove over to Rock Port early one morning and parked my car on the main street. I photographed a few of the buildings. My documentary behavior attracted the attention of a gentleman from across the street and a few doors down. He stood and watched me, curious, but not curious enough to give a friendly wave. I considered whether he sized me up as an insurance adjustor or real estate appraiser or one of the other odd outsiders who wash up from the great human river that flows along I-29. Somehow I couldn't find a way to break through that fourth wall of what felt like tourism theater to send a friendly wave his way.

I drove back into Tarkio and stopped at the local grocery store because I wanted to buy a few car snacks before hitting the road. I got there early, just as the store was opening for the morning. I wandered up and down each aisle a few times, not wanting junk food, not wanting a messy snack. Finally, I settled on a pack of string cheese. A few miles from town I tore it open with my teeth, one hand on the steering wheel as I navigated the golden dawn of farm-country corn harvest. Farming has been good here these last few years: cooperative weather, reasonable grain prices, and high prices for farmland. But farming is one of the most fickle businesses I know of, and if next year's weather is awful, prices for land and grain could drop. Just like farming and other businesses, the success of a community is in great part dependent on luck. If economic factors tilt their way, things can improve. If they tip another way—for example, if the renewable fuels standards that require ethanol to be blended into petroleum—they might not improve. If people are willing to attend continuing education programs in Tarkio, that might give the town a boost. If medical reimbursements continue to flow to small regional hospitals, things shouldn't be worse for Fairfax. If the nuclear power plant is able to renew its operating license on a regular basis, its workers might still choose to live in Rock Port.

I do not suppose people in Atchison County understand their community only in the way they'd understand a business: as something needing to be nurtured and promoted, but allowed to slip away if the time had run its course. But using that framework, what would people be willing to risk to make this place thrive? What do they want, and what would they be willing to trade for it? What do they see as the point of no return? If they attract more business and more housing, and more people, would this become a less caring place for children, a less productive place for farming, a less glorious place for watching stars? Would one be more likely to be shot or mugged while standing outside taking in the fresh air? Maybe, probably, probably, maybe. But keeping Atchison County open for business might be worth the risk.

7 NEW MADRID, MISSOURI
WHERE THE MISSISSIPPI FLOWS WEST
AND THE SOUTH BEGINS

When I decided to move to Wyoming, then to Iowa, I didn't mean to sort myself into a place that is so *white*. I didn't really think about it. The suburban Kansas City neighborhood where I grew up was almost entirely white, yet I was close enough in to notice people of color, whom I believed to be living lives similar to my own: father at work, mother at home, children in school. In spite of these parallels I sensed my parents were uncomfortable taking us to certain areas of town. We kids were instructed to lock our car door whenever we crossed north of 39th Street, though I didn't know what would happen if we did not. It didn't take me long to equate those instructions with the percentage of nonwhite faces visible through the windshield.

My childhood took place during a period of urban unrest nationwide. Symptomatic of its time, a race riot took place in Kansas City in 1968. My parents were not big on explaining complex social change to us kids. Eventually I'd understand that some whites in Kansas City, but mostly people of color, led lives inflected by poverty, inadequate education, poor access to health care, and unsafe neighborhoods. Urban demographics nationwide shifted as more middle-class whites moved into far suburbs, in part to get away from the very social conditions poor people of color had a harder time escaping. The departure of the white middle class exacerbated the problems, insofar as whites took their property-tax dollars with them. This urban disinvestment challenged the already troubled schools and neighborhoods. Divisive urban issues like white flight and racial tension aren't relics of the past, of course. Even as I write this, the St. Louis, Missouri suburb of Ferguson is dealing with the fallout from a white officer shooting and killing an unarmed black teenager.

When I picked Wyoming in which to settle, I didn't notice that the state had a black population of less than five percent. I picked it because I loved the low population density, the high elevation, and the unpretentious western lifestyle. A college town, Laramie is comparatively diverse in terms of race, ethnicity, and socioeconomic class. The University of Wyoming attracts international students from Europe, Asia, and Africa. I saw enough people of color and heard enough non-English languages spoken during my years there that it felt almost cosmopolitan.

Nationwide, the population that identifies as black or African American was 13.1 percent in the 2012 Census. In Iowa, that figure was 3.2 percent. The county where I live is 98 percent white, with the other 2 percent distributed among blacks, Hispanics, and others. But Wyoming and Iowa are not anomalous outliers. Eighteen other states have a black population under 5 percent. Most of these states are in the north, or the west. The states with the highest black populations are in the south. These demographics have historic roots. Population shifts move slowly and I don't expect in my lifetime that the mostly white states—which are actually depicted in white on the census bureau map—will change any time soon.

To find a small, rural community with a significant African American population in my area of investigation, I had to look to Missouri. The farther south in Missouri, the better my odds became. Finally, I found New Madrid County, with its African American population of just above the national average.

First, New Madrid is pronounced New MAD-rid. It is at the upper end of the Lower Mississippi River. It is at the top of the Missouri Bootheel—in other words, on the sole of Missouri's shoe. If Missouri's boot were made for walking instead of riding, New Madrid would be in Arkansas. You can credit one John Hardeman Walker, landowner in Missouri Territory who didn't want to become an Arkansan when Arkansas Territory borders were being drawn. He argued to the US Congress that the Bootheel area belonged in Missouri, for a variety of cultural and practical reasons. It's an argument he won.

The Upper Mississippi River, the region where I live, is worlds away from the Lower Mississippi River. Speaking less fancifully, that's about five hundred miles. The topography and landscape of the Upper is dynamic with limestone bluffs, the river water controlled by the lock and dam system that contains it in a sequence of pools. Locks punctuate the dams, allowing barges and other watercraft to navigate the shipping channel. The Lower is wide, too wide to span with locks and dams. Instead, river traffic navigates a shipping channel but doesn't need to line up for the dance, performing the time-consuming lock-through maneuver that they do farther north. The delta landscape of the Lower is wide and flat, with a system of levees built to trick the river into thinking it is staying within the banks it creates naturally and mercurially as it flows to the Gulf of Mexico.

I get the strong sense I'm in the South when I visit the Bootheel because of place names like St. Johns Bayou. Because when people refer to each other they use courtesy titles and first names, like Mister Ed and Mizz Sarah. Because while driving around those bayous, I see cotton fields interspersed among the corn and timber. When I hear a conversation, I have to listen carefully to understand what is being said. Just fifty-five miles north in the river slash college town of Cape Girardeau, those southern tones are present in the speech of many but not all. By St. Louis, speakers might as well be from Minneapolis.

When I put out feelers about whom I might be able to visit with in New Madrid prior to my arrival, I started with Facebook. I heard back right away from a friend I'd gone to high school with, now the warehouse shipping superintendent at Riceland Foods in Stuttgart, Arkansas. He put me in contact with Ed Williams, the plant manager there. Ed and I communicated by e-mail several times. A few weeks before my visit, he sent me a message inquiring when I'd arrive because he had a whole list of folks to introduce me to. He also planned to spend half a day with me, giving me a plant tour then guiding me on an odyssey around town.

I began said odyssey without my guide because I arrived rather late in the afternoon on a Thursday in March, the first day the weather had started to improve after an excessively wintery winter. This journey was part of a multi-purpose trip, so my husband traveled with me. One thing complicating my planning was that there is no lodging in New Madrid. This is a community of more than 3,000 people, about five miles off the interstate highway. I checked with Chamber of Commerce director, Christina McWaters, to see if Google was wrong, and that maybe there was some secret place to stay that locals could guide you to. There was not, not even at the intersection of the interstate and the two state highways one can take into town.

I begrudgingly booked a dog-friendly room at the Super 8 about seven miles away in Marston. This location would have to do, although it wasn't convenient for the sort of immersion I wanted. Nevertheless, I looked forward to New Madrid for many reasons, not the least of which was that I knew the river would be open, and not under thick ice, as it still was in Bellevue. I imagined when we got into town we'd find some little bar and grill along the river, have a light supper and a glass of wine while watching the sun settle low behind the timbered islands. We found the inviting river walk and protruding observation deck with its signage about the Civil War battle of Island Number Ten. We found a boat ramp and parking lot, and saw a few people riding ATVs along the levee that protects New Madrid from rising river waters. But no grill. No bar. No place of any kind catering to anyone of any sort who wished to socialize with others in a public place along the river.

Slow to accept what our powers of observation were illuminating, we parked at the river walk lot and strolled up the main streets. Hungry, tired, and thirsty, we were resigned to finding any place that was open and could serve us a meal. After a few blocks, just before the business district turned to residential we found a convenience store. We decided we would pick up a few snack foods and bottle of wine, and prepare a small meal for ourselves back at the Super 8, and watch March Madness basketball in our room.

Stepping into the store shot me back twenty-five years, when I last lived in Kansas City, and not every face I encountered was a white one. The presence of both white and black folks coming in and out of the store, nodding our way as we passed, gave the place an almost urban vibe. But in this setting, unlike in an urban area, we were noticed and immediately pegged as outsiders. Why else would we meander the aisles, rumpled and tired, debating the pros and cons of the processed, packaged food. Let's just say nothing looked terribly appetizing, so we approached the counter to inquire one more time about local watering holes with food service. Behind the counter stood a young man who was missing a good portion of his teeth. Along with him was a painfully thin woman who appeared middle-aged but brought to mind public service announcements on TV about methamphetamine. I reached this conclusion just from observation, not because I queried them about it directly, so my assumption could be wrong. A third young lady behind the counter suggested a local Mexican restaurant, which was no doubt delicious, but nowhere near the river. What I really craved was a public social space crowded with locals, a smooth-topped table, a plump waitress with a southern accent, one of those metal napkin holders to fidget with, and a plate full of something fried. With a river view.

Later, Ed Williams would take me to a place like that, where the only words one needed to say to the waitress were "chicken" or "fish." I'd learn that people here have a rich social life but it mostly takes place in private spaces, among friends or family. But that night, we realized we were still full from the late lunch we'd eaten in Nashville, Illinois, at Mark & Wanda's Hillbilly Barbeque. So we uncharacteristically bought two tall Lime-A-Ritas, sold to us in those brown paper bags that fit just right, and headed for the observation deck with our dog. Before leaving the store I asked if it was ok to have open containers of alcohol there. The young man assured me we'd be fine as long as we didn't have any "domestic violence" going on that would attract the notice of the police.

So there we sat, sipping our beverages, watching some folks fishing along the shore among a clutter of lawn chairs and coolers, noting some light barge traffic, letting our dog trail his leash while he bluff charged pigeons along the walkway. With my 'rita in a bag I felt dangerous, suspicious, and seedy, in the way only a middle-aged writer from a small town in Iowa can feel. Eventually a woman a bit younger than me, and a younger man who turned out to be her adult son, strolled down the pier to the observation area where we sat. They greeted our dog and we visited cordially. In this way, we had a small moment in a public space, visiting with friendly strangers, having a spot of something refreshing, and watching the sun slide down to the west.

The next morning I finally met with Ed Williams, who picked me up at the Super 8 and took me to the industrial park, home to the Riceland plant and other concerns. Our first stop was at the administration building, where we donned hard hats, safety glasses, and hairnets. Riceland Foods, Inc., is a farmer-owned agricultural marketing cooperative and the world's largest miller and marketer of rice and one of the mid-South's major soybean processors. He pointed out the railroad spur, which the mill shares with the coal-fired power plant next door. We saw the dock where barges deliver the grain and then a few days later, take it away milled, bagged, and ready to sell. Ed said the bulk of it makes its way to Haiti. What is left is trucked up Highway 57 to Chicago, and then dispersed to Chinese restaurants in the northeast.

As a person who has been on many industrial site tours, I was struck by how clean the facility was, and especially how wonderful the rice smelled as it went through the process. Ed showed me how rice was stripped of its hull, turning brown rice into white, and how little waste results from the process. The sweet aroma of warm, slightly moist rice made me think this could be a pleasant place to work. The laborers I saw, mostly African American men, were doing work that wasn't as backbreaking as it must have been in earlier times. The tasks of hand filling rice bags, and manually loading those heavy bags, had been automated many years ago. Fewer hands were required to do that work, so it was more a matter of staying ahead of the conveyor belt.

When we wrapped up at the plant we loaded up in Ed's truck and he gave me a tour of the area in about a ten-mile radius. As we drove he explained he had been working for Riceland Foods in Jonesboro, Arkansas, a town of about 70,000. He said that it was starting to feel too much like a big city. He was relieved when the job at New Madrid opened. This area suits their pace much better, he said. He and his wife live in a town of about 1,200 residents about six miles from New Madrid, called Lilbourn. He drove me by their snug corner house, yard planted with flowers, and even yucca and cactus. On the way out of town he spotted a farmer in a pickup at the edge of a field. We took a detour and caught up with that farmer. We parked door to door, tail to nose, like a pair of horses. Ed wanted a load of manure from the farmer, which he was going to mix in with his own secret gardening weapon: leftover rice hulls from the milling operation.

That business concluded, we continued our tour of the area. He pointed out the location of a couple of juke joints. He said he'd heard there was live music at these mostly black social halls, but he had never gone into one. He didn't think I should, either, but was vague about what would befall me if I did. I had romantic images of great blues or soul music and big platters of barbecue, a chance to visit with some local folks and dip my toe into the local music scene. Had I gone, I probably could have struck up some conversations and exchanged some phone numbers, as I did at the Sportsmens Bar in Niobrara, Nebraska. I might not have had to work so hard to find an individual to speak to me about the health and sustainability of their communities, from the African American point of view.

It wasn't until I returned home to Bellevue that I returned to social media, this time to LinkedIn. There, I found a professional profile, complete with photograph, for Vannessa Frazier, executive director of the Howardville Betterment Center. Howardville is about four miles from the city of New Madrid, in New Madrid County. As of 2010, there were 383 people in the town, 93 percent of whom were African American. I saw that in 2011, EPA awarded a $25,000 Environmental Justice Grant to Howardville Community Betterment Committee, and that Vannessa had written the grant. EPA's environmental justice efforts aim to ensure equal environmental and health protections for all Americans, regardless of race or socioeconomic status.

Vannessa was born in Portageville, Missouri, fifteen miles south of New Madrid. She went to school in Lilbourn. Now in her early fifties, Vannessa is too young to remember much about the officially segregated South. Yet, she attended segregated schools, even though they were declared unconstitutional with the 1954 Supreme Court ruling *Brown v. Board of Education*, well before her birth. Vanessa's school was all black, both teachers and students. Her school, what is now Howardville Elementary School, was built in the late 1950s with the intention of being segregated. If it hadn't been for her school's success in a statewide basketball tournament, no one outside of the Bootheel would have known about it at all, let alone that it was all black, she said.

That was in the early 1970s. "The state called down here and told them they needed to integrate," Vannessa said. "We're way down here, nobody really cares, nobody checked on things." Because of the communities being so close together geographically, there was a bit of musical chairs being played with which grades wound up being housed in which school buildings. Her school was opened in 1958 and graduated its first class in 1959. "We didn't do too bad. We had a brand new school, good food, all black teachers." The white classmates joined, about the time she was in junior high. "Some were afraid and timid a little, but they saw we weren't going to bite 'em and things went real well. But the black high school students had to go to school in mostly white Lilbourn. "They had riots and had to lock the black guys up in the gym," she recalled. Vannessa's mother, who was active in the NAACP, went there to pick them up. She told Vannessa she wanted her to witness what was going on. Vannessa recounts that her mother asked the principal why the black kids were locked in the gym. The principal replied it was because the white and black boys were fighting each other and he didn't know what else to do. Vannessa's mother asked, "Why didn't you call anybody? I had to find out from people on the street that you had locked them up and didn't let them come home." Vannessa recalls the boys coming out of there, running every which way, like a stampede. "As I've gotten older and looked back, I've thought 'Wow, integration was really something.'"

She and other community organizers in Howardville are working to get the school eligible for historic status, especially as pertaining to significance to black history. That designation would help fund the restoration efforts currently underway in the community, which the EPA environmental justice grant is part of funding. I had passed by the school a few times when in the area, and I could see from the broken windows and appearance of disuse that a certain section of facility was no longer open. I had noticed signage in the school lot announcing that the building was being rehabilitated as an urban brownfield site, using EPA hazardous substances grant funds. Vannessa and her group are working to remodel the school to LEED energy-efficiency standards and turn it into a community center with a place for job-training classes, an events center for special occasions, retail and office space, and extension offices for the state government.

"We need a lot of things down here that are considered basic in Kansas City and St. Louis. In those places it is just natural day to day to get up and do certain things, but we don't have it and have to drive to get it." She means things like going to a public library, or a grocery store, or a car wash. Another thing: "We don't have reliable Internet that won't kick you off." That is a problem for Vannessa, since she's the one working from home, writing grants to better Howardville, but getting kicked off the online submission system before she can get her material uploaded to the site.

Some of her work to improve Howardville was motivated by a 2009 ice storm that struck the area. Downed trees and power lines were everywhere, even on major highways. As a Red Cross disaster action team instructor, Vannessa was involved in the logistics of cleanup. She recalls watching one community after another being brought emergency generators, food, and having live power lines removed from roads and property. "But in Howardville, we were without power for eleven days." After going through numerous channels with no results, she called her congressman in Jefferson City to say they were being overlooked. "Things started jumping. A man from Jeff City came down and said we weren't overlooked, and that everyone was in dire stress." Vannessa is not too sure about that.

"It has been rough. It doesn't feel like back in 1960. You don't know you're being mistreated until something happens like that. But it taught us a lesson." That lesson is that when you prepare for disaster you need to have provisions to be on your own for three days but without assistance for eleven days, she says. "Even though we eventually got help we were not first on the agenda, not really even on the agenda. You need to have sustainable resources in place should disaster come."

Gradually, Vannessa's grant writing is paying off, and Howardville is getting funding for things like sidewalks, street lights, and painted white stripes that alert people driving along the state highway when they are about to cross onto the shoulder of the road. Vannessa remains mindful of disaster and knows her community needs a place where people can go safely if there should be an ice storm, earthquake, or tornado. The newly renovated school will provide that shelter. There's a lot to be done in this 36,000-square-foot building and not a lot of money. "In a little black community with no money it is hard to do fundraising," she said. "We need that grocery store, doctor's office, pharmacy," she says of Howardsville's plan. "Without medication, if you are sick, that can be hard in a disaster. Black people suffer a lot of chronic disease like diabetes and high blood pressure. It is just like a death sentence when you are without meds. There is nothing here. We'd like to have those things in the school so we can maintain and sustain. We'll be content with that."

Thinking about the mostly white or mostly black communities in New Madrid, and indeed in much of the rural South, made me think about race in other small towns of the Midwest and Great Plains. I haven't encountered any mostly black towns on the modern-day plains of Kansas, Nebraska, Iowa, or Wyoming that sit just a few miles from their mostly white small-town counterparts, the way they do here. The New Madrid community as a whole supports the idea of black and white children together in schools, learning and playing without segregation. Local newspapers are full of pictures of black kids and white playing sports together, encouraged on by an integrated cheerleading squad, coaches, and fans in the stands. But what about once people leave school, go to work, and choose where to live? Do they return to the sifting and sorting behavior that guides most of our choices, of preferring to be in the company of people who are like ourselves, in proximity to our families if possible, not intentionally excluding diversity, but understanding that cohesion and diversity are contrary realities?

Sally Palmer has lived most of her life in this area, and has dealt personally and professionally with a wide swath of people from all backgrounds. I met her during my tour with Ed Williams, in the Riceland break room. As production manager at Riceland, Sally's job in a male-dominated industry puts her into contact with many different sorts of people. About my age, outdoorsy-looking, and energetic, she struck me as the sort of person I'd like to hang out with after work if I lived there. Sally does hiring and firing at the plant and believes many people in the area are not equipped either with the skills or education needed to hold a good job. Sally has theories about why she has trouble finding qualified employees. "When the economy crashed, Riceland kept steady pace, but right before that occurred we started to see a huge problem getting good people. It eased up a bit from 2008 to 2012. When people were losing jobs elsewhere we began getting more qualified applicants. Now it is shifting back to what it was before, and more opportunities have eliminated our pool." So the workers already in the pipeline are harder to find, and the kids getting out of school now don't necessarily have the preparation, she said. "The schools aren't educating kids for things that would benefit them if they want to stay in the area they are from. We get kids out of high school and they don't know the practical skills."

Sally herself grew up in this area. When her father couldn't find work, he took the family to Michigan. Then, when Sally was three weeks old, the family returned to Missouri, settling in Kewanee, a few miles outside New Madrid, where she still lives. Sally looks back on that upbringing as "typical Mayberry," with a combination general store and post office, an elementary school, a place where you knew everybody and where parents were not afraid of leaving children to play outside. She married her high school sweetheart, whom she'd known most of her life, and they made that place home.

"Now we yearn to do something different. Not because we dislike it, but because we haven't lived anyplace else." The plusses are that they know everyone, but that is also the minus. By that, she means that children are so entrenched in the structures of small-town family life that they never learn how to meet new people and judge someone for themselves, and not on their history. Sally firmly states what she sees as the biggest negative. "This is a very, very racist area. You find it more and more the farther south you go. That has stuck in our craw."

She and her husband both lived through segregation during their years in elementary school and they remember it well. She doesn't think the racism is to that extreme now. "It is hard to describe. It is almost to the point that you know it is there and people try to profess they're not racist, but their actions speak louder than words." For example, mixed couples are stigmatized, and their children are as well, although mixed-race relationships are more accepted in recent years. "Ignorance in general breeds that kind of thing," Sally said. "I try to understand that when you grow up in a community that had so much segregation and hard feelings, it is generational. Sometimes attitudes get left behind, sometimes they get worse; it depends on your upbringing."

After college, Sally's kids moved to Atlanta and Charlotte, respectively. The diversity there was the drawing factor. Now Sally and her husband are ready for a community with a more diverse population, with access to things like a good park system. Since they are hoping to retire soon they might go where their kids are, maybe a suburb of Atlanta. "There is access to so many things, people of every color and race. Because everybody is a transplant they build a sense of community."

While Sally is ready to invent the next stage of her life post-retirement, I also met several young people in New Madrid in the early stages of their careers. In a display of hospitality that reminded me of Nita Jones and her crew in Sedan, Ed Williams introduced me to Sarah Ezell, Aaron Graham, and Jaime Motter during our morning together. Sarah is a young New Madridian who chose to settle in her hometown for a combination of reasons. Some of it is family, some the availability of a job, some the outdoor recreation the river affords, and in the case of Sarah and others like her, the opportunity and responsibility to keep the fires of New Madrid burning. She is the marketing director for Southeast Missouri Health Network (SEMO), which provides a variety of medical, dental, and mental-health services regardless of a patient's ability to pay. The New Madrid clinic is one of five in the network.

"As primary face of SEMO Health Network, I have my hands in a little bit of everything," Sarah explained. That means attending health fairs, reaching out to the public about their services, working with media on advertising, and developing sponsorship advertising. That includes recruiting businesses like Riceland Foods to sponsor events such as the annual Relay for Life. That was how she came to know Ed Williams, and how he came to introduce Sarah to me. I could tell when we met in the lobby of the SEMO Health Network office that she was the sort of dynamic individual who could live, or work, or go anywhere she chose.

Sarah believes in her town, which is a necessity as she helps recruit new employees, such as nursing, dental, physicians, and other medical staff. She tries to be straight with prospective employees in case they cannot simply look around and see for themselves that New Madrid is not New York. "When we recruit and hire from metro areas, we let them know that although we are in a rural county, we are close enough to city life to get there." St. Louis, Memphis, and their conveniences make good bait, it seems. As she points out, nearby Sikeston offers some of the services and conveniences handy to have on a weekly basis, like bigger grocery and hardware stores, and a movie theater. With a population just under 40,000, Cape Girardeau offers a bit more, and St. Louis and Memphis offer almost everything else a person used to city life would want.

Sarah had not intended to go to college in the area, let alone settle here. "I said, 'I'm getting out of here, no more small town. I'm moving to Florida and never coming back.'" But a scholarship to Southeast Missouri State University convinced her that a nearby college was a smart choice. Once there, she got involved with dorm life, then a sorority. She learned more about the world, traveled during spring breaks, graduated, and got a job in "Cape." Kyle, her then boyfriend, had a job offer in his hometown of Portageville. She was adamant about not returning to the area. "I'm staying in Cape, where there is life, where I can go out on a Tuesday night if I want for drinks with friends, or a movie, or to Walmart, or the mall," she told him. Eventually, Kyle convinced her returning home was the way to go. "For the first six months I was not happy about it. But my family, sisters, grandparents, cousins, aunts, and uncles were here." She and Kyle got engaged, and then married. "I hated him for a little while," she jokes. Then she realized he was right. "The older you get, the more you care about life and family. I realized New Madrid is where I'm meant to be."

Now she is trying to change the face of her community, helping bring people and business into New Madrid. "I've seen now that there is potential." She stays busy participating in all the town activities she can find. There's the Mexican restaurant with its bar, where she sometimes hangs out with groups of girlfriends. She and Kyle enjoy fishing and boating on the river, and picnicking on sandbars. "You've got to be careful with the Muddy Mississippi," she cautions. "Because of the bend in the river the current is always a challenge, it is a mystery, it is hard to tell what is on top, and what you don't see underneath." Some may hear that as a metaphor for life in general, I thought, from my perspective of twenty-five years her senior.

Sarah might not feel comfortable dodging barges on the river but that doesn't mean she doesn't enjoy the outdoors. In fact, she traces the moment she realized she wanted to stay in New Madrid to a little ride around town on the couple's Polaris Ranger. "We can ride ATVs in town as long as we have a city license, which is something you can't do in the big city," she explains. "We were riding the ATV and it hit me. I looked Kyle in the eye and said, 'I'm glad you made me move home because we couldn't do this in Cape.'" There are too many "can'ts" in the city, she said. That is something Sarah thinks her friends from college don't understand. "My friends can't believe I moved back here. Why not? The hardest thing is finding a job, and I lucked out."

During my stop at SEMO Health Network, Sarah introduced me to her colleague, who, like her, is rural by choice. Aaron Graham was born and raised in New Madrid, was valedictorian of his class, and, like Sarah, went to college at Southeast Missouri State. Now twenty-two, he is SEMO Health Network's legislative liaison, which means he studies government policies and legislation and helps SEMO implement them. He has a personal story he is quick to relate to anyone who asks because it has defined him personally and professionally.

"I am a cancer survivor," he tells me. "At age seven, I was diagnosed with rhabdomyosarcoma." That is a cancerous tumor of the muscles that are attached to the bones. It can occur in many places in the body, especially the structures of the head and neck, the urogenital tract, and the arms or legs. In Aaron's case, it meant a tumor behind his left eye. His tumor was discovered almost by chance when he was at a doctor's appointment. He went through chemo and radiation, and now is "big into cancer stuff."

He didn't want to become a doctor, because "surgeries burned me out on medical procedures." But he still wanted to help people. So he majored in political science. When we spoke he was working full time on ACA, assisting people signing up for the Affordable Care Act and making sure SEMO is in compliance. Aaron reiterated that it is politics he loves, not blood or guts, though some could construe the two together. He says of a possible political future, "If I could help people by working on health care legislation, the Affordable Care Act, and so on, I would. This is a very important time."

Hearing Aaron talk about the connection of poverty and health in his county made me consider what Vannessa Frazier had said about being prepared to deal with health situations should disaster strike. I found some telling statistics in the Missouri Foundation for Health's report—part of its Health Equity Series—called *African American Health Disparities in Missouri*. The report was based on data from the Missouri Department of Health and Senior Services, Section for Epidemiology and Public Health Practice. The report's authors state that African Americans are more than twice as likely as whites to fall below the poverty level. Americans living in extreme poverty have "more chronic illness, more frequent and severe disease complications, and make greater demands on the health care system." And the report indicates that while the relationship between poverty and health is not entirely clear, Missouri's African American population lags behind the white population on many health indicators.

A 2014 study by the Robert Wood Johnson Foundation looked at various health markers among all races in urban counties, suburban counties, and what they call non-core counties around the country. New Madrid County is non-core because it has no communities of over 10,000 residents. The study looked at health outcomes such as length of life and quality of life. It examined health factors such as health behaviors, clinical care, social and economic factors, and the physical environment. Out of the 115 Missouri counties, New Madrid ranked 109th in length of life and 112th in quality of life. It was 91st in health behaviors, 89th in access to clinical care, 104th in social and economic factors, and 112th in physical environment.

A sad reality is that having a job in health care is a recipe for a stable career in most places with a poor or aging population. That is especially true in small, rural American counties like New Madrid. As Aaron noted, "Here people don't have easy access to care, and they have trouble affording health insurance. I knew these people personally and wanted to come back and save lives, and I literally believe we are doing that. One person walks through the door, one checkup, can save a life."

People in this community are family to Sarah and Aaron and their health concerns matter to them. The well-being of individuals translates directly to the well-being of the community. As Aaron said, "This is our home, not just somewhere you live. I haven't been alive a really long time but even I've seen the town decrease and deteriorate." About half of the students Aaron went to high school with have left town, gone to college, or just moved off to other areas. The other half of the class who remain are working in agriculture, trades, or factory work. "They are still around, holding down difficult swing shift laborer jobs. Another half did move off into professional fields, but that is harder to do here in this area, since there are not a lot of those jobs," he said.

Aaron told me that maybe down the road he'll look at a political career and run for office. I wondered how hard it must be for a young person to break through the power structure in a small town. "Younger people can be looked down on a little bit, especially in politics," he said carefully. "A lot of it is older, more experienced people who have worked their way up in the system. As a significantly younger person, you just have to work through it."

Jaime Motter is another young health-care professional, born and raised in New Madrid. She's also struggling with the question of how much longer she will stay in the area. Jaime attended college at the University of Mississippi in Oxford. Then she went to pharmacy school in Kansas City, where she met her husband, Will. She was happily practicing her profession in the city, until life happened. She told me this background while we were chatting briefly in the aisles of her family owned business, Davis Pharmacy, where Ed Williams had taken me right after our stop at SEMO Health Network. It turns out that the neighborhood where she lived in Kansas City was only about a mile from my old neighborhood. As we ran down the list of familiar restaurants and hangouts, I felt a flush of nostalgia. I'd gone through that phase myself, being a young professional in Kansas City, having a good job, feeling like everything I wanted or needed was at my fingertips. I wrenched myself away because of personal wanderlust, but for Jaime it was different. Her father was operating the family business that her grandparents had started in 1938. When he fell ill, Jaime began making frequent visits back home to help. Then he died, unexpectedly. "I dropped everything and came back to help my mom. There was no time to mourn. We just had to keep the business going, not by choice, but from obligation."

Just a few days before we continued our conversation by phone, she had signed the paperwork to sell the business. "It was the hardest decision of my life," she told me. Jaime describes the new owner as "a very hometown, small market, small town, southern chain." For the time being she'll work for them and see how it goes. "The employees will all stay, and hopefully, customer service will retain high standards under new owners. Customers are treated like family in a small town, we know them by first name, we know the medications they take, we know if something wrong is called in by mistake, we go to patients' houses in winter if need be."

Jaime has noticed a shift from New Madrid being a place where people could expect to hold a steady job, to seeing the rise in mechanized farming eliminating many of the field jobs. "Mechanized farming came in, taking the jobs of the mostly African American community, who were doing farm work. People are already dealing with poor health related to poverty, like diabetes and heart disease. It is sad, there is no way out because of their lack of education. Once they complete high school there is no opportunity."

Jaime has noticed New Madrid going through a decline in recent decades, cutting across all demographics. For example, there are not as many young people as when her parents were her age. She recalls childhood summers when thirty couples would come out for twilight golf, and kids packed the pool. "Now we don't even have a golf team anymore." But in her last five years here, she's seen a small increase in people who are educated moving back.

Even if New Madrid becomes more like it was thirty years ago, it'll never be Kansas City, or even Oxford, Mississippi. "I miss city life, I miss my friends, I miss restaurants, I miss coffee shops, I miss sushi. I miss my gym. At the same time, there is a strong sense of family here, and that people care, though they are nosy to a fault." Jaime says she doesn't regret being from a small town. "There's no class system. There's more diversity in a sense because you know everyone from every class of life. There is not so much separation as there is in the city. It gives you a good perspective on how others live. At the same time I want my children to experience other things, have more opportunity to play sports, and have life experiences outside of here."

Jaime and her husband have been in New Madrid for five years of their "seven-year plan." Will has adjusted to New Madrid amazingly well, Jaime said. "He joined a band with a diverse group of people: an auto mechanic, the public defender, the heat and air guy, and a city employee. He fit right in. There are things that he really doesn't care for about a small town but does really well. But definitely he is on board with leaving."

She and Will might decide this is their forever home once out from under the business. At the same time, she is looking at her life with a longer view. "If we stay here very long we will never leave. That's what scares me more than anything. You wake up one day and you've said, 'I'm going to do this, live somewhere else,' and you look up and you haven't gone anywhere."

New Madrid resident Virginia Carlson hasn't lived here all of her life, but most of her seven-plus decades have been spent here. Some of that time has been spent preserving the ephemeral and the monumental, keeping both present for future generations. Virginia told me about how the town had weathered calamities from floods to earthquakes to Civil War battles. She told me how one day some forty years ago, she and her friend Dot Halstead were out sweeping the streets in the town's business district. While they were taking a break from their efforts, the pair stopped to ponder an old building that had been standing since before they were born. Overlooking the Mississippi River, the building started life as a saloon and eventually became an auto-repair shop. It was thick with grease and a real mess. "Dot said, 'We need to start a museum and right there is where it needs to be.'"

That pronouncement was all it took for the two to spring into action and secure the support of the chamber of commerce. The chamber purchased the building, which the newly formed New Madrid Historical Museum Board restored. Then the board purchased it back from the chamber. The nonprofit museum is now a significant tourism draw, seeing between 7,000 and 10,000 visitors a year. When the museum opened in 1975, the board was motivated by the fact that a lot of history was not being preserved. "Our original town is a mile in the Mississippi River," Virginia explained. "Nothing here is real old, because it is all out in the river." When she says "all" she means the part of town that was first developed in the 1780s. She means the part that was in ruins thanks to the series of intense earthquakes in 1811 and 1812. She even means all the small family cemeteries that provided final resting places for generations of New Madridians, her own family's included.

Because of the river's hunger, the museum started with almost nothing. They had an art showing, and "grandma's attic" items that showed how townspeople lived in the nineteenth century. They began collecting items from the Civil War, which had a local angle due to the Battle of Island Number Ten, which occurred between February 28 and April 8, 1862. Thanks to a quirk of geography, New Madrid is actually on the north bank of the Mississippi—which for most of its length flows north to south with banks on its east and west. Island Number Ten had been held by the Confederates, who used it as a location from which to pounce on Union vessels as they slowed to navigate currents in the sharp bends. To make a long and inevitable story short, the Union won the battle and the war. Now Island Number Ten has joined much else the river encounters—under water, stuck in mud, or washed away to the Gulf of Mexico.

The New Madrid Historical Museum devotes much attention to this local battle, with cases full of Civil War artifacts dug up by locals over the years. And they have items connecting World Wars I and II to local residents. But they didn't have any displays devoted to the earthquakes. "We didn't have anything 'cause nothing survived," Virginia said. "We thought nobody was paying attention to it anymore. We soon found out that was real wrong."

In fact, there was a "big scare" in 1990, when author and climatologist Iben Browning predicted strong quakes would once again shake the New Madrid Fault Line on December 3 of that year. In spite of the dire predictions of imminent danger and bodily harm, Virginia says, "people from around the world packed this little town waiting for it." The museum created T-shirts sporting the slogan New Madrid: It's Our Fault.

"We must have sold a million of those T-shirts," she said. I wasn't surprised. I'd bought one, myself.

The museum does not exactly jump out at travelers who don't already intend to go there. Neither the town nor the river can be seen from the highway. Around the time the board of directors began to promote the museum to earthquake tourists, Virginia said they placed a "big black billboard" on the highway outside of town with "shaky letters" that said Earthquake. A man who was developing the industrial park almost had a heart attack when he saw it, she told me.

I came to New Madrid with a great interest in the earthquake. It wasn't until I got to the museum that the reality of the intense fighting during the Civil War hit me. I wasn't aware of the Mississippian Indian mounds in the area either, although I knew about other cultural sites such as the Cahokia Mounds near St. Louis. The New Madrid Historical Museum has a display on local mounds that again brought that culture close to home. And of course, I spent time in the room of various domestic items, furnishings, and tools that appeal to the antique-lover side of me. Many items in the collection would fit right into my own 130-plus-year-old home a few hundred miles upriver in Iowa. But I had no idea how close to home I'd feel until I spent a few moments with museum administrator Jeff Grunwald: no doubt the only man in New Madrid at that moment drinking from a Iowa Hawkeyes coffee mug.

Jeff has lived in many cities since leaving Iowa at age sixteen, and until recently, he and his wife, Malinda, were living just a few hours away in Memphis. They decided the time had come to move closer to her family in New Madrid. Not long after, he became involved with the museum, which appealed to the history major he had been before he went into the telecommunications business. He said he never in a million years thought he'd wind up a museum director in New Madrid, Missouri. Now he works there nearly full time. Jeff estimates 60 to 65 percent of traffic is earthquake tourism, 25 percent are Civil War buffs, and the remainder a combination of folks who enjoy dropping into small towns or visiting roadside attractions.

At the time of my visit, foot traffic was starting to pick up for the season. People drifted through the door in pairs. Jeff greeted them, accepted their admission fee, asked a few questions to assess their knowledge of museum holdings, and then guided them into a small room to watch a short movie about local history. In between, he monitored the scores of March Madness basketball games from his smartphone.

Jeff has had a chance to discover some of the town's charms, and after just a few years of living there, he feels like a full-fledged member of the community. And although he and his wife are not average residents of the community, he says, "We're here for the long term, not looking to leave." In their mid-forties, the couple does not have children. "That makes us a little different." He calls children a "passport to community life." But he also thinks that is true in a bigger city, where having kids is a way of meeting people through a school system, without which one would be lost in an even bigger crowd. He says people are friendly and it is not that hard to fit in, but it helps to have someone there to introduce you. "We go against the grain in a few ways, we don't walk the same path as most people. We lived successful corporate lives, saved very well, and now have a little cushion." That's in contrast to the many who work full time at labor-intensive industrial jobs. As to the social life of a relatively young, unencumbered couple, they don't go out much. "We go to people's homes to socialize. There is a home-based way of living here."

Jeff also substitute teaches at the local school and comments on the interactions of the white children and the black children. He believes the younger kids are succeeding where older adults and past generations have struggled in terms of race, that is, "letting go of past practices and beliefs." He also confirmed what I'd heard others intimate: there is a drug problem in the area, especially with methamphetamine. "It is not like it is rampant," he said, "but it is bigger than most of us would want it to admit."

Numerous meth-lab busts and various other sorts of criminal enterprises are common enough in this area that the New Madrid Sheriff's Department communicates information through a Facebook page, along with pictures from surveillance. This example from the March 10, 2014, sheriff's department Facebook page, is typical: "As you've probably noticed by the time between updates and the long lists of arrests it has been a pretty busy and productive year for us so far. Today's release will be about the Burglaries in Lilbourn over the past several months. At the beginning of 2014 our Investigators were contacted by the Lilbourn Police Department for assistance in trying to clear up some of these cases. In the two months leading up to this request there were approximately 17 Burglaries and thefts reported."

Lilbourn is the town where Ed Williams and his wife live. These towns are not worlds away from each other. Just a few miles from Howardville, Lilbourn is 65 percent white, with most of the rest African American. Regardless of the age, race, or residence of the perpetrators, I understood why Ed might feel nervous about seventeen burglaries in a two-month span in his town of 1,200. I also had a sense of why he concluded that some of the perpetrators also spent some of their time at the neighborhood juke joint he'd pointed out to me but cautioned me against visiting. After all, this is a small town. He knows whose kids are doing what and where in his neighborhood. I needed to resist letting my view of the place be shaped by crime statistics. After all, the sheriff indicated the lists of arrest warrants and photos from surveillance cameras at locations being burglarized were helping to stop or solve crimes.

I wanted to know what civic leaders were doing not to just reduce drug-related crime, but to educate the community that crime doesn't happen because of race, but instead because of poverty. A logical place to look for answers to poverty and its effects is to the educational system. Locals take pride in their children, their schools, and of course their sports teams. But the area has a lower than average rate of adults who have graduated from high school. In the United States as a whole, among people over twenty-five, approximately 88 percent have a high school diploma, and 31 percent have a bachelor's degree or higher. Yet among adults twenty-five years of age and older in New Madrid County, only around 67 percent possess a high school diploma or higher while around 10 percent hold a bachelor's degree or higher as their highest educational attainment. These statistics made it hard to feel optimistic about reducing poverty in this community, when so far the educational achievement and the opportunities for employment were mismatched.

While money doesn't solve all problems, I considered whether an influx of cash could help the schools, could help with the poverty, could help with the crime and the poor health care that afflicted some lives. Then I learned my questions will have an answer soon, because New Madrid is about to come into some serious money. About $100 million.

I learned all about it from Ed Thomason, who, along with his wife, Linda, publishes New Madrid's paper, the *Weekly Record*. He was another on the list of local contacts Ed Williams had lined up for me. We visited in Ed's one-room newspaper office, the desks mounded with past editions, the walls filled with local artwork and memorabilia. Whereas some community papers in towns along the Mississippi River have shipping news or fishing reports, this one has a column called "Seismic Shakes," noting various microearthquakes in the area.

Ed Thomason showed me a copy of the paper that explained the extraordinary deal that has every possibility of bringing people and poten-

Newspaper publisher and editor Ed Thomason holds a copy of one of his paper's most important editions in its 150-year history. Photograph © Julianne Couch.

tial to New Madrid. The city of New Madrid used to own the coal-fired power plant that neighbors the Riceland Foods plant. Then the city arranged for Associated Electric Cooperative to purchase New Madrid Unit 1 before termination of the existing agreement between the two parties would expire.

There had been a long and complex negotiation between the city and the power company. Ed Thomason, as a community businessman, was privy to details that, though a journalist, he had not been able to publish for fear of killing the deal. He was comfortable with the position he took keeping the negotiations secret and was relieved others felt that way about their roles, too. "All it would have taken would be one alderman gone wild" and letting the story get out to kill the deal, he said. But that didn't happen. The agreement, signed in 2013, means Associated Electric will make annual option payments to the city for the right to control the future of the power plant, which includes decisions about capital improvements. The city plans to start by investing in its infrastructure, he said. That means building a new water plant, replacing water lines, developing a new industrial park, improving fire protection, building a community recreation center, and structuring utility rates to benefit residential customers, especially those on fixed incomes.

Ed thinks it might also be possible one day to use deeply discounted utility rates to attract new people to town, at least for a short period of time. That's just one of many ideas he has in his arsenal as a town booster. He is also working on ideas to acquire land that is now in agricultural production and rezone it for commercial development. "Younger farmers today are more willing to sell land to developers than the older generation," he said. He lists numerous assets the community possesses, some brick-and-mortar, some flesh-and-blood. For example, a women's botanical club raised funds to install a veteran's park on Main Street. The Dixie Theatre, though no longer showing films, has live family friendly theatrical shows showcasing mostly local talent. New Madrid is working to get on the map. Ed wishes the town was a little closer to the highway, so the billboard advertising would be more effective. What they lack in closeness, they are making up for in size and frequency of advertising. "If there is a map, we want our ad to be on it," he said.

This is not to say that New Madrid has been completely languishing, and its only hope of recovering from malaise is this power-plant deal. The difference now is potential. That's according to Don Lloyd, economic development director of New Madrid County, who was city administrator for almost nineteen years. "For a small town of 3,000 plus people, now we have a little bit of cash on hand," he said. That gives them a chance to take a different approach to attracting new business and industry. "We have always been more reactive than proactive, and have depended on the economy and the State of Missouri partnerships to avail us of companies looking for places to go. We haven't gone out and actively searched. But now we have that capability, and are hoping to go into proactive mode." And it helps that leaders from the city and the county work "tremendously, unusually well together." The city has invested part of the electrical plant sale income to buy 212 acres in the county with rail service to the area, he said. "We have a lot to offer. I see only bright days ahead."

I asked about issues related to economic development other than location, such as the availability of a skilled workforce and adequate affordable housing for those workers. Don sounded confident that those issues would not stop a new business from joining companies like Rice-land Foods or Miranda Aluminum. "With today's economy, if there are jobs to be had then people will move. We get very few questions from prospects regarding labor supply."

I also wondered about the quality of life in an area that might boom suddenly. It seemed like New Madrid was smartly addressing that issue by diversifying its industrial economy. But what about planning for steady growth and not stomping the life out of other reasons people come to town, such as the quiet lifestyle, the strong sense of family connection, and the access to outdoor recreation the river provides. Don acknowledges that a focus on quality of life and amenities was not part of the first phase of spending the town's new bounty. Again accentuating the positive, he focused on what the area has rather than what it lacks. What it doesn't have itself, it can easily access. The small towns and villages in the county won't directly receive funding, but it could certainly mean jobs and intangible benefits flowing from a sense that the area was headed in the right direction.

Don itemized the tangible and intangible reasons he enjoys living in New Madrid. "The area has a fascinating geologic history," he explained. "The Gulf of Mexico used to extend up here, and in fact the six county area of the Bootheel is the beginning of the Mississippi River delta. It is a different topography from the rest of the state. It was once a two-and-a-half-million-acre swamp. In the 1920s they developed a drainage district and drained the delta. Now this is some of the best farmland in the world."

Not only is the farmland fine, but the water supply is almost endless, thanks to the river and the high water table in the area. The river isn't valued only for practical reasons but because, with its ever changing colors and textures and mysteries, it is a connection to the beautiful natural world. "I have to drive by and check on the river every day," Don told me. "Most people do."

That reminded me of my patch of river upstream in Bellevue. Residents of Mississippi River towns upstream or down love their river. But I thought about Sarah Ezell, who was nervous about what was beneath the surface of that water. And about Jaime Motter, who had told me about data suggesting the local high cancer rate could be traced to the environmental pollutants in the area. And about cancer survivor Aaron Graham, who mentioned he enjoyed fishing but did not eat the river fish because of the industrial and agriculture pollution in the waters. In spite of the Clean Water Act, much of the country's agricultural runoff and lawn fertilizer and industrial pollution winds up in the waterways, flowing to the Mississippi River and on to the Gulf of Mexico, where it pools to create a dead zone the size of a small New England state. Naturally, Don believes the view from his town is superior to anywhere else, because it isn't just a straight line, he points out. It is a tight loop. And it's not just the view that he appreciates, it's what the river signifies about the region and New Madrid's place in it.

"This is where the South begins."

EMMETSBURG, IOWA

8

ADD A COLLEGE, STIR IN A CASINO

Until I moved to my home along the Mississippi River, I'd always lived in a town with at least one college. The greater Kansas City area has numerous community colleges, technical schools, and branches of state universities. Colleges and college students had been so omnipresent in my environment I hardly noticed them. It was 1977 when I went away to school in Emporia, Kansas. This town of about 25,000 was just over a hundred miles from home, far enough away that I felt I'd entered a new world. College campus, college friends, college bars, jobs that hired college kids were all I noticed. I don't think about anything that affected townies, like plant closures or rising taxes or farm crises, penetrated my self-involved brain.

By the time I graduated for good in 1984, however, I was sorely tempted to stay. Had the phone call for a job interview at the *Emporia Gazette* come a few days before I'd already hauled a trailer of stuff to Kansas City and a job at the newspaper there, my life would have taken a very different path.

Fast forward seven years and I was off to Wyoming. During my first several years in Laramie, the University of Wyoming campus was the place I'd go to watch sports, or see a play, or attend lectures. Once I started teaching there, I fell under the spell of university life. Stately limestone buildings, cloistered around an open green area, bell-tower clock chiming the hours as the skies darkened on late semester fall afternoons — this was college as I never noticed it being when I was a student. The university was its own small town that had everything I craved: a sense of both inclusion and separateness, an air both solid and ethereal, a place where first-generation college kids from the antipodes of Wyoming could share classes with kids from Japan, China, Norway, Kenya, Russia, and speak a common language of learning. And we, the professors, instructors, and staff, were the foundation of all these things I loved. I could sit in my poet-garret office and look out at a spacious grassy area ringed in pine trees bordered by boulders. Some days a man in a kilt would stand on the green and play his bagpipes. You could feel breathing stop in this part of campus as people listened to his music.

I write about these things with nostalgia but I'm not investing them with more meaning now than they had at the time. More than anything else about Laramie, I miss university life. Make no mistake, I was ready to move on from the actual work I did there. But crossing campus, even when the sidewalks were sheets of ice and wind blew snow parallel to the ground, gave me a sensation of being in situ I hadn't realized had sunk so deep into my personal geography.

Now that I'm in Iowa, I wonder what my new town of Bellevue will be like with another 1,500 or so people living in town, if those people will include the students, faculty, and staff of a college. I wonder how these extra people will affect the economic, cultural, and civic life of a small town. Will it form the hub of what cultural scholars such as Richard Florida call the creative class, capable of attracting young people and creative types of all ages, nailing down the foundation of a town? Or will it be only one of the cultural currents that define a place?

Being new to Iowa, I had to ask around about towns in the state with fewer than 5,000 people that had a college town "vibe," as I put it. A friend who teaches at Iowa State told me that Emmetsburg had the sort of youthful energy and hip nightlife associated with college towns, and it might just be the place. Emmetsburg is in Palo Alto County, in northwest Iowa, about forty miles south of the Minnesota border. The town tends to be overshadowed by the larger communities of Spencer to the west, Algona to the east, the Iowa Great Lakes region to the northwest. But because Iowa Lakes Community College (ILCC) operates one of its two main branches there, I set off to see what it was like.

I made the five-hour drive from Bellevue to Emmetsburg on the Friday of a hot Labor Day weekend, motoring alone along the monotony of the divided four-lane highway through row-crop country. Highway 20 was designed to go around, not through, small towns. There are no highway rest stops along the route, so it is best to keep the mind occupied. In my case, my thoughts turned to the impressions I'd formed about Iowa before I moved here. Growing up a midwesterner, I had long been aware that Iowa had good school systems and was considered progressive in terms of social justice and politics. Those were some of the things that drew me to move here.

When I moved here from Wyoming, none of my friends understood my choice because "progressive" is not how Iowa reads to most westerners. All they saw was the shortcomings of its outdoor spaces. It was flatland country, they said, hot and humid in summer, gray and snowy in winter. And what was I going to do without access to public lands, they asked. And with all that corn?

I decided I'd learn some things about agriculture. I paid attention to the debate about the Farm Bill and the conflict between the agricultural-subsidies faction and the entitlement-benefits faction. I also learned about another piece of the Farm Bill that was not widely discussed. As part of the Farm Bill, the USDA is developing programs to assist veterans starting or continuing farming and ranching operations. The Department of Labor data shows that 45 percent of armed service members are from rural America. Iowa has its own effort underway. Formed in 2012, the Farmer Veteran Coalition of Iowa helps veterans figure out how to start a farm, how to get a farm job, or even find new customers for farm products.

I also learned about the work of Practical Farmers of Iowa. This organization doesn't simply focus on yield and grain prices, although that is part of it. They work to be inclusive, representing a diversity of agriculturists. Members farm everything from corn and soybeans, hay, and livestock, to fruits and vegetables, to cut flowers and herbs, and more. Some farm conventionally, others organically. They come together in this group because, as they say, they believe in nature as the model for agriculture and they are committed to moving their operations toward sustainability. Through their lens I have learned about the financial incentives for farmers to remove timber and prairie in order to plant fence line to fence line, and I understand why putting conservation first is a tough call. I also learned about the agricultural laborers working in various links along the food chain. Some are what one would picture as "average Iowa farm families." There are still plenty of farmers, descendants of nineteenth-century European settlers who busted Iowa sod and established communities like those they'd left behind in Germany or Ireland. There are also workers from Mexico and other parts of Latin

America here, planting and harvesting the corn and beans that mostly become livestock feed. And those same sorts of folks are working in Iowa's slaughterhouses and packing plants, preparing chicken and beef as part of Iowa's effort to feed the world.

Iowa has been a welcoming place for immigrants over its history. In some instances, that has gotten people into trouble, as was the case with the Agriprocessors Plant, a kosher slaughterhouse in Postville, Iowa, in the northeast part of the state. Its practice of hiring undocumented workers not only changed the culture of this small town—it brought notoriety to the community when the plant was raided by federal, state, and local officials in 2008. These incidents were documented in the book *Postville U.S.A.: Surviving Diversity in Small Town America* by Mark Grey and others. They describe the way hundreds of illegal immigrants were arrested, imprisoned, and then deported. Postville lost a huge piece of its population, through no fault of its own. It still bills itself as Hometown to the World and proudly reminds people it is a diverse community, "rich in industry and culture."

Like most places, people in Iowa try to do the right thing by others. But the definition of "right thing" varies depending on what each individual perceives to be at stake. While Iowa has welcomed migrant workers and even refugees from Southeast Asia and from Central America, it has trouble with African Americans within its mostly white borders. At least, that's the way it appears, considering that although just over 3 percent of Iowa is black, they make up 17 percent of Iowa's prison population. Many of these prisoners were incarcerated because of marijuana convictions. At least Iowa has started the conversation to change sentencing for this sort of offense.

I knew that Iowa wasn't all Grant Wood and wholesome county fairs but it was good to remind myself of some realities before heading to Emmetsburg. This is a town that, in fact, is doing pretty well. Mostly white but with some diversity of age and race due to the college, it also has economic diversity. Emmetsburg does not depend too much on tourism, or industry, or entrepreneurship. Other than during the devastation of the 1980s farm crisis, Emmetsburg has had a stable population, gaining or losing no more than a few percentage points annually. It appeared to me before my visit that the various subgroups of the community function well together, from the college administrators to the casino operator to the farmers to the shopkeepers on Main Street. I was ready to walk the streets and visit the public spaces, and imagine myself an Emmetsburger for a few days.

When I reached my destination it was too early in the day to go to my motel, which was near Iowa Lakes Community College. Instead, I drove around a bit and got my bearings: Wild Rose Casino on the east edge of town on Highway 18, the downtown area at the intersection of Highways 18 and 4, and just to the north, the bottom tip of Five Island Lake. A visitor who did not consult a map might guess this lake was a reservoir formed by damming the nearby west fork of the Des Moines River, but that visitor would be wrong. Like the Iowa Great Lakes, this natural lake was formed by departing glaciers. It is about a thousand acres in size, long and thin, slip-stitched by houses with individual boat docks, those boundaries punctuated here and there by public access to fishing or boating, a little swimming beach zippered along one edge. On this hot late summer day, the lake is where I headed in lieu of an air-conditioned motel. I kicked off my sandals and waded up to my shins along the edge of the water. Problems of sand and towel presented themselves later — for the moment, I made myself at home.

Eventually, I picked my way from one shady spot to the next, found my shoes, and walked three blocks back uptown, leaving my car parked in the shade by the lake. I stopped at the combination Chamber of Commerce/Iowa Visitor Center/KEMB-LP radio station building. The chamber uses a low power station to broadcast music programs, news, and information about local events. The radio broadcast provides the audio for the town's local-access cable station. College students help run the controls. I visited for a few minutes with Deb Hite, the chamber director, who was staffing the office when I arrived. Her family moved to Cylinder, a few miles from Emmetsburg, when she was six years old. Her local school consolidated with Emmetsburg's when she was in sixth grade. She went away to college for a couple years and returned to work at the local John Deere Equipment dealer. She left that job to have a child and later started a retail business in Emmetsburg, which she ran for twenty-nine years. "Five years before closing my store, a number of us who were retailers saw the value of organizing to try to attract traffic to town. We started the Emmetsburg Retail Association and I co-chaired that until I had the opportunity to become director of the chamber," she said.

I asked what was going on in town this three-day weekend, thinking there might be a local holiday event, but there was not. However, in a tone suggesting I was in luck, Deb told me the high school football team was playing a home game that night. In parting, she gave me a handful of brochures and some ideas about where to have lunch.

I took one of her suggestions and walked a block to New Shoots Farm Store, Café, and Bakery. Oversized brightly stylized paintings of chickens and cows hung from brick walls. The latte machine burbled and the smoothie machine whirred. Wait staff were college-aged women I took to be students. They were waiting on thirty- or forty-something folks who sat in small groups wearing professional work clothing sipping nonalcoholic beverages with their midday meals. I was interested in a small group of women about my age, seated at the table next to me. I thought about how I'd go about meeting them, if I were new in town and wanted to make friends. As they passed my table on their way out the door, one smiled and commented about my lunch choice of the panini special, and how good hers had been. It was nice to be acknowledged, even through the transient intimacy of adjacent tables.

Stepping outside after lunch, I noticed how people passed up and down the sidewalk with their eyes focused in front of them, not extending a greeting to me, or even a curious look. I conducted a social experiment: if it didn't seem too awkward to greet someone, I did so, and was acknowledged in return. But if I didn't initiate a greeting, I was not greeted. This said to me not that people in Emmetsburg were unfriendly, but simply that they were used to encountering people on the street who were unknown to them, who were perhaps in town for any number of reasons a nonresident of Emmetsburg might walk the streets of their town.

People here might not be excited by newcomers, but they seem enamored by the old-timers who settled here. Many white settlers coming into this country were European immigrants seeking land to farm. In the case of Emmetsburg, many of those folks were from Ireland, but others were from Germany, Denmark, or Poland. According to local history, in 1856 a group of Irish immigrant families established a frontier Irish colony in Palo Alto County on the banks of the Des Moines River near the present site of Emmetsburg. In 1858, several families staked out a town on the west bank of Five Island Lake. They agreed to name the town Emmetsburg, after Robert Emmet, the Irish patriot who, in 1803, was executed by the British government for rebelling against British rule in Ireland.

I wondered why Palo Alto County was named for a place in Mexico, rather than Ireland. The reason is that the county was named for a battle in the Mexican–American War, which the United States won at about the time the county was settled. But in the context of today, it feels rather nice to have a county name that can be construed as inclusive. It made me think about a young man I'd recently met who lives in northwest Iowa, in a town delightfully called Orange City. Eduardo Rodriguez works for a northwestern Iowa nonprofit called Justice for All. The organization brings together Christians from various denominations to work together for the good of people in need, in their area.

Eduardo is in his mid-twenties now. When he was a student at Northwestern College in Orange City, he held an internship at a nonprofit organization in Chicago and could have stayed on at that job. But he was contacted by Justice for All about a job and took it. He was glad to come back, he said. "Living in Chicago was really cool, to experience different lifestyles and cultures, to be someplace where things are open later at night." But those things are still there if he wants them. Meanwhile, he says, he's developed a passion for working with underserved youth in northwest Iowa.

In addition to his work with children from immigrant families, Eduardo mentors students at his alma mater through a group called Hispanics of Northwestern. Part of its purpose is to help students fill in gaps in their preparation for college. Another part of it is about mentoring. "We want students to know their options and what is possible, to help them knock down barriers. We want to make sure they have a support network and they have people who are willing to invest in them."

Eduardo himself understands the position these kids are in. He came from Mexico with his parents as a first grader and entered school in Orange City. Some of his family remained in Mexico, and his parents make occasional trips to visit. He noted the way community heritage celebrations are viewed by those from outside that heritage. Orange City is a community of about 6,000 and growing. Each May its Tulip Festival marks the city's Dutch heritage. "The festival is fun and entertaining, but a little odd for some individual Orange Citians," Eduardo said.

"Growing up Mexican American here can be difficult because you can't be as open in celebrating your culture, creating that space for it. You don't want to be ostracized because of it, but you want to celebrate your culture and feel good about where your family came from," Eduardo added. That desire to feel good about one's family history is one of the main motivations for Eduardo's efforts on behalf of immigrant children.

I myself came from a culture that was eventually accepted and embraced by mainstream America. Like much of Emmetsburg, I am Irish, though four generations removed from the Emerald Isle known to my Brennan ancestors. Still, I feel that sense of privilege—peculiar to Americans who claim Irish descent—to wear green and rail against the British overlords at certain times of the year. In that spirit I paid my respects to the statue of Robert Emmet. It was hard to look at Emmet's bronze likeness rising high above the green grass in front of the courthouse—bare-headed, romantic, and righteous—knowing the end that was to greet him, executed for treason against the British government. But it was also hard not to look at him, tall on the lawn, visible from just about every vantage point of downtown Emmetsburg, and hope those traits would stand for all.

I was schooled in the history of Irish settlement in Palo Alto County by Julia Nixon, an Emmetsburg native. As the descendant of pioneers, Julia seems personally connected to the idea that the United States was founded by a plethora of nationalities, and she celebrates the mix that remains in her town today. When we spoke, she was midway through reading a history of Palo Alto County. It came as no surprise then that when I inquired of her where to go and what to do in town, she steered me to the Mexican and Chinese restaurants, and the Irish store, in order to highlight the western Iowa melting pot. She told me about the annual three-day St. Patrick's Day celebration in town, which is a centerpiece of Emmetsburg identity.

Now in her seventies, Julia has seen a goodly percentage of Emmetsburg's history through her own eyes. That history has included lots of changes to her small town. "Some of the changes have been nice changes, but it is like any small town: downtowns tend to diminish. As a kid in the 1940s I remember there was a grocery store on every corner, now there are a few larger grocery stores," she told me. "Twenty-five miles away there is a Walmart, and that has made the neighborhood stores go away. There were shoe stores, men's and women's clothing stores, but those are all gone now." On the plus side, she said, about fifteen years ago Emmetsburg received a grant "to spiff up downtown." So,

Dublin-born Robert Emmet was executed at age twenty-five for leading a rebellion against the British in 1803. This statue evokes the cultural heritage for some, though not all, of the townspeople. Photograph © Julianne Couch.

even though the center of town is not thriving with businesses, "at least there are sidewalks, curbs, and gutters that look nice," she said.

Julia's husband, David, was for many years the executive dean of ILCC and served as the chief administrative officer of its Emmetsburg campus. In 2003 he took a job as president of a community college in Monroe, Michigan. When he retired in 2013, the couple moved back to Emmetsburg. Now they enjoy many of the amenities he was partially responsible for creating in town. He led the fundraising campaign for the campus wellness center, which includes an indoor Olympic-sized pool, handball court, gym for events, and a combined college and public library. "Those are nice changes, good for the town," Julia said.

Other positive changes resulting from the college in general has to do with diversity among the college population. ILCC draws students from rural Iowa, but also from urban areas in other states and even other countries. "We see African Americans and Hispanics in town and are happy to see that diversity," Julia said. Although Julia and David's circle of friends share this attitude, she is not sure whether the sentiment is universally held in Emmetsburg. "After all, not everyone thinks that President Obama is a good thing." Her tone suggested mystification, but then she brightened, noting that many presidential candidates come through Emmetsburg during presidential campaigns, because of Iowa's early caucuses.

When I began to research small towns in Iowa with some type of college, I found an astounding number of choices. Had I been willing to visit a larger college town and not worry about geographic diversity for my research, I could have gone to Grinnell (pop. 9,000), Decorah (8,000), Lamoni (2,500), Pella (10,000), Forest City (4,000), Mt. Vernon (3,390), or of course Orange City. The sixty colleges and universities in Iowa include two research universities, nine universities that include master's programs, and nineteen four-year colleges, as well as twenty-one associate's degree-granting colleges. I wanted the towns I visited to be small enough so that not everyone would know each other, but that everyone would at least know of each other, or of the place one another worked, or went to school, or to shop. Possibly the college in Emmetsburg has kept the town's population from decreasing, making the community fairly stable.

Bill Lapczenski, director of auxiliary services at ILCC, agrees with that thesis. In his position, he oversees the campus bookstore, housing, food service, the wellness center, and in his spare time is student senate advisor. I found him after spending time on social media trying to whittle down Iowa college towns to visit. On a LinkedIn site for those interested in Iowa, I posed a question about what I was looking for and what my parameters were. It wasn't long before Bill posted his reply, that Emmetsburg was the place, and that he'd be happy to help me in any way he could.

I asked him which he thought was most important to the town's growth and viability, the college, or the presence of the tourist-destination casino. "In towns this size, all the pieces of the puzzle are important," he said. As it turns out, Bill is an instrumental figure in both.

Originally from Buffalo, New York, his family moved to Ohio when he was a child. When he was seventeen he went on a road trip to check out Emmetsburg with a friend who was planning to attend community college there. Bill said he had no thoughts of doing so himself, until he got there and found that he liked it. With his parents' blessing, he enrolled and majored in hotel management. After graduation he began working for various colleges, running their food-service departments. Then about thirty years ago the position at Emmetsburg came open. He applied, got the job, and has become a leader in the town's economic and civic development.

"Students at Emmetsburg are a big part of the community," he said. They major in programs including automotive, diesel, welding, administrative assistance, veterinary technology, hotel and restaurant management, and wind-farm technology. There is even an extracurricular athletic program, with the Lakers excelling at swimming. "The swimming program has attracted international students who compete on the team," Bill told me. "And the nursing program is especially attractive to African American students from urban areas like Minneapolis where there is a waiting list to get into nursing programs." Bill believes the diversity of students has been good for Emmetsburg. "The culture has changed. We were a small rural town, full of white farm kids. Now there is some cultural diversity in town. The little community college I went to in the 1970s has grown up."

My holiday weekend visit to campus was poorly timed for seeing a lot of students. I drove past the dorms, where a few students were drooping limply on porches, looking about as lively in the ninety-five-degree heat as the soybeans in the farm field across the street from campus. I saw no one hanging around in the shade, no little group of students clustered on park benches talking about Chaucer or thermodynamics. In spite of this town's Celtic heritage, no one was playing a bagpipe, dressed in a kilt. I took refuge in the air conditioned wellness center and saw a few students working at the front desk who looked very glad to be indoors. I stepped into the library, which serves both the campus and the community. A glass-walled computer room fills the center of the space. I couldn't tell for certain which of the individuals at the computers were students and which were townies, but all seemed devoted to their tasks. Over in the periodicals section I eased around a young man with a backpack who, sprawled on the floor, was resting. I also noticed a cluster of individuals I took to be international students, both by their whispered, accented English and their willingness to work in the library on the Friday afternoon of a three-day weekend.

ILCC student Cassie Malm was not among those in the library that day. Cassie is majoring in agriculture, and during the two years she spends there she'll take one agriculture course per semester, with other courses being the required general education studies. Then she'll be set to transfer to Iowa State University, where she'll major in agricultural education and minor in agricultural communication.

Cassie's father and uncle farm 800 acres outside Spencer, a town of 11,000, where the Walmart that Julia Nixon mentioned is located. Cassie's dad is an ILCC graduate who then transferred to ISU to earn a degree in agricultural communication. In addition to farming, he is a regional manager at an agricultural corporation. Her mother, on the other hand, went straight to college for the full four years to major in agricultural education and now teaches school in Spencer. Cassie has seen both routes to earning a degree and chose the two-year-then-transfer route for herself. It wasn't simply a matter of following in her father's footsteps, however. "All my friends were going to ISU so it was hard to decide. But I was offered a golf scholarship to ILCC that brought the cost of college down. That made the decision easier," she told me.

Cassie says the golf team is fun, if time consuming. The team carpools thirty minutes each way to practice four days a week and travels to golf meets. She takes classes with many of the young women on the team, which gives the group a lot of time to get to know each other. They also spend time together during late summer and fall harvests.

"Most students are working all the time," Cassie said. "This is a small farming community so students have to be gone now and then to work on farms. The teachers understand that the farmers in the area need help. I think this school is more forgiving of those sorts of things than a large university would be." There are also job opportunities for students in town, Cassie added. She cites the casino, restaurants, and the grocery stores that have locations throughout Iowa and which will transfer students to the Emmetsburg location if they already work for the store elsewhere. There's also light industry that hires students. Then of course there are the off-hours. Tuesday is wing night at the Corner Stone Bar and Grill, Cassie told me. There's outdoor recreation, too, and students spend warm nights on the lake, floating on rafts. The school also provides plenty of structured activity for students, she said. They volunteer for civic events like blood drives and pancake breakfasts. There's the wellness center gym and swimming pool. There are regular activities like Zumba classes, root-beer festivals, and Western Night, complete with a mechanical bull.

If all of this wasn't enough to keep Cassie busy, she is still involved with 4-H at home in Spencer. She and her sister show feeder hogs at the state and county fairs, and they have their own little herd of goats. Plus there's the broiler chickens to show and care for. Cassie would like to stay in Iowa after her graduation from ISU but she knows that might not be possible right away. "Most companies I am looking at expect maybe five to seven years of moving around when you are first hired, and you don't get to choose. As long as it isn't Hawaii or someplace like that very far away I'd be willing to go." Then she hopes to return and start her life near home.

I was reminded of Atchison County, Missouri, which lost Tarkio College decades ago and still has not recovered. Here in Emmetsburg, students have places to work and can walk or bike to get there if they choose. They have fun night spots that cater to college kids. They all live on campus, so there is no friction between landlords and young renters, as in many college towns. ILCC draws many of its instructional staff from the local area. For these reasons, the college seems integrated into the town in a way that Tarkio College never will be again.

States like to tout their community colleges as economic development engines for the regions they serve. These schools can be nimble enough in their course offerings and programs that they can meet industry needs for variously skilled workers, as trends develop. For instance, Iowa has been a national leader in recent years in wind-energy production, and some of its community colleges were early to train students in this technology. And for students and industries better suited to four or more years of education, community colleges can capture promising individuals, get them in the education/workforce pipeline, and produce skilled individuals who not only contribute to the tax base but have the civic maturity that a well-rounded educational experience can develop.

A great deal has been written about "brain-drain"—the phenomenon in which young educated people leave the community where they were educated for the greener pastures of better urban opportunities. Authors Patrick J. Carr and Maria J. Kefalas write about this issue specific to Iowa in *Hollowing out the Middle: The Rural Brain Drain and What it Means for America*. They conclude with suggestions for not simply trying to placate the group of students they call super-achievers into remaining in Iowa, but to invest more in the average students who, with a little encouragement, will push themselves academically and find enough within Iowa's borders to keep them happy and content. Brain drain, known more formally as out-migration, is one focus of the Rural Renaissance program at Iowa State University.

ISU researchers contend that many college-educated young people are drawn to an urban location whether in state or out by a larger salary, only to find it's not worth the cost to one's quality of life. "Housing is exceedingly expensive; the daily commute is costly, stressful, and time consuming; school systems are poor; crime is a concern, there is little green space for recreation; and the air may be cut with a knife. Smaller communities within Iowa offer opportunities for enhanced quality of life," they say. The Rural Renaissance program has developed an interactive website to help people who wish to stay, return, or become a first-time resident of Iowa. The Rural Renaissance Community Index rankings are based on population, educational attainment of residents, racial diversity, the open presence of gays and lesbians in a community, age, gender distribution, and the presence of singles. Other ranking data touch on economy, cost of living, health, transportation, quality of life, cultural tourism, community and business support, recreational opportunities, and Internet access. The 128 locales were selected based on strong economic activity. All county seats were included because those communities usually have jobs, access to resources and services, and opportunities for social, leisure, and civic activities. Also, they looked for communities that met some of the above criteria but also had unique features to offer, such as a college or university, art and cultural events, scenic areas and natural amenities, shopping and dining venues, and community festivals and activities. Iowa communities included in the Index range in population from 727 to 27,740.

In 2014 researchers were undertaking a revision of some of the statistics, last developed in 2008. It was in that year that Emmetsburg was ranked dead last in the category of public transportation and for the presence of sports clubs and spectator sports. It ranked 125th for the presence of biking and hiking trails. It ranked 97th for the commitment of residents to the future of the town, and 95th for providing business assistance, services, and opportunities. In a ranking study where lower numbers are better, there are two categories in which Emmetsburg scored in the single digits: it ranked 8th for safety, and 9th for its high percentage of non-married residents.

In spite of the mixed findings from Rural Renaissance, people I spoke to in Emmetsburg stated their belief that theirs was a thriving community where positive things were happening. People indicated, when I asked, that the presence of ILCC was good for their community. But when I asked in an open-ended way how the town was managing to stay economically viable, their first answer was "the casino." Maybe I'd been looking for the wrong sort of vibe.

When I drove by Wild Rose Casino on my way into town, I saw that its parking lot was full of cars with license plates from all over this area of Iowa and into Minnesota. In Iowa, as with many states, casino gambling was legal as long as the casino was on a boat and the boat was on the water. Then in the early 1990s, changes were underway, with the gaming industry expressing interest in evolving into something land-based. Various gaming industries began courting the state to set up a procedure for placing casinos on land. That done, a nonprofit board formed in Emmetsburg to look into getting a gaming license for their community. Bill Lapczenski from ILCC was one of its members. The town of Emmetsburg put a referendum on the ballot about whether its citizens would want a casino in the community. It voted yes, by 71 percent, even before voters knew where it would be located. Bill says he isn't a gambler. "But I was for more jobs in town. More jobs mean families come in, those families have kids in schools, and they buy homes. That's basic economic development."

Bill explained how the relationship works. The nonprofit board promoted the idea around the county and got the gaming license from the state. The owner/operator is required by law to give 3 percent of its profits back to the community, but this owner gives 6 percent to nonprofit organizations in the city. The board reviews around a hundred applications for funding from nonprofits each year and gets to give away money. The casino provides the town the hotel, ballroom, restaurant, buffet, and entertainment amenities, Bill said. Furthermore, there are part-time jobs for students there, providing valuable experience especially for those in the hotel/restaurant program. The casino's general manager is on the advisory board for that program at the college. The state gaming board continues to balance requests from other communities to have a revenue-generating casino of their own with the reality that there is only so much space in the room. There is a saturation point at which all potential casino customers are being served. Any new casino would only draw business from a neighbor, hurting its economy.

Jane Whitmore has seen how the town has morphed from one just hanging on to its population to one where generously funded nonprofit agencies serve the needs of many. Jane is the editor of the *Emmetsburg Reporter-Democrat*. She grew up in West Bend, Iowa, just a few miles down the road. Because Jane planned to be a teacher, she did not attend journalism school. Instead, she has been at the paper for close to forty years. She has a small staff and puts out two editions weekly of what is technically two separate papers. Jane explains why the casino referendum was passed convincingly, from her perspective.

"People had seen the benefits of it. Some thought it would bring increased crime, all the negatives you hear about. All the bad things we thought were going to happen haven't happened. It is a small enough community and casino that there are more benefits than negatives." For example, she said, $1.9 million came back into the county from the casino in March 2013, though the amount fluctuates each year. "Without grants, a lot of projects would not be done. That's the biggest upside."

She explained that the entertainment offerings draw good crowds. "It is pretty fun to go there, and now local people don't have to drive to Des Moines or Minneapolis. Instead, those people come here." Jane doesn't know how often tourists visiting the casino come the extra mile into town to shop or eat at the restaurants, especially since the casino has restaurants, bars, and a hotel of its own. She does know that the paper hasn't covered anything negative about the casino in its pages. "We've had a few police cars or ambulance calls out there, mostly medical things because of elderly visitors who go there. Nothing negative. Sometimes I forget it's there."

I, too, wanted to forget it was there—not because I have reservations against gambling but simply because I greatly dislike casinos. I can tolerate the eighty-decibel *boop bloop szinnngg bloop boop ba deep zooooop* for about four minutes before my breathing goes shallow, my blood pressure rises, and my head starts to spin. Lucky for me, four minutes is as long as it took me to walk past the security guard—whom I took to be a student—stroll past the perimeter doing a theatrical rendering of trying to locate a friend, glancing at my watch once or twice in a broad gesture to telegraph that motive, and walking back out with a chagrined stage glance at the young guard expressing that, *Oh well, I can't find my friend so I may as well leave.*

I did this ridiculous errand on two separate days during the course of my stay in Emmetsburg so I could see if there was any difference in the atmosphere on a Friday afternoon at 4:00 p.m. and a Saturday evening at 9:00 p.m. There was not. It was still full of older white people, with a few younger groups who looked like they were doped up on hope. Nobody looked very happy. A female casino employee about my age who'd been standing near the same guard on my second visit told me they were especially busy because they were open extra hours for the holiday weekend. She and I commiserated for a moment about the air quality, since smoking is still allowed in Iowa casinos, though not in most other indoor spaces. The young guard just smiled and nodded, he himself apparently sharing our pain. On the way out, I picked up a business card advertising a service to call if one felt gambling was taking over one's life. 1-800-BETS-OFF is the number to call for "gambling responsibly." I wondered if there was a number to call for irrational gambling phobia, such as what gripped me.

Deb Hite of the chamber of commerce had characterized the community's challenges not about gambling or other addictions, but in terms I've heard from people in small towns across the Midwest and Great Plains. Change is difficult for any community, and this was a community dealing with change on several fronts, although not tectonic. Although Emmetsburg is holding its own, some people struggle to think progressively and be forward thinking, in Deb's view. "Not everyone realizes that today there is no status quo. If a community isn't moving forward, it is going backward." Deb noted that Emmetsburg's infrastructure had been in decline for a few decades, meaning the current generation of citizens has a lot of work to do. As in most small communities, it takes a few key citizens to move ideas forward. Deb said that in 1990, concerned citizens realized Five Island Lake was a good attraction, but needed to be maintained, in part through regular dredging to make it navigable. "It was at this point that Emmetsburg started moving forward," she said. There is a new trail system being paved in the northwest part of town, but its committee has had many hurdles to jump as some members of the community have fought it. There is a community center being built on the shore of Five Island Lake to give another option as a place to gather for weddings, family reunions, as well as business conferences. "This too has met with opposition by the public to the point that concerned citizens worked to derail a large state grant by appearing before the state board asking that the grant not be awarded to our community," Deb told me. Their main concern was that it would compete with businesses already operating for those purposes.

There is nothing new in the argument that governments at any level should not be in competition with private entrepreneurship. That's what was at the root of this argument. I'd also heard this long ago in Laramie, when the town passed a bond issue to build a recreation center. People who already operated gyms in town were very upset by being asked to compete against a taxpayer-funded businesses. In all my conversations with people in Emmetsburg, I did not find anyone who directly spoke to me about their opposition to the community center, only that they knew that opposition existed. I had spent some time walking the lake path, just a tourist mentally projecting myself across the water into one of the homes along the opposite shores. I knew that if I lived in Emmetsburg, I'd go hang out at a community center on the lake. And no doubt that's where I'd want to find a home. Real estate ads in the paper showed that prices for some of the newer properties would be at the high end of a professional person's budget. But, many older, modest homes were also available in a price range I expected wouldn't shut out younger working families.

In addition to considering how people live, work, and play in Emmetsburg, I wanted to spend time downtown to see how they shopped. Though there is some new construction, many of the old brick buildings still stand, retaining architectural detail from their nineteenth-century construction. Some of the buildings were shuttered, with For Sale signs in the window. Antique malls, thrift shops, junk shops: most of the shopping was for items that people only buy when they go out of town and want to bring a little keepsake back with them. I knew I wanted to buy something from the Irish store, operated by volunteers to fund the Emmetsburg St. Pat's Association. I rummaged for ten minutes seeking an item "for that special Celtic someone." I decided that "special someone" was myself and traded twenty dollars for a cute beaded shamrock purse.

My next stop was at the Mainstreet Memories Mall, which fills half a city block. One of the co-owners, Ardell Conner, was in the store that day, along with her employee, Carol Simonsen. Just by coincidence, I was wearing a University of Northern Iowa Panthers T-shirt. It was an excellent conversation starter, especially since that night UNI was scheduled to play Iowa State. The area around Emmetsburg is ISU Cyclone country, so any college football fan not wearing red and gold is met with a good-natured yet slightly suspicious smile. I explained that I liked both ISU and UNI just fine, but that really, my team was the University of Wyoming Cowboys. Then I had to explain why. Then Carol said, "My son lives in Cheyenne. He works in economic and business development for the city there. I wonder if you know him. Dave Simonsen."

Obviously, I wouldn't be relaying this story if the answer had been no. But know him I did. After a few minutes exclaiming over the coincidence, Carol and I asked Ardell to snap a photo of the two of us together. I sent it on to Dave through our LinkedIn channels. He messaged me right back, though he did not seem surprised that I'd randomly bumped into his mother in an antique shop three hundred miles from my home.

Ardell and I left Carol in the shop and walked a few doors down the block to her other store. This was the higher-end antique stuff, things she'd purchased from estate sales or was unloading from her own personal household inventory. "You can't be too sentimental about these things," she told me, pointing to an old record player of hers she'd refinished to sell. "You have to face facts." We walked from room to room, while she pointed out old Hoosier cabinets, iceboxes, and various domestic and farming implements. She asked if I knew what each was and I hazarded a guess. She seemed satisfied when I applied the right terms to the physical specimens I was seeing, even though I couldn't always calculate what a clamp and a wheel and a buffed wooden surface might add up to. The purpose of the object was secondary to what she always said it was: "A piece of Iowa history."

Like in many small towns, the past gets herded into antique stores like this, or auctions or flea markets, or even town museums like the one in Norton, Kansas. Each time a piece is sold, the owner has a little extra cash in the drawer. And the object is in the hands of someone new, waiting to see what the next phase of its life will be. Feeling philosophical, I reminded myself of one of my other goals on my visit, which was to track down an informal men's coffee group. In small towns, this group is usually composed of farmers, retired businessmen, and men who like to confab on local news one-to-one, without their wives. Universally, they assemble in town cafés, or even fast-food restaurants. I hadn't bothered to ask anyone in Emmetsburg where a group of this type might be found, for I figured I'd wake up Saturday morning, reconnoiter around town a few minutes, and spot the right café on the edge of town by its parking lot full of pickups.

I'd already identified one likely suspect and headed there first. No pickups. No "Open" sign. Turns out it was only a lunch and dinner joint. Fortunately, I found a man out on the street setting up a produce stand, and asked him what folks do for breakfast around these parts. He sized me up immediately as an outsider, possibly even a refugee from the casino, and directed me to a bakery down the block. I refined my query, telling him I wanted breakfast with the farmers. "In that case," he said, "you'll need to go the café." That sounded just up my alley, until he directed me to the Food Pride, one of three groceries in town. I was dubious I'd be able to get anything like a decent farmer-philosopher experience in a grocery store, but I headed over anyway. I was heartened to discover that in addition to the vehicles likely bearing Saturday morning family shoppers, several road-dust-covered pickups sat in the lot.

I stopped in the entryway first to get my bearings by reading the bulletin board. Here is a sampling: Weight Watchers; Kathy's Hilarious Hypnosis; free appliance pickup; For Sale: mini jazz electric chair; Think You're Irish, German, Native American, South African? Find out! Professional Genealogist; 5 Chihuahua puppies, purebred but no papers; Fender guitar; Dining Room Set; 141 John Deere Tandum disc; 10 percent off first pest service; Toy Show; Farmers Market; weight loss; church chicken supper; Found Dentures (uppers) Inquire at Food Pride customer service; Preservation of Rural Iowa Alliance to stop unnecessary electrical transmission line.

I followed my nose to the part of the store where hot food was being served, and honestly, it smelled pretty good. I took the lead of an athletic-shorts- and T-shirt-clad man in front of me and ordered the ham and cheese omelet special with wheat toast. I found a booth by the window with a yellow bench seat and plastic white tabletop and tucked in. In a cluster of tables in the room's center was a group of men I guessed to be the fellows I sought. But the room was in a bit of a hush, because at a booth just down from mine, another man sat with radio broadcast equipment and a microphone. He began to speak into the microphone in the voice of a trained announcer, which meant we could all hear what he said. This was Scott Nolte, sports director of the local radio station. The athletic man I was in line behind turned out to be the local high school football coach, whose E-Hawks had lost badly the night before to the Spencer Tigers. This was Coaches Corner.

Everyone in the place chewed quietly and leaned in to better hear Coach Mike Dunlap murmur about the "positives we took away in spite of having a hard time matching up" in the 44–21 loss. After a short break, Scott interviewed a coach from a nearby town whose eight-man football team had won big. Then the broadcast ended, the coaches and sportscaster packed up to assurances from the men, like, "Don't worry, Mike. It'll get better." I started cleaning up my table and was hailed by the group. "Who are you?" one asked, curiosity getting the better of him. "The volleyball coach here for an interview?"

I cleared up for them that I was just visiting town, and that I was a writer from eastern Iowa interested in what the rest of my new state was like and what the big issues were here in Emmetsburg. One fellow asked if someone was paying me to do this, and I reluctantly admitted the answer was no. Another fellow said he was a pig farmer, then mentioned the transmission tower I'd seen mentioned on a flyer in the store entrance. He stated his views in three words: "We're against it." He asked rhetorically why Iowa should have to deal with everything that goes into building a transmission tower when all the electricity in it just goes to Chicago. "It doesn't benefit Iowa," he said, carrying his breakfast remains to the trash receptacle.

"Your pigs go to Chicago, too, but that doesn't seem to bother you," another man at the table pointed out, to laughter. The real issue, said the teasing gentleman, is that even though farmers will be reimbursed for the land they cannot plant because it is in the right-of-way for the transmission towers, the difficulty lies in farming that other land, the part between the towers and the fence. The space is too tight for the huge planting and harvesting equipment used on farms today. That means the farmer either has to lose time by switching to other equipment to work those rows, or lose money by not planting them at all. In either case, they see this as losing to the power company.

I'd picked up a copy of the *Emmetsburg Democrat* that weekend and read an article on the issue written by reporter Dan Voigt. The headline read: "Supervisors Withdraw Support." He writes: "While admitting that any gesture they made would have little effect, the Palo Alto County Board of Supervisors rescinded a resolution of support during action Tuesday Aug. 27 [2013]. The resolution of support for the Rock Island Clean Line Transmission project was originally adopted in January this year by the board." Not supporting it doesn't mean being against it, the reporter explained. It just shows the Iowa Utilities Board they are neutral.

One reason local farmers are so eager to grow as much corn as they can is the price they get for selling it, not just as a grain, but as a feedstock for ethanol. In fact, the South Dakota-based biorefining company POET operates a plant in Emmetsburg. It has begun working with the Dutch company DSM to make advanced biofuels. "Project LIBERTY" will process 770 tons of corn cobs, leaves, husks, and stalks daily to produce 20 million gallons of cellulosic ethanol per year, with plans ramping up to 25 million gallons per year. That is a lot of non-food parts of the corn finding another use. Some people think the main use of corn stover is a pretty good one: keeping topsoil and nutrients in place over the long winter months before a fresh crop is planted. Still, POET-DSM plans to license this technology to companies across the United States and around the world. That should help the company remain a stable employer in this area of Iowa. Unless, of course, the federal government does not continue Renewable Fuel Standards that have helped Iowa become the number one ethanol producer in the country. In that case, agriculture could be in for another rocky ride.

Another issue material to daily life in Emmetsburg is the debate on whether the city should join a consortium of nearby small towns that already have fiber-optic systems for cable, Internet, and telephone. One of the men gathered at the regulars table at the Food Pride on this morning was a city councilman. He seemed happy to explain to me how this might affect Emmetsburg residents. First, he said that people indicated in an election they'd like this to happen, but it was only now becoming possible to join an existing group of municipalities. "We will have to borrow money through a bond issue, and property taxes might go up a bit," he explained. "Hopefully that cost will be offset by what people will save by subscribing, and ditching existing services." That isn't as straightforward as it sounds, the other men pointed out. Sure, they are willing to invest in their community. But what about the people in town who work for the Internet and cable companies that the city system would displace? Those people have families and might wind up losing their jobs and leaving town with their families in tow, if the measure passes.

I listened to this discussion thinking about how complicated everything gets when you open the door a crack and let information about it come in to your mind. Farming, energy, the role of local government, all seem like they should have the complexity threshed out of them in a small town on Iowa's fertile plain. But complexity and confusion are a natural byproduct of both striving for something better and struggling to keep things afloat.

I'd been searching for the difference an influx of college students and a formally educated faculty and staff would make in a small town. But what hit home for me in Emmetsburg wasn't that simple. I discovered the key is to understand that the epicenter of a small, rural town is through its public school. If an epicenter can have a nucleus, it is the high school football team. Emmetsburg is lucky: many small towns across Iowa have already closed their schools, consolidating with neighboring towns to form a hyphenated educational home. Doing so can diffuse, or at least confuse, cross-section sports rivalries, like football.

In its purest form, football is remarkably simple. Its complexity lies in its execution, as I'd heard from the football coach at the café. The reason the Emmetsburg E-Hawks lost was that, after their initial exciting play and long run leading to a score, the Spencer Tigers played great defense and scored quickly on almost every offensive possession, especially in the first half. The E-Hawks got themselves back together in the second half a bit but the other team, with older, bigger kids gathered from Spencer's larger population, were just better players. In fact, I had been there that night, thanks to Deb Hite's suggestion. I sat alone on the grass near the stands, moving every few minutes so the tall utility poles could shield my eyes from the blinding hot setting sun. Cars were parked all around the stands and in the high school parking lot. Boosters arrived early for $5 rib-eye sandwiches to support the team and marching band. The home team entered the field beneath an archway inscribed with the words *Tradition Matters*. Little kids played their version of football on the grass along the fringes of the stands, with parents secure in their children's well-being as they ran at large. I'd never been to this town before, or sat in this stadium before, or seen this team before. But when that E-Hawk running back swept around the corner and ran sixty yards for a touchdown, I felt the same thrill as I cheered that kid down the sidelines as if he were a player on my own town's team. All of a sudden, and for just moment, I belonged.

I couldn't authentically see Emmetsburg through the eyes of a resident, of course, only as an interested observer trying to guess at the sustainability and viability of a small town over the long haul. My consumption patterns over the holiday weekend were that of the average visitor. I ate in a few restaurants. I picked up inexpensive items at a few shops. I paid admission to a public event. I tried to spend money at the casino. And of course, I paid for accommodations for two nights at a local motel, room rate plus lodging tax.

The Suburban Motel is a single-story mom-and-pop style of lodging, the kind with one row of rooms whose doors opened on its designated parking spot. It is operated by an East Indian couple named Manny and Debbie Patel. Being around them was one of my first opportunities since moving to Iowa to converse with someone who spoke in accented English, and it was charming to my ears. I had plenty of chances to hear the melodic tones of Mr. Patel, who roamed the grounds searching out guests whose needs might be unmet in the realms of air conditioning or snack machine. I had no troubles in terms of either of these things, but then, because there were so few guests the Patels had plenty of time to be sure those who were staying there were completely satisfied.

The morning I checked out, I'd gone to the lobby for the continental breakfast of coffee and a roll, and was seduced by the aroma of East Indian cooking coming from their apartment kitchen. Between the intoxicating curry and Mr. Patel's constant checking on me and whether I was leaving so he could immediately dispatch the maid to my humble room, I got rattled. Which is why I drove off forgetting to pack my cellphone charger. Which he called me to report almost immediately upon my departure. But I, not one to talk on the phone while driving, didn't get his message for several hours. Which is why he put the charger in the mail for me. No charge.

Thanks, Iowa neighbor. I knew I'd like it here.

BELLEVUE, IOWA

9

FITTING IN

"What brings you to Bellevue, then?"

I get that question a lot. Residents of this community under-standably wonder why someone with almost twenty years of Lara-mie, Wyoming, under her belt would suddenly pull up stakes and plop her tent down in a river town on the Mississippi River where she has no job, no connections, and no ties except her husband and their dog.

I had found myself thinking more about my native Kansas after a trip to the northwest part of the state, in Cheyenne County. A long-time friend from Kansas City has some wheat acreage there, which has long been in her family. We met up for harvest on a Fourth of July weekend, spending time with her family in St. Francis. I was baffled to find I still felt this emotional connection to the Midwest. I know that trip planted a seed in my mind that Wyoming might not be the only place for me. At about that same time, my mother, in Kansas City, was deteriorating with age. My siblings were there to care for her but I had difficulty traveling to see her as often as I wanted. Lastly, though transience is normal in a college town, in a period of about a year, several of my best girlfriends left Laramie, up and moving to New Jersey, Nevada, North Carolina, or Indiana. I felt like a starter pistol had fired while I stood still on the starting line, laces undone, watching them go.

My husband was happy where we were, but he too was facing the reality of aging parents, and was even farther away from them than I was from my family. Ron was moving toward retirement, converting his identity from an artist who worked mostly for others to an artist who created work for himself. That signaled to me he was open to new experiences. So when I came home after an espe-cially harrowing travel experience, which saw me stalled in the Den-ver airport for twelve hours, I explained to him in a voice choked with frustrated tears that I'd had enough. I'd had enough of endless wind, nearly endless winters, and the steady march of friends to distant locations. Seeing my long-widowed mother's decline foreshadowing my own rather predictable end, I didn't like this version of how my final years might unfold. I told my husband I'd like to think about making a change. He said if we did something that allowed me to put creative projects ahead of the same routine but in front of different scenery, he'd be willing to try something new, too.

Rather accidentally, on a road trip about this time, we'd happened upon Bellevue, tucked between high limestone bluffs and the wide Mississippi River. To make a short story long, we found a Victorian home that had great bones and original features but had fallen on hard times as a two-apartment rental. We purchased it, kept the tenants for just over a year, and then began the restoration process. Our home in Laramie sold quickly, so we moved into a literal construction site in June 2011. The people we spent the most time with in those early months were our remodeling contractors, the Sieverding "boys," who are in their sixties and part of a very large family so well-established a local road bears their name. Joining them were the plumbers, the Kieffers, who've been in their line of work for three generations and also have a street in town named after them. Regular visits from the electricians and painters rounded out our social life for months. And every new person we met would sooner or later utter those colloquially expressed words: "What brings you to Bellevue, then?"

We wanted to be closer to family. We thought it would be fun to try something new. We wanted to garden closer to sea level. We wanted the opportunity to restore this potentially beautiful home before it was too far gone. We wanted to root for the Bears and the Cubs and eat bratwurst. We wanted to see the sunrise over the river each day. We wanted to boat. We wanted wood ducks, coots, pelicans, pheasants, mockingbirds. We wanted humidity. We wanted warmth.

But that's a longer answer than most people want to hear.

I love my new town, but in many ways I am a tourist, forever explaining where I'm from and what I'm doing here. I feel content being in the Midwest, being in Iowa, most of the time. Other times I look in the mirror and see somebody with wind-leathered skin who will probably wind up in the West again, one day, even if it is just as ashes scattered across the Laramie basin. Or maybe even back in Kansas City as an old woman, living in a derelict cabin on one of the high hills that overlooks the confluence of the Kansas and Missouri Rivers. Although my mind is a work in progress, my body has de-adapted to the West. It is back to requiring moisture, and oxygen—both in short supply in the high country. Still, I straddle both worlds, telling people I'm from neither Iowa nor Kansas nor Wyoming. I say I'm from "Wy-owa." In my mind, that's the truth.

————————

People in this town of around 2,100 can be divided into two sorts. The main sort are extended families that go back several generations, where certain families hold reunions so large the local bowling alley slash reception hall can barely contain them. One woman of our acquaintance joked that she had so many relatives in Bellevue she had to go to a town twenty miles away to meet someone she wasn't related to, in order to find a husband.

Of the less numerous sort are people like us, here from somewhere else. Some are retirees from the Quad Cities of Moline, Rock Island, Bettendorf, and Davenport. Others are escapees from Chicago. A few have moved here from distant locales in order to form a generational trinity of their children, their parents, and themselves.

Most people who relocate to a new place have some practical anchor, or at least magnet, attaching them socially or economically to a place. Although we didn't have a *reason* to be here, we had an unexpected guide to instruct us through some of the social nuances and tangled families. That guide came in the form of our local newspaper editor, Sara Millhouse.

In a coincidence of the "meant to be" variety, I had connected with Sara a few years previous to moving to Bellevue. She was the editor of a newspaper in western Wyoming, and I saw a piece she'd written about a woman who owned a bar where my husband and I had spent some time, and about whom I'd written. I contacted Sara to compliment her on her article, and we communicated a bit over the months. Then, about a year later, I was putting out some feelers to see if there was any work I might land as a freelancer once I arrived in Bellevue. I saw the position of newspaper editor advertised, so I responded, just as an opportunity to introduce myself to the local journalism community. A woman there wrote back to welcome me (in advance) to the area. Then she added, "We've hired someone for the job from Wyoming. Maybe you know her. Sara Millhouse."

Just like the Dave Simonsen episode in Emmetsburg, I wouldn't relate this story except for one reason. Of course I knew her.

Then again, lots of people know Sara Millhouse. Most editors of small-town weekly newspapers make an effort to know their communities. People want to know the editor, too, so they can put in a good word for their club, sport, business, or cause. But with Sara, those connections are more than just professional. Late twenties, cheerily colored red hair, with a little nose stud and flip-flops, she looks more like an American Studies PhD student than a newspaper editor. But her ability to learn everyone's name, to know how they connect to this place, and to write about them fairly, has earned her many friends and the community's respect. Combined with her love of staying out late at Bellevue's various watering holes, laughing so loudly she can be heard above the jukebox, she became a local favorite almost immediately.

Sara graduated from Grinnell College in Iowa and after bouncing around a bit, came to Bellevue in 2010. She was originally from Galena, Illinois, which is just across the Mississippi River from Bellevue, as the crow flies. There is no bridge across the river at Bellevue, though, so unless one is a crow or has a boat, one must drive twenty-three miles north to Dubuque to get to the bridge, cross the river, then head back south. With a population of about 3,500, Galena is the average size of the places Sara has lived. That is, outside of some stints studying abroad in New Zealand, Australia, and India, and, more locally, in Madison, Wisconsin.

Fueled by a thirst for new things that I suspect will never fade, Sara decided to take the job in Wyoming in part to check out a different part of the country. However, her parents were entering their sixth decade, and her father has had health difficulties. She figured she'd stay in Wyoming about five years and then return to the Galena area to be "a good daughter." Journalism jobs don't come along often. She was prepared for the possibility of taking a job outside of journalism if need be, to be able to live within a reasonable distance of her parents. So when the job in Bellevue opened up, she knew she'd need to at least apply.

For Sara, an economic opportunity to move to a small town presented itself, and it worked out. She works hard as the editor and only news reporter at her paper. Her salary isn't going to make her rich and she doesn't have much time off. On the plus side, she was welcomed into the community, found a decent place to live just a few blocks from work, and quickly made friends. Sara said she doesn't feel the urge to live in a large city. "I enjoy anonymity once in a while, but I think, realizing how my life has gone life so far, I am happiest in a community where I know most of the people."

We sat in her Second Street apartment one warm summer afternoon, raising our voices to be heard over the occasional rumble of a passing freight train. Mature houseplants and an upright piano filled the space, while a solar-powered Queen Elizabeth II action figure waved at passersby from the windowsill. Together we pondered the relationship between rootedness and mobility.

"A lot of people are tied to where they are from," she said. "But people who are professional think they have more options to go elsewhere. They think they are making a more conscious choice on their part based on what they *think* their options are." That makes them more mobile, she said, lending credence to the suggestion that once educated, people are more likely to leave their hometowns and pursue other options.

One thing that encourages people who are from Bellevue to remain in the area, in Sara's view, is having the means to do so. "Money helps. Not having scads but having enough that you don't have to go outside the area to look for work, whether your goals are blue collar, white collar, or something else, you can find work in Bellevue and not have to leave the area."

The "area" still might mean driving half an hour each way to a job in Dubuque where there are plenty of stable employers, such as John Deere, IBM, numerous colleges, and the casino, to name a few. Work is also available in Maquoketa, about twenty miles to the southwest, which is the county seat. There are employers in Bellevue including small manufacturing, agricultural suppliers, a nursing home, the school district, an insurance company call center, and a variety of retail and service industries.

Sara points to the importance of strong institutions that "create a community where people want to live, who make big families, which grow kids who want to come back and live here." But when those institutions slip, a community can be in trouble. "When communities lose schools, churches and other institutions, that decreases people's sense that theirs is an important place," she said. "Once people stop believing their town is important, that their community cares about them, that they are part of the fabric that makes their town pleasant and comfortable, that's when they start to look elsewhere. They look beyond proximity of family and friends and look for practicalities."

When people in a community start to doubt their relevance, how long can they keep resilience alive? The recent national recession has cast doubt in the minds of many rural communities regarding their futures. The Bureau of Labor Statistics reveals that as our national economy slowly recovers, rural counties have been slower to recover than their urban counterparts. There are simply fewer jobs in rural counties than there used to be and therefore, the number of unemployed is steady. Jackson County, where Bellevue is located, had a lower unemployment rate in May 2013 than it averaged in 2007, but the county had 147 fewer jobs to fill.

The population of Bellevue decreased by 159 people between 2000 and 2010. However, the fringes of town have grown, with more people living in unincorporated areas, either on farms or in housing developments along the Mississippi River. Although they don't live in town, these people identify as being from Bellevue. For many, that identity is tied to the community school district. In recent years closures of some rural school districts have meant that children from those small communities and outlying areas now attend school here. Not only does Bellevue serve public-school students, it has a small but flourishing Catholic grade school and high school.

Each spring the *Bellevue Herald-Leader* runs a special section featuring photos of high school seniors with captions that indicate their plans after graduation. One can't assume that an eighteen-year-old's vision of their future is highly correlated with reality later on. But assume their hearts are in the right place and they have a reasonable opportunity to achieve their goals. There were fifty-five graduates from Bellevue Community High School, and thirty-five from Marquette Catholic School, in 2013. Of these ninety high school seniors, forty-eight stated they planned to attend a four-year college. Nineteen planned to attend a two-year college. Of those who indicated either a two- or four-year program, all but four had selected an in-state school. One had selected a college just over Iowa's western border in Nebraska. Three planned to attend school in neighboring Wisconsin. Three planned to enroll in a technical school, while seven planned to enter a trade. Two planned to work the family farm full time, while a few others indicated they intended to farm while also attending school. Five graduates were headed for the military, and one planned to move to France. Remarkably, only two students were "undecided."

It is possible students' expressions of a future involving higher education was a placeholder for something else they weren't prepared to think about or make public. Regardless, there is clearly an expectation that young people will grow up and do something to make themselves employable, comfortable, and able to make choices about where to settle down. Yet, statistics based on 2006–2010 figures show that the only educational achievement category for which Bellevue ranks above the national average was in the percentage of residents with a high school diploma. Some 43 percent of people in Bellevue have that education level. Twenty-seven percent have some college. Thirteen percent have a bachelor's degree. Five percent have a master's or some other professional degree. Still, the town ranks somewhere around the top third of educational achievement compared to other locations in Iowa.

The rather low number of graduates who go on to college does not correlate with how they present themselves in the annual graduate round-up. It may be that ambitious local high school kids lose their enthusiasm between May and September. Or it may be that the ones who head for college decide not to return to Bellevue to become statistics. They may join the rural exodus to larger cities like Des Moines or Chicago and not return.

Yet, strong family connections and a stable population make remaining in Bellevue possible for its young people. So many natives stay here it isn't hard to notice that there is little ethnic or racial diversity. In fact, the town is 99 percent white. In Sara's job as newspaper editor, and simply from being acquainted with a wide cross-section of Bellevue, she has seen how people's attempts to grapple with diversity play out.

"It is easier for a community to be unified when it is less diverse," she said. "Yet, when people's very limited experiences with diversity are that it causes problems, that perception can lead to expressions of racism."

People here comment with pride that Bellevue is a safe community, that most houses are left unlocked, that keys are left in cars, that children roam freely to play with only a bedtime curfew to tether them to home. And these things are true. I wonder if a dominantly white community's pride in safety is a polite way of saying they feel safer simply by virtue of the fact that everyone looks like them. I wonder what would happen should there be a sudden influx of Latinos arriving to work in agriculture or food-processing, the sort of migration that has taken place in other small mostly white farming towns around Iowa. Would local people begin to perceive they are less safe, even if crime statistics did not change?

Sara's thinking about this issue is more nuanced than my own. "Being welcome here isn't about racial diversity but perceived cultural diversity. That's a bigger divider, which gets expressed crudely and racially sometimes." And she adds that even though others "code" her as mainstream, when she notices the exclusionary tendency of some here she feels less welcome, even though she is not the one being excluded. Sara is white, straight, outgoing, and friendly to people of all ages and walks of life in Bellevue, yet she is not a mainstream individual in some ways. She is educated and not afraid to show it. She is childless, and is neither married nor in a domestic partnership. She shows no desire to embrace those markers of the mainstream middle class any time soon.

Sara says she is living a socially fulfilling life here, having fun, meeting stimulating and interesting people. However, most of her friends are much older than she is, myself included. That's because most people her age are married with children. "What part of their schedule isn't kid-based is mostly filled up," she said. And even locals who are near her age and single have existing friendships and connections that take up their time.

It is critical to make good first impressions as a newcomer, to think about how you want to present yourself when you arrive. Do you want to make friends right away? Do you want to keep to yourself? Those choices affect how you relate to people in your community. It is a truism that people in small towns tend to be friendlier than their urban counterparts, more willing to pitch in when a neighbor has trouble. My explanation for this is that work is a social experience in farming communities like Bellevue. People see a storm-downed tree limb as little more than an excuse to visit with neighbors while they chop and stack the resulting firewood. That, and getting together to talk about the river.

The Mississippi River is a life force here, just like I'd found it to be in New Madrid. People fish and eat the fish they catch, although on a recommended limited basis. People can, and do, boat, and swim, and water ski. In the summer, people come to Bellevue because of the river, either to admire its beauty from afar or to stay at one of the campsites that offer direct access to the water.

My husband and I bought a thirty-five-year-old fishing boat within a few months of moving here and we use it frequently. We knew that leaving behind a state in which more than half of the land was public, we'd need to do something about the claustrophobia. That is, we'd need recreation that took us away from people, into nature, where we could troll quietly in our fishing boat or even take our canoe down the backwaters. Wildlife is abundant here, especially the winged variety. Bald eagles, great blue herons, American white pelicans, geese, cormorants, various gulls, and anything you can think of that comes out after dark to sing or shriek, ribbit, or sting abounds in the fertile plain of the Mississippi River.

Boating the river is more than a hobby for some people here. It is a living for commercial fishermen and for boat captains. One of these, Bellevue-based boat captain Mike Blitgen, has been in turn a pilot of towboats pushing barges, a casino boat captain, a water-taxi captain, and even a steam-powered paddle-wheel boat captain. When I put in a call to him, he was in the wheelhouse of a boat he was piloting, pushing barges full of asphalt up the Illinois River. We decided to meet in person when he returned home after this hitch on the river.

He called one early August afternoon and suggested that instead of meeting at some location in town, maybe I'd like to take a ride on his twenty-foot pleasure boat to the downhill ski resort across the river. One can simply tie up the boat, ride the lift chairs to the top of the hill, and relax over food and beverages on the patio of Chestnut Mountain Resort. So it was with sprawling views of the sparkling blue Mississippi River, braided by islands and framed by limestone bluffs, that we sat with digital recorder and umbrella drinks. Mike told me his life story with the garrulousness of someone who spends most days and nights in the wheelhouse of a towboat in the company of a small crew of men.

Now in his mid-fifties, Mike was born on a farm near Springbrook, about ten miles from Bellevue. He recalls walking across fields to neighbors' places a few times a month for barn dances and other get-togethers. "It was a real Mayberry RFD feeling. We swam in the creeks, fished in the ponds, made forts in the cornfields. It was pure wholesome country living."

When Mike was in the fifth grade, his dad started working on the river and the family moved into town. He spent many summers taking his dad's flat-bottom boat and exploring the islands just south of Bellevue, packing a lunch, leaving early in the morning, and not coming home until dark. Yet, he and a close childhood friend pledged they weren't going to get jobs working the river the way their fathers did. "It is no life for a family man," they asserted. Yet the minute they finished high school, that friend took a job on the river.

Mike said he never considered going to college. For one thing, he said, the family didn't have the money. For another, Mike didn't consider himself college material, and apparently neither did the folks at the high school. "Every senior got five minutes with the guidance counselor," he recalled. "The counselor reviewed my records, looked up at me, and said, 'Looks like you are going to work, Mike.'"

So Mike found himself working part-time jobs like delivering newspapers, unloading grocery-store trucks, and working on the grease rack at a local garage. Eventually he figured he needed something more steady and succumbed to a river trade. He worked for three years for the Ingram Barge Company, on the river thirty days, then thirty days off. That schedule didn't help his social life much. A charming and entertaining guy, Mike had little trouble meeting girls to take on dates, go to the movies, and have a nice time. Then he'd head back to the river for a month. "By the time I got back, somebody else had also figured out she was a fun date and I'd have to start over." Eventually he got another job off the river, as a bellboy at the Dubuque Holiday Inn. He met Elaine, the woman who would become his wife, and worked a series of steady jobs on land. After about seven years and with a growing family, it occurred to him that river-boat pilots made a better wage than his factory job paid, and that he'd be able to bring his river experience back into play and eventually qualify for that job. Which is what he did.

Since those early years he's worked for a variety of companies on rivers from the Mississippi to the Alleghany, the Illinois, the Intracoastal Canal, and more. He's always called Bellevue home. The company pays for him to get to the boat's departure point on the river. People have asked him why he doesn't move somewhere south, where winters are warmer, since he could live anywhere he wanted.

"I do think about places to live, but Bellevue has everything I need. There are lots of great places, and I can visit them any time I want to. All of my roots are here, my family has been here for generations, and I know everybody. If times got hard I could make it here, there's support here. I could even throw a Help Mike fundraiser and people would probably donate!"

Mike says he doesn't mind a slow steady increase in outsiders coming in because he realizes that the same people and families don't last forever. He also knows that new businesses have to come in so people can have employment. But over the years he's heard some talk that what Bellevue needs is industry. We tried to picture how smokestacks would affect our view from the patio of the ski hill's balcony. Had it been dark, we could have seen the lights of Bellevue twinkling modestly across the water. Instead, we saw trees, and limestone, and more trees.

Bellevue residents appreciate the tourist dollars that flow in because of the river and can tolerate the modest uptick in motorcycle or RV traffic. Unfortunately, summers when high water floods the campground or low water curtails pleasure boating, Bellevue takes a hit. In terms of new residents, Mike has heard locals grumble about "Chicago people" with lots of money who pay inflated prices that locals find laughable for riverfront property. "But there are a lot of cool people who come here," Mike said. "This is called growth."

I hoped Mike had mentally filed me as one of the "cool people." I hoped others in town felt that way about us, too. We started out as absentee landowners and from 900 miles away, turning the wheels of snow removal and lawn maintenance was hard pushing. But after we moved to Bellevue we made enormous and rapid strides in remodeling and restoring the home. We did some of the work ourselves, but for most of it used local contractors and materials. We sat on our front porch each warm-weather evening and greeted anyone who passed. Eventually those strangers became acquaintances, and we were grateful when they would say something like, "We are so glad you are working on that house. It is really starting to look great."

Thank you so much for that, neighbors. It is very nice to be noticed and appreciated.

Bellevue isn't exactly Mayberry today, and maybe it never was. The general atmosphere here is that of a prolonged family reunion, where you know everyone or at least recognize everyone, and each day is some form of rolling merrymaking. People here don't honk their car horn because someone is in their way. They honk because they see a friend or neighbor, maybe the same one they just said hi to an hour ago on the sidewalk. Friendliness aside, back when I found myself itching for a life change and had made that fateful trip through Bellevue, I gathered data to see if it was just love at first sight, or if this town could work for me.

I knew I was going to be self-employed, doing a combination of writ-

Renovating a town landmark, the Setzepfandt House, brought the author and her husband notoriety, free advice, and eventually friendship to share on the home's wide front porch. Photograph © Ronald K. Hansen.

ing, editing, and teaching online courses. In order to do those things, I'd need a reliable infrastructure. Bellevue purchases electric power through a co-op, but if the need arises, can generate its own power. Bellevue has the capacity to generate approximately 165 percent of the power needed to supply the community at peak demand. Power can be supplied within thirty minutes of an outage, the city assures us. Having sat through many dark hours during midwestern ice storms in my earlier days, I liked the idea of a town being self-sufficient. I'd also need better than average Internet service. Bellevue was the first city in Iowa to construct and operate a fiber-to-the-home network. This service is super fast and reliable. Both city officials and local businesses view the infrastructure as vital to the central functioning of the community and necessary for building a strong sustainable population. I am case in point that it works. So: able to keep the lights on and get work done here. Check. Possible to fit in socially. Check. But like most other potential modern settlers, I wanted an appealing setting and conveniences I could walk to.

Bellevue is a pretty good walking town. It mostly stretches north and south along the Mississippi River, along the Great River Road National Scenic Byway, which has a brick walkway along the river through town. Also known as Highway 52 or Riverview, or Main, or Front Street, or Water Street, or First Street, the two-lane road is lined on one side with nineteenth-century buildings, some functioning as shops or restaurants, others vacant and sporting For Sale signs. On the other side is the river. On summer weekends scores of motorcyclists drone through, stopping for a meal or staying the night. Pleasure craft, fishing boats, and barges pushed by towboats fill the waters all passing through Lock and Dam No. 12. A bike trail juts out of Bellevue's northern reaches and to the campground and marina. There are a good variety of businesses here and when considering whether Bellevue was the town for me, I had to think about what services were essential, and which were fine twenty-three miles away in Dubuque. There is a medical clinic here with a full-time physician and nurse practitioner. There is a dental practice, an eye doctor, several chiropractic offices, and a few massage therapists. There is a veterinarian and two banks. There is no hospital but there is a volunteer ambulance and fire department.

There is a grocery store, three gas stations, a pharmacy, a dry cleaner, and several places to get a haircut. There is an auto dealership and other car repair businesses. If you want to buy paint or hand tools or eyeliner, you head to the hardware store. There is a public library. There is no movie theater. There are no stop lights. There are specialty boutique shops and an independent bookstore, but no shopping mall or big box store. There is a gym where you pay for membership and they give you a door combination. There is a bike shop providing sales, service, and accessories. There is a swimming pool and a bowling alley. There is a music store. There are marine shops and a bait store. If you are Catholic, Lutheran, or Presbyterian, there is a place for you to worship and a place to be buried when the time comes, and a funeral home to aid in the process. There are some good restaurants. There is only one fast-food place, a Subway. There is a post office with part-time hours. You have to call an 800 number if you want FedEx or UPS service. One day a month, the folks from the county courthouse set up in our city hall building. That's when you can go get your driver's license renewed. There are several fun bars, an American Legion, a Masonic lodge.

I suspect this list reveals me to be a person of quiet tastes. Others are more willing to endure urban sprawl and long commutes for the amenities I readily acknowledge only larger cities provide. Yet I'm not the only one now in Bellevue who saw the chance to jump ship from a larger town to this smaller one, thanks to the combination of technology, a sense of community, pleasing scenery, and adequate services. Bellevue's Chamber of Commerce director Deanna Cook grew up in Davenport, Iowa, and graduated from the University of Iowa. She had spent her career in the finance industry, working in Kansas City, Chicago, and New York City. A few years ago she attended a class reunion and bumped into a former classmate who'd purchased some land on the edge of Bellevue. On that land he started a small urban farm. She came to visit her friend, who lives in Bellevue during the summer, and the rest of the year in the Los Angeles area, working in the film industry.

"I was struck at how beautiful it is here," she said. "The farm, the river, downtown: just so beautiful." She visited a few more times over the course of a few years. Single and in her mid-forties, she started feeling the itch to try something new. "When it came time for me to leave New York, I thought about the Quad Cities and living closer to home. In a weird way the 'QC' is too big. New York is huge city, but each neighborhood is like a small town. It has its bank, post office, library, dry cleaner, restaurants, and coffee shops: you never have to leave the neighborhood. The Quad Cities has those things too, but you can't easily walk to them."

On a whim, she contacted her friend and asked if she could come to Bellevue and work at his farm for the summer. He said she was welcome to come, but that he couldn't pay her. That took the wind out of her sails a bit but she found another way to tackle the problem. "Finding a job in a town of 2,000 is not easy. My biggest wish was to live and work here, walk to work, have a job and house in the downtown area." She didn't want to drive to a job in Dubuque, come home at night and sit in her house, then drive to work in Dubuque each morning. So, she sent some feelers out.

"One benefit of a small town is that all you have to do is say 'This is what I want, need, am looking for.' Say what you want and it will come to you, through word of mouth." While Deanna was searching for housing she was asked to apply for the job with the chamber of commerce. The house she purchased was for sale by owner, who happened to be the departing chamber director. Locals seemed to get a kick out of Deanna's apparent absorption into the life of the previous director.

But she made her own space in town, quickly. She made an early social splash at an art gallery event on Halloween, very convincingly as Audrey Hepburn from *Breakfast at Tiffany's*, the ultimate New Yorker, complete with pearls, cigarette holder, and little black dress. Most of the other costumed women came as witches.

Now Deanna is steady at the helm of the chamber, supporting local businesses and serving as a starting point for tourists to the area. She said that recently an older man from Illinois stopped by and explained that the city where he lived was getting "really bad" with crime. He and his adult son were determined to get out, and they decided to explore Iowa. He approached Bellevue's south bluff and turnout to the state park with its butterfly garden, hiking trails, and river overlooks and said he felt like he was driving into a resort. He asked what it was like to live in Bellevue and she told him about the highlights of the area. Then he asked for directions to the nearest realtor.

"It is my job to extol Bellevue's virtues, but that is easy for me to do," Deanna acknowledged. The story illustrated by the man from Illinois is one of many and it is hard to know how many people actually follow up on that initial urge for greener grass. They might follow up within six months, as I did. Or it might be a twenty-year retirement plan. Or it might be a passing whim, the urge to appropriate something because it is beautiful, until you realize how impractical it is to do so.

Many of our friends, especially those who already commute out of town for work, spend a lot of time in Dubuque for shopping, dining, and other urban pastimes. Ron and I have to remind ourselves occasionally that we really ought to make a run up there to see a friend's art opening, or to get Italian food. I sometimes joke about having "gone to seed," by which I mean I no longer have appropriate clothing for really nice events, I don't know the names of current pop-culture icons, I am way behind on figuring out why I need to acquire consumer goods I see advertised on commercials I view during my non-DVR television watching. It isn't because I live in Bellevue that I've reached that state. I think it is just a fact of being a middle-aged, self-employed, stay-at-home writer. And while it generally takes a day longer than if I were in a city, I can order the material goods I want online and have them shipped to me, if they aren't available in town. Of course, one's personal desires for close relationships are not so easily met.

Deanna acknowledges that being an outsider can be a hurdle, socially. "Because of my job I'm welcomed into the community," she said. "Lots of people go back to the founding families of Bellevue, and if you aren't in one of those you are considered an outsider. I'm fine with that because I've moved around a lot, and in my job I meet a lot of people."

Similar to Sara Millhouse's experience, having a public role in town has put Deanna into contact with many people. She's had people shovel her walks unbidden, leave bags of homegrown vegetables on her porch. She extrapolates these actions to the way other newcomers are welcomed to town, but that might not be the experience for those whose arrival isn't heralded by an article and photo in the local paper, as hers had been.

Having slipped in more quietly, I have noticed that one has to make a strong effort to meet others, like joining civic organizations, being visible in public by supporting local restaurants, attending fundraisers, and the like. I know it is important to me to be known and accepted by others. I have made friends among Bellevue's native set. But when I look at the group of people I spend most of my time with, I notice we are mostly from someplace else. When I walk into a public place I still feel the buzzing around the room as people whisper to their companions the most often spoken words in Bellevue: "Who is that?" I've chosen mild notoriety over invisibility, now playing up being one-half of "that couple from Wyoming" as my husband and I have come to be known.

One Bellevue businessman and civic leader who is a native but not a lifelong resident is Allen Ernst. He comes from one of eastern Iowa's original families and is the unofficial caretaker of family history in photographs and stories. He, his wife Brenda, and their three children recently moved into the home where he grew up, from which his father operated an insurance business for many years. The elder Ernst was among an informal group of community leaders who began Bellevue's volunteer ambulance service when the mortician who was doing it wanted out.

Allen graduated from Marquette Catholic School and went to college for one semester to study art. But then he dropped out and moved to Chicago. He got a job as a runner at the Chicago Board of Trade. "It taught me immeasurably that you have to be wealthy to live in Chicago. I was broke, like I've never been broke before or since." He realized he needed a degree to afford the lifestyle he wanted, so he enrolled in Loras College in Dubuque. Upon graduation, he worked in various insurance and financial companies in larger cities around Iowa. Then his father passed away, and Allen's brother, also living away from home, got caught up in the hometown conversation about what Bellevue's future should be. He came to Allen with a long list of ambitious ideas. "He's my brother and I only have one of those. Of course I was going to help," Allen said.

Together they purchased several buildings and started various new businesses. Of this venture, Allen said, "Hopefully it'll work on its own and then I can get back to my real life." "Real life" means not sitting at his desk in the office at the back of the restaurant and art gallery space he operates with his wife, but selling Bellevue by developing businesses, which is the part he loves the most. He sees his service on the board of the Bellevue Arts Council, on the city council, and the Jackson County Economic Alliance, as ways to do just that.

Allen agrees with Deanna that the beauty of the town is what initially draws tourists and potential residents. But he doesn't think that tells the whole story. "Bellevue is a special little jewel, partly because we're on the river, which is the first thing that catches your eye. If you talk to most people they'll tell you the river is beautiful, but how much time do you really spend on the river, or even looking it? But if you dig a little deeper, you'll see there is an ingrained sense in Bellevue people of what a great town it is and that they want to take care of it."

He uses language reminiscent of Sara Millhouse's comment about strong institutions being central to people's sense that their town is important. Allen believes Bellevue is full of people who love it as much as he does and take care of it. "That means being a good citizen, taking care of your home, your yard, your stuff, and being part of the community," he said.

I have observed that no matter how many civic activities are scheduled, from blood drives to Cub Scout popcorn sales to holiday festivals, there are volunteers, and they are not always the same faces. Allen's long experience with Bellevue confirms my observation. "It is rare to see the community involvement we have here. People understand that's part of the deal to live here. It is not like that every place." He notes that people are more inclined to stay in an attractive place that seems to function well. But they won't stay if they can't make a living.

Allen points out that on paper, Bellevue's revenues are rising, but looking at inflation, the town is losing ground by 5 percent a year. If you're not doing something you are falling behind already, he explains. "We need careers for people to stay if they don't want to go to college, or to go and then come back so they can start a family."

Small businesses can be a great community addition, especially if the business started out of someone's passion for their hobby. But the failure rate for small businesses is very high. Anchor employers are better for new and existing residents. They offer stable employment, allowing people to buy or build homes, to shop locally, pay taxes, and send their children through the local school system.

By "anchor business," Allen does not mean smokestack industries, as Mike Blitgen had feared. What Allen feels is needed is technology based business like Sedgwick, an insurance company call center, already operating in Bellevue. Or a manufacturer like Rockwell-Collins, the Iowa-based global avionics business that has operated a plant in Bellevue since 1968. It employs around a hundred people and hires workers of various educational backgrounds, including engineers. A hundred employees working for a company translates into a lot of families.

"Those are the kind of employers that would really help the town," Allen said. "Our location is such that we will never have major industry here, we're not on a major highway, and we're landlocked because of the river. But the way the world is changing, we could attract little job shops, little parts suppliers, little technology business: that's the sort of thing that can work in a small town."

Allen has had enough experience working and living in larger places that he is able to bring a critical vision to Bellevue's future. After all, he has lived approximately half of his life thus far someplace else. He has the perspective to consider whether this place he loves is insular, as some have said, or if it welcomes newcomers.

"We hear people say it is tough on people coming to town. I have never seen that. It is true some people have come ~~have~~ and tried to open a business that ended up failing. It wasn't because locals didn't like them. It just didn't work." Allen has noticed that when things go wrong, most people look for a reason. He describes a certain mindset that affects how people perceive life. "If you see good people around you, that's all you see. If you see things negatively, that's what you'll see. If someone says people in Bellevue don't like them, maybe people don't like them somewhere else, too. It isn't our job to *like* everyone—that's true of every community."

It is also true everywhere that you have to get off the porch and introduce yourself to people. One of Allen's most visible ways of "getting off the porch" has been through the restaurant. The cuisine there is much more creative than what is found in typical small town cafés. In the adjoining coffee shop, customers can purchase specialty coffee drinks and baked goods. On the second floor of the building is an art studio that was the brainchild of local artist, photographer, and retired high school art teacher, Dave Eischeid. The idea of forming the Bellevue Arts Council developed in part because of Dave's vision that local artists could offer programs for Bellevue's school kids. Allen was sold on the idea when he realized those programs could take place in the second floor of his building. "I would love more than anything if every kid in town could walk through a coffee shop and see what a coffee shop is like before they get to college or the real world. Then they walk through an art gallery on their way up the stairs to see a working art studio. Then when they went off to college they would understand what it looked like, what it did, and not be afraid."

But why should Allen use his space for these non-money-making endeavors? His answer is a phrase that comes out of his mouth with frequency: "Somebody has to do it."

The Bellevue Arts Council's programs have had good support in its short life. Allen sees that support as an extension of the way the community has rallied around theater groups and various arts festivals over the years. Even though not everyone is an art lover or theatergoer, people in town take pride in the talents of their extended family, friends, and neighbors.

Allen's vision for the community in the short term includes an affordable housing program that could bring in young families. He sees affordable housing as essential for keeping the town vibrant and the schools working. He believes that Bellevue would be an even better community with 3,000 people, instead of 2,100. The most important step, Allen says, is that the town's key players have put together an incentive package for developers that is offered to all new business developers. "It takes the politics out. We offer this package to anybody who walks in the door, not just if you are from here or if someone likes or doesn't like you. That change of mindset has been tremendous. It's the main thing that'll make a difference in the next years. It has already started to make a difference."

Allen's three children may or may not be in the mix of Bellevue's future. "At least one would do well here. The others have a potential in different ways that might be better served someplace else," he said carefully. His youngest wants to be an architect and Allen says he has the skill set and personality to accomplish that goal, if he wants to. But you don't become a great architect in Bellevue, or even Dubuque or Davenport. "For him to fully realize himself he should probably be somewhere else. I'd encourage that. I'd love them to be close enough for me to be 'grandpa' but I don't want them to regret being here."

You never know what shade of green the grass is until you've seen it up close. In spite of my admitted propensity for rose-colored glasses, I know Bellevue is a real place with occasional problems, not simply a Mayberry of imagination. For starters, the town had a rough start, established on land that the Black Hawk Native Americans called home until the Black Hawk Purchase of 1836 opened it to white settlers. Bellevue's early history was marked by skirmishes and squabbles that led to a sequence of violent acts known now as the Bellevue War of 1840, resulting in the death of four townspeople and three of the lawbreaking gang. With law-enforcement officers days away, residents of Bellevue had to decide together whether to hang or whip those surviving ruffians. By a small margin, whipping and running out of town prevailed.

Through the decades there have been other unpleasant events of the sort that can be expected to take place among humans anywhere. In 2001 a murder was committed over Civil War antiques one person possessed but that other persons wanted. After the murder, the killers used a chainsaw to dismember the victim's body and deposit parts of it into the Mississippi River. Another murder in 2009 involved a pair of brothers who kidnapped and killed a member of a local farm family.

Most of my connections with law enforcement involve waving hello as officers drive down our block, a subset of waving hello at everyone who drives down our block. We had our only official contact with local law enforcement—so far—in the summer of 2013. That's when three young men moved into a house down the street. This trio was soon joined by numerous other young men and a few teenage girls for parties on the lawn and the sort of squealing tires, fistfights on the lawn, and beer-bottle garbage one might expect. We neighbors made allowances for youthful summer fun. After all, the Fourth of July was just around the corner. But one day a man living across the street had enough and went to visit the group. He explained he was taking down their license plate numbers because he'd need those when he called the police after their next display. They apologized and begged him not to call the police, because they'd been in trouble before and worried things wouldn't go well for them if they were in trouble again. But the next day two of them proceeded to set off a "sparkler bomb" in the alley behind the man's house. Things went downhill from there but the situation eventually righted itself. By which I mean the young men dispersed, and the house, which they'd trashed, was purchased and completely gutted. The resulting remodeling job means a new family with children will likely move in soon.

I was confident all along that the transgressive behavior of this group of young men would be straightened out by the social-norming machinery that is a small town's greatest tool. Yet I understand that intense and immediate social judgment can also be the thing that makes people feel excluded. That machinery is the reason some young people who have interests outside farming, blue-collar work, or small business entrepreneurship move away as soon as they are able. For cultural nonconformists—like kids trying to figure out how to live in a way that puts creative passion in front of making money—I can imagine Bellevue would be stifling.

I know Bellevue is not for everybody, and frankly, there are days I'm not sure it will be for me, forever. Nevertheless, you know you are becoming part of a place when you are actually invited to take part in activities, rather than hoping a fallen tree limb presents you an excuse to join in. Or when people begin to recognize you enough that they introduce themselves to you, rather than the other way around. Or when you start to note familiar names in the obituary section of the newspaper. Or when friends you've made pack up and move away.

Inevitably, Sara Millhouse accepted a job at a newspaper in a town about an hour away from Bellevue. She is still approximately the same distance from her parents' home, but the job is a professional step up for her. I miss having a friend I could always count on to be there when I'd say words like, "You know what we should do? Let's . . ." It wouldn't matter how that blank was filled in, Sara would respond with, "Okay!"

The new editor moved into her old apartment for a time. It took the new editor a few weeks to discover that people had already decided he was going to be their friend even before they'd met him. That's the way Bellevue works.

I still expect to see Sara striding along the riverwalk, camera dangling over her shoulder and reporter's notebook in the back pocket of her jeans. But she's not on the other side of the universe—she's just on the other side of Dubuque. Her departure was my first loss of this sort since coming to Bellevue. She was the person who introduced me to most of the friends I've made here. Her transition away from our orbit has been gradual, because she's close enough that it can be. She's happy in her job, has found a nice place to live (this I know because I helped her move), and has quickly made connections. She's going in with the attitude of one practiced in breaking new trails. "I haven't quite found my tribe," she said. "But I've found some people who *are* going to be my friends. They just don't know it yet."

AFTERWORD

When I reflect on the people and places I've become acquainted with during this exploration, they aren't scattered across nine towns and counties in five states. Instead, they are unified as residents of one community, going about their business in the theater of my mind. Some aspects of this created place are factual, and some are invented. For example, I know for sure that today's New Madrid has better sidewalks, lighting, sewer systems, and other infrastructure improvements, thanks to monies from its power plant sale. I know that the Tarkio College Alumni Association continues to restore the buildings, develop education programs, and raise funds with the goal of purchasing the campus. In Norton, Lori Shields reports she is doing well: her husband found a good welding job and the family is thriving, now that he has been released from the correctional facility. She still works at the school, takes online classes, and of course, runs the Haven. Judy Tolbert has left Sedan to move with her new husband to Georgia, and the plans for the public library have lost momentum, for now. Nancy Waldman Taft and her husband are still in Centennial, waiting for the right buyer for their home. Brian and Dana Eberhard have moved back west to Spearfish, South Dakota, for a university teaching job that gets them closer to Laramie, and of course, Centennial.

Within the invented scenes of my town, I've put New Madrid's Jeff Grunwald in touch with Norton's Lee Ann Shearer, to talk about promoting cultural-attraction tourism. Sedan's Jack Newcomb and Sue Kill are great cohorts for Chuck Karpf in Bridgeport. In my mind, they've formed a regional roundtable to discuss rural entrepreneurship and economic development. I imagine Santee Sioux Reservation radio host Jim Hallum has been cast in one of Bliss Ragsdale's films, which will be viewed widely on computer screens across the country. Newspaper editors Rudy Taylor, Valorie Zach, Sara Millhouse, and the rest are trading ideas on enhancing community news via print and online publication. Diane and Calvin Krupicka of Niobrara are touring Bellevue with boat captain Mike Blitgen around their part of the Missouri River, areas he can't reach in his larger boats. In Emmetsburg, college students are going about their day, planning to study and then meet up later to watch some Big 10 football with the gang in Niobrara. At the end of the day in my created town, a barred owl calls *who cooks for you*. Instantly, I'm transported, sipping a glass of wine with Mark Palmer and Mary Kurtis on the porch of a house aligned with the North Star in the timber of the southern Flint Hills.

These people aren't just in my mind of course: they are in the pages of this book and very feasibly could pick up the phone, call one another, and have the kind of conversations I imagine each would benefit from and enjoy. People in these towns and in towns like them have a lot to give to one another, and to the country at large. I recall Scottsbluff newspaper editor Steve Frederick's comment that the tide of rural population loss can't go out forever. Eventually, people on the crowded coasts are going to look at what Nebraska and places like it have to offer and think they look pretty good. That's why so many communities are hopeful about what they'll look like in five years, or twenty.

Yet in spite of amenities or location or planning, sometimes no amount of good intentions can protect a town from people's need to live someplace else. Taken to the extreme, sometimes a town literally dissolves itself and turns its functions over to the county where it resides. So-called disincorporation might happen when the town no longer has the tax revenue for services for police and fire protection, or for street lights and snow removal. Or when no one is willing to run for council, or to be the mayor. Just because a town dissolves its government doesn't mean it cannot carry on, though in an ad hoc way. Yet people who've been through disincorporation report it brings a profound sense of loss, with residents feeling they were poor stewards for the hopes of long-gone town founders, who still keep watch from the quiet hilltop cemetery.

Like other forms of life, communities have a cycle and transition naturally from hopeful beginning, to thriving, to struggling, to ending their days as vessels for nostalgia and reflection, but also for rebirth. Every day, through acts of stubborn resilience, this region seems poised to reinvent itself, to grow new hope, to teach new lessons. Those lessons may be as simple as finding resilience through thinking locally but acting as a collective, being mindful that even long traditions are not infinite. Taking steps like investment in education, housing, entrepreneurship, infrastructure, and civil public discourse are important everywhere, in communities of all sizes—possibly nowhere more than in the rural areas of this region, which by many measures is in deep trouble. But the world has always been full of rooters and rangers: people who plant themselves in one spot permanently and people who make a sail out of their mobility and let the wind be their guide. It will be a fine thing when this region finds a way to sustain those rooters, and tempt some of those rangers to settle here, at least for a time.

A NOTE ON SOURCES

To research this book, in addition to travel and interviews, I relied on many books, reports, articles, and online information. These are noted within the text. Among the most valuable were the following.

Bishop, Bill. *The Big Sort: Why the Clustering Of Like-Minded America Is Tearing Us Apart*. New York: Houghton Mifflin, 2008.

Brown, David L. *Rural People and Communities in the 21st Century: Resilience and Transformation*. New York: Polity, 2011.

Carr, Patrick, and Maria J. Kefalas. *Hollowing Out the Middle: Rural Brain Drain and What It Means for America*. Boston: Beacon Press, 2010.

Flora, Cornelia Butler, and Jan L. Flora. *Rural Communities: Legacy and Change*. Boulder, CO: Westview Press, 2012.

Grey, Mark, Michele Devlin, and Aaron Goldsmith. *Postville U.S.A.: Surviving Diversity in Small-Town America*. Boston: GemmaMedia, 2009.

Health Equity Series: African American Health Disparities in Missouri. April 2013, http://www.mffh.org/mm/files/13AfrAmDisparities.pdf.

Longworth, Richard C. *Caught in the Middle: America's Heartland in the Age of Globalism*. New York: Bloomsbury USA, 2009.

Popper, Deborah Epstein, and Frank J. Popper. "The Great Plains: From Dust to Dust." *Planning*, December 1987, n.p., http://www.planning.org/25anniversary/planning/1987dec.htm.

Price, John T. *Not Just Any Land: A Personal and Literary Journey into the American Grasslands*. Lincoln: University of Nebraska Press, 2004.

Reding, Nick. *Methland: The Death and Life of an American Small Town*. New York: Bloomsbury USA, 2010.

Smart Growth America. Measuring Sprawl 2014. http://www.smartgrowthamerica.org/documents/measuring-sprawl-2014.pdf.

Western, Sam. *Pushed Down the River, Sold Down the Mountain: Wyoming's Search for its Soul*. Jackson, WY: Homestead Publishing, 2002.

Wood, Richard E. *Survival of Rural America: Small Victories and Bitter Harvests*. Lawrence: University Press of Kansas, 2008.

Woodard, Colin. *American Nations: A History of the Eleven Rival Regional Cultures of North America*. New York: Penguin Books, 2012.

Wuthnow, Richard. *Small Town: Finding Community, Shaping the Future*. Princeton, NJ: Princeton University Press, 2013.

INDEX

IOWA AND THE MIDWEST EXPERIENCE